YOUR CHINESE HOROSCOPE 2005

NEIL SOMERVILLE

What the Year of the Rooster holds in store for you

TO ROS, RICHARD AND EMILY

Element
An Imprint of HarperCollins*Publishers*
77–85 Fulham Palace Road
Hammersmith, London W6 8JB

The website address is: www.thorsonselement.com

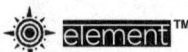

and *Element* are trademarks of
HarperCollins*Publishers* Limited

Published by Element 2004

10 9 8 7 6 5 4 3 2 1

© Neil Somerville 2004

Neil Somerville asserts the moral right to
be identified as the author of this work

A catalogue record for this book
is available from the British Library

ISBN 0 00 717700 3

Printed and bound in Great Britain by
Clays Ltd, St Ives plc

All rights reserved. No part of this publication may be
reproduced, stored in a retrieval system, or transmitted,
in any form or by any means, electronic, mechanical,
photocopying, recording or otherwise, without the prior
permission of the publishers.

CONTENTS

Acknowledgements	v
Introduction	vii
The Chinese Years	ix
Welcome to the Year of the Rooster	xiii
The Rat	2
The Ox	30
The Tiger	58
The Rabbit	88
The Dragon	116
The Snake	144
The Horse	172
The Goat	200
The Monkey	228
The Rooster	256
The Dog	282
The Pig	310
Appendix:	
Relationships between the Signs	338
Your Ascendant	340
How to Get the Best from your Chinese Sign	
and the Year	343

ABOUT THE AUTHOR

Neil Somerville is one of the leading writers in the West on Chinese horoscopes. He has been interested in Eastern forms of divination for many years and believes that much can be learned from the ancient wisdom of the East. His annual book on Chinese horoscopes has built up an international following and he is also the author of *What's Your Chinese Love Sign?* (Thorsons, 2000), *Chinese Success Signs* (Thorsons, 2001) and *The Ultimate Book of Answers* (Element, 2004).

Neil Somerville was born in the Year of the Water Snake. His wife was born under the sign of the Monkey, his son is an Ox and daughter a Horse.

ACKNOWLEDGEMENTS

In writing *Your Chinese Horoscope 2005* I am grateful for the assistance and support that those around me have given.

I wish to acknowledge Theodora Lau's *The Handbook of Chinese Horoscopes* (Harper & Row, 1979; Arrow, 1981), which was particularly useful to me in my research.

In addition to Ms Lau's work, I commend the following books to those who wish to find out more about Chinese horoscopes: Kristyna Arcarti, *Chinese Horoscopes for Beginners* (Headway, 1995); Catherine Aubier, *Chinese Zodiac Signs* (Arrow, 1984), series of 12 books; E. A. Crawford and Teresa Kennedy, *Chinese Elemental Astrology* (Piatkus Books, 1992); Paula Delsol, *Chinese Horoscopes* (Pan, 1973); Barry Fantoni, *Barry Fantoni's Chinese Horoscopes* (Warner, 1994); Bridget Giles and the Diagram Group, *Chinese Astrology* (HarperCollins Publishers, 1996); Kwok Man-Ho, *Authentic Chinese Horoscopes* (Arrow, 1987), series of 12 books; Lori Reid, *The Complete Book of Chinese Horoscopes* (Element Books, 1997); Paul Rigby and Harvey Bean, *Chinese Astrologics* (Publications Division, South China Morning Post Ltd, 1981); Ruth Q. Sun, *The Asian Animal Zodiac* (Charles E. Tuttle Company, Inc., 1996); Derek Walters, *Ming Shu* (Pagoda Books, 1987) and *The Chinese*

Astrology Workbook (The Aquarian Press, 1988); Suzanne White, *Suzanne White's Book of Chinese Chance* (Fontana/Collins, 1978), *The New Astrology* (Pan, 1987) and *The New Chinese Astrology* (Pan, 1994).

As we march into a new year
we each have our hopes, our ambitions and our dreams.

Sometimes fate and circumstance will assist us,
sometimes we will struggle and despair,
but march we must.

For it is those who keep going,
and who keep their aspirations alive,
who stand the greatest chance of securing what they want.

March determinedly,
and your determination will, in some way, be rewarded.

Neil Somerville

INTRODUCTION

The origins of Chinese horoscopes have been lost in the mists of time. It is known that Oriental astrologers practised their art many thousands of years ago and even today Chinese astrology continues to fascinate and intrigue.

In Chinese astrology there are 12 signs named after 12 different animals. No one quite knows how the signs acquired their names, but there is one legend that offers an explanation.

According to this legend, one Chinese New Year the Buddha invited all the animals in his kingdom to come before him. Unfortunately, for reasons best known to the animals, only 12 turned up. The first to arrive was the Rat, followed by the Ox, Tiger, Rabbit, Dragon, Snake, Horse, Goat, Monkey, Rooster, Dog and finally Pig.

In gratitude, the Buddha decided to name a year after each of the animals and that those born during that year would inherit some of the personality of that animal. Therefore those born in the year of the Ox would be hard-working, resolute and stubborn, just like the Ox, while those born in the year of the Dog would be loyal and faithful, just like the Dog. While not everyone can possibly share all the characteristics of a sign, it is incredible what similarities do occur and this is partly where the fascination of Chinese horoscopes lies.

In addition to the 12 signs of the Chinese zodiac there are five elements, and these have a strengthening or moderating influence upon the sign. Details about the effects of the elements are given in each of the chapters on the 12 signs.

To find out which sign you were born under, refer to the tables on the following pages. As the Chinese year is based on the lunar year and does not start until late January or early February, it is particularly important for anyone born in those two months to check carefully the dates of the Chinese year in which they were born.

Also included, in the Appendix, are two charts showing the compatibility between the signs for personal and business relationships, and details about the signs ruling the different hours of the day. From this it is possible to locate your ascendant and, as in Western astrology, this has a significant influence on your personality.

In writing this book, I have taken the unusual step of combining the intriguing nature of Chinese horoscopes with the Western desire to know what the future holds and have based my interpretations upon various factors relating to each of the signs. Over the years in which *Your Chinese Horoscope* has been published I have been pleased that so many have found the sections on the forthcoming year of interest, and hope that the horoscope has been constructive and useful. Remember, though, that at all times you are the master of your own destiny. I sincerely hope that *Your Chinese Horoscope 2005* will prove interesting and helpful for the year ahead.

THE CHINESE YEARS

Snake	4 February	1905	to	24 January	1906
Horse	25 January	1906	to	12 February	1907
Goat	13 February	1907	to	1 February	1908
Monkey	2 February	1908	to	21 January	1909
Rooster	22 January	1909	to	9 February	1910
Dog	10 February	1910	to	29 January	1911
Pig	30 January	1911	to	17 February	1912
Rat	18 February	1912	to	5 February	1913
Ox	6 February	1913	to	25 January	1914
Tiger	26 January	1914	to	13 February	1915
Rabbit	14 February	1915	to	2 February	1916
Dragon	3 February	1916	to	22 January	1917
Snake	23 January	1917	to	10 February	1918
Horse	11 February	1918	to	31 January	1919
Goat	1 February	1919	to	19 February	1920
Monkey	20 February	1920	to	7 February	1921
Rooster	8 February	1921	to	27 January	1922
Dog	28 January	1922	to	15 February	1923
Pig	16 February	1923	to	4 February	1924
Rat	5 February	1924	to	23 January	1925
Ox	24 January	1925	to	12 February	1926
Tiger	13 February	1926	to	1 February	1927
Rabbit	2 February	1927	to	22 January	1928
Dragon	23 January	1928	to	9 February	1929

YOUR CHINESE HOROSCOPE 2005

Snake	10 February	1929	to	29 January	1930
Horse	30 January	1930	to	16 February	1931
Goat	17 February	1931	to	5 February	1932
Monkey	6 February	1932	to	25 January	1933
Rooster	26 January	1933	to	13 February	1934
Dog	14 February	1934	to	3 February	1935
Pig	4 February	1935	to	23 January	1936
Rat	24 January	1936	to	10 February	1937
Ox	11 February	1937	to	30 January	1938
Tiger	31 January	1938	to	18 February	1939
Rabbit	19 February	1939	to	7 February	1940
Dragon	8 February	1940	to	26 January	1941
Snake	27 January	1941	to	14 February	1942
Horse	15 February	1942	to	4 February	1943
Goat	5 February	1943	to	24 January	1944
Monkey	25 January	1944	to	12 February	1945
Rooster	13 February	1945	to	1 February	1946
Dog	2 February	1946	to	21 January	1947
Pig	22 January	1947	to	9 February	1948
Rat	10 February	1948	to	28 January	1949
Ox	29 January	1949	to	16 February	1950
Tiger	17 February	1950	to	5 February	1951
Rabbit	6 February	1951	to	26 January	1952
Dragon	27 January	1952	to	13 February	1953
Snake	14 February	1953	to	2 February	1954
Horse	3 February	1954	to	23 January	1955
Goat	24 January	1955	to	11 February	1956
Monkey	12 February	1956	to	30 January	1957
Rooster	31 January	1957	to	17 February	1958
Dog	18 February	1958	to	7 February	1959
Pig	8 February	1959	to	27 January	1960

THE CHINESE YEARS

Rat	28 January	1960	to	14 February	1961
Ox	15 February	1961	to	4 February	1962
Tiger	5 February	1962	to	24 January	1963
Rabbit	25 January	1963	to	12 February	1964
Dragon	13 February	1964	to	1 February	1965
Snake	2 February	1965	to	20 January	1966
Horse	21 January	1966	to	8 February	1967
Goat	9 February	1967	to	29 January	1968
Monkey	30 January	1968	to	16 February	1969
Rooster	17 February	1969	to	5 February	1970
Dog	6 February	1970	to	26 January	1971
Pig	27 January	1971	to	14 February	1972
Rat	15 February	1972	to	2 February	1973
Ox	3 February	1973	to	22 January	1974
Tiger	23 January	1974	to	10 February	1975
Rabbit	11 February	1975	to	30 January	1976
Dragon	31 January	1976	to	17 February	1977
Snake	18 February	1977	to	6 February	1978
Horse	7 February	1978	to	27 January	1979
Goat	28 January	1979	to	15 February	1980
Monkey	16 February	1980	to	4 February	1981
Rooster	5 February	1981	to	24 January	1982
Dog	25 January	1982	to	12 February	1983
Pig	13 February	1983	to	1 February	1984
Rat	2 February	1984	to	19 February	1985
Ox	20 February	1985	to	8 February	1986
Tiger	9 February	1986	to	28 January	1987
Rabbit	29 January	1987	to	16 February	1988
Dragon	17 February	1988	to	5 February	1989
Snake	6 February	1989	to	26 January	1990
Horse	27 January	1990	to	14 February	1991

Goat	15 February	1991	to	3 February	1992
Monkey	4 February	1992	to	22 January	1993
Rooster	23 January	1993	to	9 February	1994
Dog	10 February	1994	to	30 January	1995
Pig	31 January	1995	to	18 February	1996
Rat	19 February	1996	to	6 February	1997
Ox	7 February	1997	to	27 January	1998
Tiger	28 January	1998	to	15 February	1999
Rabbit	16 February	1999	to	4 February	2000
Dragon	5 February	2000	to	23 January	2001
Snake	24 January	2001	to	11 February	2002
Horse	12 February	2002	to	31 January	2003
Goat	1 February	2003	to	21 January	2004
Monkey	22 January	2004	to	8 February	2005
Rooster	9 February	2005	to	28 January	2006

Note: The names of the signs in the Chinese zodiac occasionally differ in the various books on Chinese astrology, although the characteristics of the signs remain the same. In some books the Ox is referred to as the Buffalo or Bull, the Rabbit as the Hare or Cat, the Goat as the Sheep and the Pig as the Boar.

For the sake of convenience, the male gender is used throughout this book. Unless otherwise stated, the characteristics of the signs apply to both sexes.

WELCOME TO THE YEAR OF THE ROOSTER

With his shrill cock-a-doodle-do, the Rooster heralds the start of many a morn. And having woken everybody up, this busy bird struts around his territory surveying everything, his beady eyes ever alert. The Rooster has a commanding presence and his year too will be a dramatic one.

One of the key features of the Rooster year is that it is very much a time for commitment and hard work. Good organization, efficiency and attention to detail will be paramount and for those who slack or infringe the law, the Rooster year can be unforgiving. Illegal actions, protests and lack of respect for authority will be quickly and effectively dealt with. This will be no year to stray outside accepted boundaries. It was, for example, in the last Rooster year that the Russian authorities crushed the revolt in the Russian parliament, that President Clinton sent warships to enforce UN sanctions against the military-led regime in Haiti and that Iraq's refusal to obey a no-fly zone resulted in the bombing of strategic sites. Similarly, in 2005 the flouting of laws and directives, whether national or international, will be dealt with firmly *and* forcefully. The current war against terrorism will also continue with considerable vigour.

The year will also see the coming together of leading nations and organizations in an attempt to bring peace to troubled areas as well as for general economic benefit. Significant meetings and summits will be held throughout the year, sometimes leading to landmark agreements. It was in the last Rooster year that the Maastricht Treaty came into force, creating the European Union, that the North American Free Trade Agreement was ratified, that the Downing Street Declaration was given on the future of Northern Ireland and that Israeli and Palestinian leaders signed the Peace Accord to end 45 years of fighting. As time so often shows, not all agreements will be successful, but the sentiments will be there and the world will certainly benefit from some of the measures taken during the Rooster year.

Economically, the Rooster year will be one of steady but slow growth, with market conditions most favouring companies which are sleek, efficient and producing quality goods and services. In addition financial malpractice and inefficient or uneconomic procedures could come under close scrutiny, with some major investigations taking place.

The year is also likely to be marked by some historic achievements, often coming as the culmination of many years of effort and planning. It was in previous Rooster years that man conquered the moon and Concorde made its first supersonic flight. Further achievements this year will also mark the advance of mankind. In particular, discoveries in space and new information about our solar system could be dramatic and significant.

The Rooster year also favours pageantry and display, and 2005 will see some major events and spectacles. Events in the British Royal Family often feature strongly in Rooster years. Past Rooster years have seen Queen

WELCOME TO THE YEAR OF THE ROOSTER

Victoria's Jubilee, the Investiture of Prince Charles as Prince of Wales and also his marriage to Lady Diana Spencer, an event which had an estimated worldwide audience of 1,000 million viewers and listeners, or almost a quarter of the world's population. This year is also likely to see events with royal connections generating worldwide interest.

For the individual, the Rooster year can often be beneficial and rewarding. Many people are likely to pay more attention to their lifestyle and well-being over the year, and interest in disciplines such as yoga, *t'ai chi*, aerobics and other forms of exercise will increase. Many governments around the world will back this, making funds available for sports and fitness programmes and encouraging health initiatives. Attention will also be given to the importance of diet. Health awareness will be a major feature of the year.

Also, for those prepared to work hard and to use their skills well, the Rooster year can be rewarding on a personal level. This is a year which favours dedication and effort and, as the Chinese proverb states, *Diligence leads to riches*. In the Rooster year, it is the diligent who will fare the best.

And this does sum up the nature of the year. It is a time for positive action and commitment rather than for letting talents, ideas and opportunities go to waste. For those prepared to make the most of themselves and put in the effort, the year can bring many rewards. Use it well and may you enjoy good fortune over the next 12 months.

YOUR CHINESE HOROSCOPE 2005

18 FEBRUARY 1912 ~ 5 FEBRUARY 1913	*Water Rat*
5 FEBRUARY 1924 ~ 23 JANUARY 1925	*Wood Rat*
24 JANUARY 1936 ~ 10 FEBRUARY 1937	*Fire Rat*
10 FEBRUARY 1948 ~ 28 JANUARY 1949	*Earth Rat*
28 JANUARY 1960 ~ 14 FEBRUARY 1961	*Metal Rat*
15 FEBRUARY 1972 ~ 2 FEBRUARY 1973	*Water Rat*
2 FEBRUARY 1984 ~ 19 FEBRUARY 1985	*Wood Rat*
19 FEBRUARY 1996 ~ 6 FEBRUARY 1997	*Fire Rat*

THE RAT

THE PERSONALITY OF THE RAT

> Every individual has a place to fill in the world and is important in some respect, whether he chooses to be so or not.
>
> *Nathaniel Hawthorne, a Rat*

The Rat is born under the sign of charm. He is intelligent, popular and loves attending parties and large social gatherings. He is able to establish friendships with remarkable ease and people generally feel relaxed in his company. He is a very social creature and is genuinely interested in the welfare and activities of others. He has a good understanding of human nature and his advice and opinions are often sought.

The Rat is a hard and diligent worker. He is also very imaginative and is never short of ideas. However, he does sometimes lack the confidence to promote his ideas and this can often prevent him from securing the recognition he deserves.

The Rat is very observant and many Rats have made excellent writers and journalists. The Rat also excels at personnel and PR work and any job which brings him into contact with people and the media. His skills are particularly appreciated in times of crisis, for the Rat has an incredibly strong sense of self-preservation. When it comes to finding a way out of an awkward situation, the Rat is certain to be the one who comes up with a solution.

The Rat loves to be where there is a lot of action, but should he ever find himself in a very bureaucratic or restrictive environment he can become a stickler for discipline and routine.

THE RAT

He is also something of an opportunist and is constantly on the lookout for ways in which he can improve his wealth and lifestyle. He rarely lets an opportunity go by and can become involved in so many plans and schemes that he sometimes squanders his energies and achieves very little as a result. He is also rather gullible and can be taken in by those less scrupulous than himself.

Another characteristic of the Rat is his attitude to money. He is very thrifty and to some he may appear a little mean. The reason for this is purely that he likes to keep his money within his family. He can be most generous to his partner, his children and close friends and relatives. He can also be generous to himself, for he often finds it impossible to deprive himself of any luxury or object he fancies. The Rat is very acquisitive and can be a notorious hoarder. He hates waste and is rarely prepared to throw anything away. He can also be rather greedy and will rarely refuse an invitation for a free meal or a complimentary ticket to some lavish function.

The Rat is a good conversationalist, although he can occasionally be a little indiscreet. He can be highly critical of others – for an honest and unbiased opinion, the Rat is a superb critic – and sometimes will use confidential information to his own advantage. However, as the Rat has such a bright and irresistible nature, most are prepared to forgive him his slight indiscretions.

Throughout his long and eventful life the Rat will make many friends and will find that he is especially well suited to those born under his own sign and those of the Ox, Dragon and Monkey. He can also get on well with those born under the signs of the Tiger, Snake, Rooster, Dog and

Pig, but the rather sensitive Rabbit and Goat will find the Rat a little too critical and blunt for their liking. The Horse and Rat will also find it difficult to get on with each other – the Rat craves security and will find the Horse's changeable moods and rather independent nature a little unsettling.

The Rat is very family-orientated and will do anything to please his nearest and dearest. He is exceptionally loyal to his parents and can himself be a very caring and loving parent. He will take an interest in all his children's activities and will see that they want for nothing. The Rat usually has a large family.

The female Rat has a kindly, outgoing nature and involves herself in a multitude of different activities. She has a wide circle of friends, enjoys entertaining and is an attentive hostess. She is also conscientious about the upkeep of her home and has good taste in home furnishings. She is most supportive to the other members of her family and, due to her resourceful, friendly and persevering nature, can do well in practically any career.

Although the Rat is something of an extrovert, he is also a very private individual. He tends to keep his feelings to himself and while he is not averse to learning what other people are doing, he resents anyone prying too closely into his own affairs. He also does not like solitude and if he is alone for any length of time he can easily get depressed.

The Rat is undoubtedly very talented, but he does sometimes fail to capitalize on his many abilities. He has a tendency to become involved in too many schemes and chase after too many opportunities all at once. If he can slow down and concentrate on one thing at a time, he can become very successful. If not, success and wealth can elude him. But the Rat, with his tremendous ability to charm, will rarely, if ever, be without friends.

THE FIVE DIFFERENT TYPES OF RAT

In addition to the 12 signs of the Chinese zodiac there are five elements and these have a strengthening or moderating influence on the sign. The effects of the five elements on the Rat are described below, together with the years in which the elements were exercising their influence. Therefore those Rats born in 1960 are Metal Rats, those born in 1912 and 1972 are Water Rats, and so on.

Metal Rat: 1960
This Rat has excellent taste and certainly knows how to appreciate the finer things in life. His home is comfortable and nicely decorated and he likes to entertain and mix in fashionable circles. He has considerable financial acumen and invests his money well. On the surface the Metal Rat appears cheerful and confident, but deep down he can be troubled by worries that are quite often of his own making. He is exceptionally loyal to his family and friends.

Water Rat: 1912, 1972
The Water Rat is intelligent and very astute. He is a deep thinker and can express his thoughts clearly and persuasively. He is always eager to learn and is talented in many different areas. He is usually very popular, but his fear of

loneliness can sometimes lead him into mixing with the wrong sort of company. He is a particularly skilful writer, but he can get side-tracked very easily and should try to concentrate on just one thing at a time.

Wood Rat: 1924, 1984

The Wood Rat has a friendly, outgoing personality and is popular with his colleagues and friends. He has a quick, agile brain and likes to turn his hand to anything he thinks may be useful. His one fear is insecurity, but given his intelligence and capabilities, this fear is usually unfounded. He has a good sense of humour, enjoys travel and, due to his highly imaginative nature, can be a gifted writer or artist.

Fire Rat: 1936, 1996

The Fire Rat is rarely still and seems to have a never-ending supply of energy and enthusiasm. He loves being involved in the action – be it travel, following up new ideas or campaigning for a cause in which he fervently believes. He is an original thinker and hates being bound by petty restrictions or the dictates of others. He can be forthright in his views, but can sometimes get carried away in the excitement of the moment and commit himself to various undertakings without thinking through all the implications. Yet he has a resilient nature and with the right support can often go far in life.

Earth Rat: 1948

This Rat is astute and very level-headed. He rarely takes unnecessary chances and while he is constantly trying to improve his financial status, he is prepared to proceed slowly and leave nothing to chance. The Earth Rat is probably not as adventurous as the other types of Rat and prefers to remain in familiar territory rather than rush headlong into something he knows little about. He is talented, conscientious and caring towards his loved ones, but at the same time can be self-conscious and worry a little too much about the image he is trying to project.

PROSPECTS FOR THE RAT IN 2005

The Chinese New Year starts on 9 February 2005. Until then, the old year, the Year of the Monkey, is still making its presence felt.

The Year of the Monkey (22 January 2004 to 8 February 2005) is a generally positive one for the Rat and the closing months will bring some good opportunities for him to make progress as well as enjoy himself.

On a personal level the Rat will find himself in demand, with his domestic and social life set to become busier in the last quarter of the year. And with his sociable nature, he will often revel in the activity. In addition to receiving invitations to various gatherings, he will often be tempted out to meet friends or attend events that appeal to him. In some cases, meeting colleagues on a more informal basis will lead to building some good contacts.

Work-wise, the last quarter of the Monkey year will bring some interesting opportunities, with September being a particularly positive month. At this time the Rat may find himself taking on additional duties or following up openings that appeal to him. By making the most of the chances that come his way, he can greatly enhance his future prospects.

In money matters, many Rats will enjoy some good financial fortune at the end of the Monkey year. However, as the Rat will want to do and buy a great deal, he would be wise to keep track of his general level of spending.

Overall, though, with his resourceful and sociable nature, the Rat can make much of the closing months of the Monkey year and will enjoy himself as well as place himself in a good position to make greater headway in the next Chinese year.

The Year of the Rooster starts on 9 February and will be a busy and important one for the Rat. While the speed with which certain events may happen may disconcert him, he does thrive on activity and both personally and professionally, the year holds exciting prospects for him.

The speed of events is a key feature, though, and throughout the year the Rat will need to be alert to unfolding situations and be prepared to move swiftly. Opportunities could arise suddenly, particularly at work, and if the Rat sees an opening he feels well suited for, he should act quickly and put himself forward. He will often find his initiative and earnestness being rewarded. Also, he could find that one opportunity leads to another. Setting about his activities in his usual enthusiastic manner will also help him when further opportunities arise. This is very much a year to advance, with April, May, September and November containing some particularly good possibilities.

For those Rats seeking work the Rooster year also holds interesting prospects. Again, though, these Rats need to be swift in making applications and need to remain persistent as well as be prepared to contact companies directly about possible openings. This is a year when initiative *can* make a difference. Even if certain applications do not go his way, the Rat should not lose heart. With determination and resolve, he may well secure a suitable position, and one which offers the chance of further development. Workwise, this can be an eventful and often significant year.

The progress the Rat makes in his work will also lead to a welcome increase in income, but throughout the Rooster year he would do well to manage his money carefully. In addition to his existing obligations, he will be keen to carry out accommodation and travel plans, and other purchases will be sure to tempt him. While the Rat is one who enjoys the fruit of his labours, in the Rooster year he would be wise to watch his spending and avoid risks. Succumbing to too many temptations could prevent him from doing all he would like. He would also find it helpful to save towards certain requirements as well as consider setting something aside for the longer term.

The Rooster year will also see much activity in the Rat's domestic life. The Rat always takes a fond interest in the activities of his loved ones and likes to be involved. As a consequence, he will find himself very busy this year. When those close to him have problems and pressures, he will be there to advise and assist, and similarly, whenever there is good news, he will be at the forefront of the celebrations. As always, he will do much to help others, but he should not hesitate to seek help himself should he feel under pressure. Should any problems raise their head, he will find that a willingness to talk them through will lead to the easing of tension. Once more, the Rat's ability to empathize with others and communicate so effectively will prove useful over the year.

Also, while the Rat and his loved ones may lead busy lifestyles, he should make sure family activities do not suffer as a result. By suggesting occasional family treats as well as enjoying time spent together on mutual interests, he will find his input into family life will again be appreciated.

The Rat's social life will also see much activity in the Rooster year. The sociable Rat knows a great many people and will often find himself with parties and social occasions to attend as well as regular opportunities to meet up with friends. On a social level he will be in great demand. And any Rats who may have had recent personal problems or be feeling lonely will find the Rooster year can bring an important new person into their lives, with a significant friendship or romance being forged. Late March to June, August and September will be favourable times for meeting others.

Although the Rat will have much to occupy himself with during the year, it is also important that he sets time aside for his own interests and recreational pursuits. Not only will these help him to relax and unwind but they can also be a good way for him to have a break from his everyday concerns. In some instances, too, the Rat's interests will give him the chance to get out of doors, take additional exercise or meet other enthusiasts. Whatever he does, his personal interests can help bring balance to his lifestyle.

It is also important that he does not neglect his own well-being, and over the year he should try to make sure he eats a balanced diet as well as takes sufficient exercise. To make the most of such a busy year, he does need to keep himself in good form.

Overall, the Rooster year holds much potential for the Rat. In his work there will be excellent chances for him to make progress, while on a personal level the year will see much activity, with the Rat enjoying a busy but often rewarding domestic and social life. And for some, important new friendships and romance beckon. The Rat is certainly a sign that lives life to the full and the Rooster year will give him the opportunity to do so.

The Metal Rat

This will be an eventful year for the Metal Rat. With his many skills and considerable experience, he is set to make impressive strides. However, events will move quickly and he will need to be flexible in outlook and prepared to make the most of prevailing situations.

This will be a particularly important year as far as the Metal Rat's work is concerned. Although he will have achieved a great deal in recent years, he may well feel that he could be making more of himself. As a result, he will be keen to make the most of any opportunities that arise, including becoming involved in new initiatives and taking on other work as well as putting his talents to more effective use. And his efforts *will* bear fruit. Not only will his industry and commitment be noted, but in many cases what he does now will put him in an excellent position for promotion or duties which will extend his experience and move his career forward. In some cases the opportunities offered may be different from those the Metal Rat was envisaging, but by being flexible and willing, many Metal Rats will make important headway over the year as well as feel more fulfilled in their new role.

While many Metal Rats will remain with their present employer and profit from their in-house knowledge and contacts, for those who feel there may be better opportunities elsewhere or who are seeking work, again the Rooster year will bring some interesting opportunities. However, to benefit, these Metal Rats will need to show some flexibility in what they are prepared to consider. In the Rooster year, it is a case of making the most of situations as they arise and being prepared to build on them. As the Metal Rat will discover, events will move fast and one opportunity can often lead to another. April, May and the months from September to November could see important developments work-wise.

Another positive feature of the year will be the way it will allow the Metal Rat to spend time on personal development. By taking advantage of training opportunities and chances to add to his experience, he will help his future prospects. However, he should not restrict his development to work matters but include his personal interests as well. He will find that taking them further can add to the pleasure they bring.

THE RAT

As far as the Metal Rat's domestic life is concerned, this will be a busy year. Those around him will often look to him for advice and support, particularly with important decisions they may have to take. For some Metal Rats there could also be domestic changes in store, as relations move on for the purposes of education, work or marriage. Again, the Metal Rat will do much to ensure any change goes smoothly and well. As always, his thoughtfulness and empathy will be appreciated.

However, while his input into family life will be valued, with so much going on there will be times during the year when he will feel under pressure. When this happens, he should try not to become too preoccupied or uncharacteristically uncommunicative, but let others know how he is feeling and ask for help if necessary.

This will also be an active year socially. The Metal Rat will receive many invitations to go out and can look forward to some particularly pleasant occasions. His circle of contacts is set to grow, with many people being impressed by his genial manner. For the unattached Metal Rat, someone he is introduced to could quickly become important. The Rooster year will bring romance for quite a few unattached Metal Rats. For socializing, the months from April to June and August and September are most favourable.

As far as money matters are concerned, the progress the Metal Rat makes in his work will lead to an improvement in his situation, but to benefit he should manage his money well and avoid risks. This is a year for care, for moderation and if possible for building up long-term savings and reducing borrowings. With good management and control the Metal Rat's financial position can be much improved by the year's end. This is, though, not a year for risks.

Overall, the Rooster year will be a busy one for the Metal Rat, but it will certainly bring opportunities for him to develop and progress. By making the most of the situations that arise and being his resourceful self, he can do himself much good as well as find greater fulfilment.

TIP FOR THE YEAR

While you will enjoy the activity and opportunities the year will bring, do keep things in perspective and make sure your lifestyle has balance. This includes setting time aside for those important to you and for spending on activities that help you relax and unwind. In 2005, do aim to balance your activities.

The Water Rat

This year will contain many positive developments for the Water Rat, bringing change but also considerable opportunity.

A key feature of the year will be the speed with which events occur. Particularly at work, offers to take on new responsibilities could be made suddenly and with little warning, or opportunities could arise by chance. Also, there could be factors at work which the Water Rat may not always be aware of. Colleagues who know of his strengths could put in recommendations for him or those he meets during the course of his duties could be impressed and speak highly of him. Many Water Rats will find their reputation serving them well over the year, sometimes in unexpected ways. And by taking advantage of the opportunities that come his way, even if they represent quite a change, the Water Rat will not only advance his career but also add to his experience.

For those Water Rats seeking work, there could also be some surprises in store. Often the Water Rat will obtain a new position which is completely different from what he has previously been doing but which will not only be an excellent new opportunity for him but also have the potential for further development. The Rooster year is capable of opening up some exciting new doors for the Water Rat, even though he may have to face some uncomfortable moments or disappointments on the way. For work opportunities, late March to May, September and November are most favourable.

As far as financial matters are concerned, this will be a generally positive year. In addition to an increase in income many Water Rats could enjoy a bonus, financial gift or even find a way to supplement their income. However, while this is an encouraging year for financial matters, the Water Rat will still need to be prudent. With his existing obligations, as well as some of the plans he is hoping to carry out, he will have much outlay over the year. In view of this he should keep a close watch on his financial position, making allowances for known commitments and setting funds aside for plans he has in mind, as well as (if possible) his longer-term future. With good management, though, he can find himself in a much improved financial situation by the year's end.

In view of his often active lifestyle, it is also important that the Water Rat pays attention to his well-being in

2005. He should ensure he eats a healthy and balanced diet, gives himself the chance to relax and, if sedentary for much of the day, takes sufficient exercise.

This will also be a busy year domestically. As well as the changes likely in the Water Rat's own work, those around him could also see many changes or have pressures of their own. Throughout the year, the Water Rat would find it helpful to encourage a spirit of openness between family members, with everyone helping out at demanding times. Being willing to talk about current activities and concerns will also lead to a greater understanding and rapport. In addition, the Water Rat should set time aside for mutual interests as well as for home projects that can be tackled together. By playing a full part in family life, he will find the year containing many rewarding occasions. Those Water Rats who may be parents, or who become parents in 2005, will also delight in the progress of their children. The Water Rat will also do much to assist more senior relations during the year, and while he may experience some pressures on his time, the support he gives will often mean a great deal.

To add to the activity of the year there will also be some Water Rats who decide to move to more suitable accommodation. Again, this will put considerable pressure on the Water Rat's time, but with the help and co-operation of all involved, he will be pleased with how the move works out and the benefits it brings.

The Water Rat will also value his social life over the year and will find it a good way to relax and have a break from everything else that is going on. For Water Rats who are unattached and would welcome new friends or perhaps romance, someone met during the Rooster year could quickly become important and help make this already eventful year all the more special.

Generally, the Rooster year will be a significant one for the Water Rat and by making the most of himself and the opportunities that come his way, he can make important progress.

TIP FOR THE YEAR
Make the most of the opportunities that arise. As the saying goes, *There's no time like the present*, and the present will certainly bring chances worth pursuing.

The Wood Rat

This will be an eventful year for the Wood Rat with almost all areas of his life seeing much activity. By making the most of his talents, he can look forward to making important progress as well as enjoying some fine personal achievements.

The Wood Rat's personal life is especially well aspected. For those enjoying romance, the Rooster year will certainly bring some memorable moments, with many marrying or settling down together. And many currently unattached Wood Rats will meet someone who will quickly become important to them. Sometimes a chance meeting could change their life. Also, for any Wood Rat who may have experienced recent difficulty in their personal life, this is a year for moving forward. Many will see much more promising times, especially if they make the effort to build up a new social circle. For the affairs of the heart, the year is splendidly aspected.

The Wood Rat will also enjoy his social life and will often find himself in demand, with many parties and other occasions to attend. Also, as many Wood Rats will move or see changes in their circumstances over the year, they will find themselves getting involved in a range of different activities and new social groups.

There will also be quite a few Wood Rats who decide to travel during the year and again this can go well, with many Wood Rats getting to see some awe-inspiring sights. However, before setting out, the Wood Rat should plan his itinerary carefully as well as seek medical guidance if travelling to anywhere particularly exotic or remote. The care and precautions he can take can make his travelling that much easier.

This will also be a significant year as far as the Wood Rat's work is concerned. Whether he is already in a position or seeking one, he will be thinking a great deal about the direction he would like his future career to take. However, while he may have his own ideas, he may need to build up his experience first, and this is something most Wood Rats would do well to focus on over the year. There will certainly be some good openings which can provide valuable experience, even if they do not quite relate to what the Wood Rat is hoping to do in the longer term. Work-wise, 2005 can be a very constructive year and it can also have surprising developments too. Opportunities could arise at short notice, or the Wood Rat could decide to switch to a different type of work altogether and find his plans moving more swiftly than he had envisaged. Whenever opportunities arise, it is a case of 'striking while the iron is hot' and by making the most of rapidly

THE RAT

unfolding situations, the Wood Rat can do his prospects considerable good.

In addition, all Wood Rats should take advantage of any training opportunities that may be available to them. The skills they can learn now will not only prove helpful to what they are currently doing but also aid their future prospects. Those Wood Rats who are studying for qualifications will find that by remaining focused on what they need to do and keeping the end results in mind, their achievements will be of long-term value. The significance of what the Wood Rat accomplishes during the year should not be underestimated.

As far as financial matters are concerned, this will be a reasonable year, with the Wood Rat's resourceful and thrifty nature enabling him to do a great deal. However, the year does call for care and he should avoid financial risks, committing himself to schemes he knows little about or entering into agreements without checking the full implications. In money matters he needs to be thorough and careful. Wood Rats, take note.

Overall, the Rooster year holds excellent prospects for the Wood Rat, allowing him to extend his experience and skills, while on a personal level, romance, new friendships and a rewarding social life will mean a great deal. This will be a busy year, but one the Wood Rat will enjoy.

TIP FOR THE YEAR
Events will happen quickly and to benefit you will need to act quickly too. With a positive and keen attitude, though, a great deal is possible. Also, what is accomplished now will often be helpful in the longer term.

The Fire Rat

The Fire Rat likes activity and there will certainly be activity aplenty in 2005. This is a year for action and for change.

One area which the Fire Rat will pay much attention to over the year will be his home. For some time he will have reflected on certain changes he would like to make and as the Rooster year begins, he will set about his ideas in earnest. Some Fire Rats will decide to move to accommodation more suitable for their present needs and will spend time considering various possibilities as well as tackling all the sorting and preparation that needs to be done. As these Fire Rats will find, there will be lots to do, but with a concerted effort and help from others, they will be satisfied with what they accomplish. Also, if the Fire Rat should have any uncertainties over any aspect of the moving process or require assistance with more strenuous activities, it is important that he seeks help.

Those Fire Rats who remain where they are will also embark on making alterations to their home, both in adding new comforts and improving décor. They will also spend time considering the choices open to them as well as taking pleasure in seeing their ideas unfold. In addition, many will be keen to improve the running of their home and will decide to rid themselves of some of the paperwork and clutter that has accumulated over the years. Not only will this make their home tidier but also more efficient. As so many Fire Rats will find, this is very much a year for getting things in order!

In so much of what he does, the Fire Rat will be helped by those close to him, and by involving others he will find

THE RAT

that many hands do indeed make light work. In addition to the practical activities of the year, he will follow the progress of younger family members with much interest and will often be glad to help if they need advice or support. Family bonds are important to all Rats. Over the year the Fire Rat will also enjoy any activities that can be shared with loved ones, and whether these are trips out or time spent in the garden or on shared hobbies, they will bring him many pleasurable moments.

The Fire Rat too will value the time he sets aside for his own interests. With his inquisitive nature, if there is a particular subject that has been intriguing him or a skill he feels it would be useful to learn, this would be an excellent year in which to follow it up. Whether through personal study or enrolling on a course, the Fire Rat will take much satisfaction from new interests. The one word of warning that does need to be sounded, though, is that if he gets involved in any strenuous activities, he does need to take care, follow the recommended procedures and, if necessary, seek help. This is not a year to risk his well-being. Fire Rats, take note.

The Fire Rat's social life will also bring him pleasure over the year. Any Fire Rats who may be lonely or have experienced recent personal difficulties will find that going out and immersing themselves in different activities – perhaps joining a local society or helping in some sort of charitable work – can lead to new friendships as well as new interests. The Rooster year *is* supportive of the Fire Rat, but the initiative does rest with him.

Travel is favourably aspected and the Fire Rat should consider going away for a break at some time during the year. If he receives invitations to visit family and friends, he should follow them up. Again, this is a year to make the most of the opportunities that arise.

As far as financial matters are concerned, this will be an expensive year, particularly with all the activities and plans the Fire Rat will want to carry out. However, provided he is careful and budgets for what he has in mind, he will be pleased with what he is able to accomplish. If, though, he has doubts over any financial matter or is involved in any important financial transaction, he should seek advice rather than take risks. This is a year for watchfulness and control.

Overall, this will be a busy year for the Fire Rat, but whether he is moving, tackling domestic projects or pursuing family or personal interests, it will bring him a great deal of satisfaction. This is a time for him to act – and to enjoy his achievements.

TIP FOR THE YEAR
Seize the moment! Follow up your ideas and carry out your plans. With the support of others and the opportunities that will arise, you can accomplish a great deal.

The Earth Rat

The Earth Rat is a good judge of situations and often has a canny knack of gauging how certain events or actions are likely to work out. And his talents will serve him well over the Rooster year.

Although many Earth Rats will have made good progress in their work in recent years, many will still have certain ambitions or goals in mind. In the Rooster year the Earth Rat will decide to act upon these, feeling that if he does not aim for them now, some fine opportunities could be lost.

For some Earth Rats their goal will be to move to a more senior position, and in addition to pursuing any openings that become available, these Earth Rats could find it helpful to offer to do more in their current position. By showing initiative, taking on a greater role and making effective use of their experience, their efforts could count for a great deal. Also, throughout the year, the Earth Rat will find some of his contacts helpful to him and should make the most of any chances to meet others in his line of work. With his fine qualities, he will impress many people and this too will help his progress. For work opportunities April, May, September and November are most favourable.

This also applies to those Earth Rats who feel in a rut or sense they are getting nowhere in their current position. It rests with them to act, and act they will. Although moving away from a position they know well will lead to some uncomfortable moments, by making the decision to do something different, they will not only feel invigorated by the challenge before them but also be pleased to use talents that may have lain dormant for many years. For some, the year can bring a complete career change, but one they have been yearning for for some time. The Rooster year can bring the Earth Rat some excellent new opportunities, though it does rest with him to take the initiative.

Those Earth Rats seeking work can also fare well. While securing a new position will require persistence, once they have done so they will not only make the most of it but also find it an important platform to build upon. Workwise, the Rooster year *is* an encouraging one and by making the effort, putting himself forward and overcoming the knocks and occasional rejection, the Earth Rat will find he *is* able to advance his career as well as obtain greater fulfilment from it.

The progress the Earth Rat makes in his work will lead to an increase in his income, and financially he will fare well in 2005. However, to benefit he does need to manage his finances carefully, setting funds aside for known expenses as well as making allowances for his plans. The more control he has over his finances, the more he will be able to do. Also, if he is able to set some funds aside for the longer term, he could find savings made now could prove useful in a few years' time.

Another gratifying area will be the Earth Rat's personal interests and despite the many demands of the year he should aim to set a regular time aside for activities he enjoys. Whether he prefers creative, practical or more outdoor pursuits, interests that provide a break from his everyday concerns really can benefit him, as well as bring him a great deal of pleasure. Many Earth Rats will find that setting themselves a particular project to do or skill to learn, perhaps by enrolling on a course, will be especially satisfying.

As with all Rats, though, the Earth Rat does need to take care with his well-being over the year and ensure he has a balanced diet as well as regular exercise. To keep on good form, he does need to give consideration to himself and seek guidance, if necessary, on what is most appropriate for him.

THE RAT

The Earth Rat will see much activity in his domestic and social life over the year and can look forward to some important family events, possibly a wedding or the birth of a grandchild. In addition he will often find others looking to him for advice, and his willingness to help will be valued. Family bonds are precious to the Earth Rat and his love and care will certainly be appreciated over the year. He will also take pleasure in some of the joint family activities he gets involved with and many of the practical activities, particularly those that enhance his home or garden, will be especially satisfying. He may, however, need to allow plenty of time to complete them. With everything else that will be happening over the year, practical activities could take longer and involve more effort than anticipated. Earth Rats, take note.

The Earth Rat too will value his social life over the year, not only enjoying meeting up with friends but also some of the social occasions he goes to or even hosts himself. His social life can provide a necessary balance to his lifestyle and be a good way for him to relax and unwind. Any Earth Rats who may have let their social life lapse or feel their lifestyle is out of balance should try and address this, perhaps by joining a special interest group or making sure they go out more regularly. As the Earth Rat will find, positive action in the Rooster year *can* make a difference.

Overall, this is a year of opportunity for the Earth Rat and by acting upon his ideas and the opportunities the year will bring, he can make good progress and feel satisfied with what he accomplishes.

TIP FOR THE YEAR

Give yourself time to develop your personal interests. They will not only be pleasurable and beneficial but can sometimes lead you to discover other talents you will be keen to take further.

FAMOUS RATS

Ben Affleck, Alan Alda, Ursula Andress, Louis Armstrong, Charles Aznavour, Lauren Bacall, James Baldwin, Shirley Bassey, Kathy Bates, Irving Berlin, Silvio Berlusconi, Kenneth Branagh, Marlon Brando, Charlotte Brontë, Jackson Browne, George H. W. Bush, Glen Campbell, David Carradine, Jimmy Carter, Maurice Chevalier, Aaron Copland, Chris de Burgh, Cameron Diaz, David Duchovny, T. S. Eliot, Queen Elizabeth the Queen Mother, Eminem, Colin Firth, Clark Gable, Liam Gallagher, Gareth Gates, Hugh Grant, Geri Halliwell, Daryl Hannah, Thomas Hardy, Prince Harry, Vaclav Havel, Haydn, Charlton Heston, Buddy Holly, Mick Hucknall, Henrik Ibsen, Jeremy Irons, Samuel L. Jackson, Jean-Michel Jarre, Gene Kelly, Avril Lavigne, Lawrence of Arabia, Gary Lineker, Lord Andrew Lloyd Webber, Claude Monet, Nana Mouskouri, Richard Nixon, Roy Orbison, Ozzy Osbourne, Sean Penn, Terry Pratchett, Ian Rankin, Lou Rawls, Vanessa Redgrave, Burt Reynolds, Rossini, William Shakespeare, Tommy Steele, Donna Summer, James Taylor, Leo Tolstoy, Henri Toulouse-Lautrec, Spencer Tracy, the Prince of Wales, George Washington, the Duke of York, Emile Zola.

6 FEBRUARY 1913 ~ 25 JANUARY 1914	*Water Ox*
24 JANUARY 1925 ~ 12 FEBRUARY 1926	*Wood Ox*
11 FEBRUARY 1937 ~ 30 JANUARY 1938	*Fire Ox*
29 JANUARY 1949 ~ 16 FEBRUARY 1950	*Earth Ox*
15 FEBRUARY 1961 ~ 4 FEBRUARY 1962	*Metal Ox*
3 FEBRUARY 1973 ~ 22 JANUARY 1974	*Water Ox*
20 FEBRUARY 1985 ~ 8 FEBRUARY 1986	*Wood Ox*
7 FEBRUARY 1997 ~ 27 JANUARY 1998	*Fire Ox*

THE
OX

THE PERSONALITY OF THE OX

The great thing in this world is not so much where we stand as in what direction we are moving.
Oliver Wendell Holmes, an Ox

The Ox is born under the signs of equilibrium and tenacity. He is a hard and conscientious worker and sets about everything he does in a resolute, methodical and determined manner. He has considerable leadership qualities and is often admired for his tough and uncompromising nature. He knows what he wants to achieve in life and, as far as possible, will not be deflected from his ultimate objective.

The Ox takes his responsibilities and duties very seriously. He is decisive and quick to take advantage of any opportunity that comes his way. He is also sincere and places a great deal of trust in his friends and colleagues. He is, nevertheless, something of a loner. He is a quiet and private individual and often keeps his thoughts to himself. He also cherishes his independence and prefers to set about things in his own way rather than be bound by the dictates of others or influenced by outside pressures.

The Ox tends to have a calm and tranquil nature, but if something angers him or he feels that someone has let him down, he can have a fearsome temper. He can also be stubborn and obstinate and this can lead him into conflict with others. Usually he will succeed in getting his own way, but should things go against him the Ox is a poor loser and will take any defeat or setback extremely badly.

The Ox is often a deep thinker and rather studious. He is not particularly renowned for his sense of humour and

THE OX

does not take kindly to new gimmicks or anything too innovative. He is too solid and traditional for that and prefers to stick to the more conventional norm.

His home is very important to him and in some respects he treats it as a private sanctuary. His family tends to be closely knit and the Ox will make sure that each member does their fair share around the house. The Ox tends to be a hoarder, but he is always well organized and neat. He also places great importance on punctuality and there is nothing that infuriates him more than to be kept waiting, particularly if it is due to someone's inefficiency. The Ox can be a hard taskmaster!

Once settled in a job or house the Ox will quite happily remain there for many years. He does not like change and he is also not particularly keen on travel. He does, however, enjoy gardening and other outdoor pursuits and he will often spend much of his spare time out of doors. The Ox is usually an excellent gardener and whenever possible he will always make sure he has a large area of ground to maintain. He usually prefers to live in the country rather than the town.

Due to his dedicated and dependable nature, the Ox will usually do well in his chosen career, providing he is given enough freedom to act on his own initiative. He invariably does well in politics, agriculture and in careers which need specialized training. The Ox is also very gifted in the arts and many Oxen have enjoyed considerable success as musicians or composers.

The Ox is not as outgoing as some and it often takes him a long time to establish friendships and feel relaxed in another person's company. His courtships are likely to be long, but once he is settled he will remain devoted and loyal to his partner. The Ox is particularly well suited to those born under the signs of the Rat, Rabbit, Snake and Rooster. He can also establish a good relationship with the Monkey, Dog, Pig and another Ox, but he will find that he has little in common with the whimsical and sensitive Goat. He will also find it difficult to get on with the Horse, Dragon and Tiger – the Ox prefers a quiet and peaceful existence and those born under these three signs tend to be a little too lively and impulsive for his liking.

The female Ox has a kind and caring nature, and her home and family are very much her pride and joy. She always tries to do her best for her partner and can be a most conscientious and loving parent. She is an excellent organizer and also a very determined person who will often succeed in getting what she wants in life. She usually has a deep interest in the arts and is often a talented artist or musician.

The Ox is a very down-to-earth character. He is sincere, loyal and unpretentious. He can, however, be rather reserved and to some he may appear distant and aloof. He has a quiet nature, but underneath he is very strong-willed and ambitious. He has the courage of his convictions and is often prepared to stand up for what he believes to be right, regardless of the consequences. He inspires confidence and trust, and throughout his life he will rarely be short of people who are ready to support him or who admire his strong and resolute manner.

THE FIVE DIFFERENT TYPES OF OX

In addition to the 12 signs of the Chinese zodiac there are five elements and these have a strengthening or moderating influence on the sign. The effects of the five elements on the Ox are described below, together with the years in which the elements were exercising their influence. Therefore those Oxen born in 1961 are Metal Oxen, those born in 1913 and 1973 are Water Oxen, and so on.

Metal Ox: 1961
This Ox is confident and very strong-willed. He can be blunt and forthright in his views and is not afraid of speaking his mind. He sets about his objectives with a dogged determination, but he can become so involved in his various activities that he can be oblivious to the thoughts and feelings of those around him, and this can sometimes be to his detriment. He is honest and dependable and will never promise more than he can deliver. He has a good appreciation of the arts and usually has a small circle of very good and loyal friends.

Water Ox: 1913, 1973
This Ox has a sharp and penetrating mind. He is a good organizer and sets about his work in a methodical manner. He is not as narrow-minded as some of the other types of Ox and is more willing to involve others in his plans and aspirations. He usually has very high moral standards and

is often attracted to careers in public service. He is a good judge of character and has such a friendly and persuasive manner that he usually experiences little difficulty in securing his objectives. He is popular and has an excellent way with children.

Wood Ox: 1925, 1985

The Wood Ox conducts himself with an air of dignity and authority and will often take a leading role in any enterprise in which he becomes involved. He is very self-confident and is direct in his dealings with others. He does, however, have a quick temper and has no hesitation in speaking his mind. He has tremendous drive and willpower and has an extremely good memory. The Wood Ox is particularly loyal and devoted to the members of his family and has a most caring nature.

Fire Ox: 1937, 1997

The Fire Ox has a powerful and assertive personality and is a hard and conscientious worker. He holds strong views and has very little patience when things do not go his own way. He can also get carried away in the excitement of the moment and does not always take into account the views of those around him. He nevertheless has many leadership qualities and will often reach positions of power, eminence and wealth. He usually has a small group of loyal and close friends and is very devoted to his family.

Earth Ox: 1949

This Ox sets about everything he does in a sensible and level-headed manner. He is ambitious but also realistic in his aims and is often prepared to work long hours in order to secure his objectives. He is shrewd in financial and business matters and is a very good judge of character. He has a quiet nature and is greatly admired for his sincerity and integrity. He is also very loyal to his family and friends and his views and opinions are often sought.

PROSPECTS FOR THE OX IN 2005

The Chinese New Year starts on 9 February 2005. Until then, the old year, the Year of the Monkey, is still making its presence felt.

The Year of the Monkey (22 January 2004 to 8 February 2005) will have been a busy one for the Ox and as he likes to proceed steadily, he will certainly have felt ill at ease with the pace of some of it. And the closing months indicate little respite in the general activity.

In his work the Ox could find developments taking place with little warning, but by being prepared to make the most of the situations that arise, he can do his prospects much good. August and October 2004 could see some interesting work opportunities.

The closing months of the Monkey year will also see much activity in the Ox's personal life. Domestically, he will have a lot to do, particularly in helping others and arranging family activities as well as carrying out certain plans of his own. In all his activities, he does need to liaise closely with others. As he will find, it is better to benefit from the support others can give rather than keep his thoughts to himself and plough on alone. And in the last quarter of the year he will enjoy some fine family get-togethers.

Socially, too, the Ox will find himself in demand, with many chances to go out and meet up with friends. August, November and December will be especially active socially, and for the unattached, a new friendship or possible romance could add special meaning to this time.

The Year of the Rooster starts on 9 February and will be a much improved one for the Ox. The Rooster year is all for method and order, and this suits the Ox well. Over the next 12 months he will feel more in control of his situation and able to follow through his plans. This is a year for action and achievement.

In his work the aspects are especially encouraging. Although many Oxen will have made good progress in recent years, this may not always have been in the direction they wanted and they may not have been allowed to make the best use of their skills. The Rooster year will give the Ox more chance to progress in the way that *he* wants.

Over the year many Oxen will find themselves well placed to take on greater responsibilities. With their contacts and experience, many will be able to make good progress with their present employer, but will take on duties more in line with the work they have wanted to do for some time. Those Oxen who feel there may be better opportunities elsewhere too should actively follow up any openings that appeal to them. With persistence and

THE OX

determination – two qualities already strong in the Ox – many of them will be successful in securing what can be an important new position. For work opportunities the months from March to early June and October are significant, but generally, with the aspects as they are, whenever the Ox sees a suitable opening he should act quickly.

Often the changes that take place at work will allow the Ox to develop his skills, but if he is offered the chance of further training or sees any courses which he feels could benefit him, he should follow them up. By extending his skills, he will do his prospects much good, and his accomplishments over the Rooster year can be both positive and far-reaching.

As far as money matters are concerned, the Ox will, however, need to be careful. Although the progress he makes in his career will often lead to an increase in income, this is not a year for risks. In particular, if he is thinking of moving or entering into any major financial undertaking, he needs to check the details and obligations he may be taking on as well as obtain appropriate advice. Without vigilance he could find himself losing money or committed to greater expense than necessary. He should also be wary about accepting all that he is told, especially when there are financial implications. This is a year when he should scrutinize important paperwork and be his thorough self.

The Ox's personal life is, though, more positively aspected. In his home life the Ox will value the love and support shown by others, and by being forthcoming with his thoughts and ideas, he will gain a great deal of encouragement. He will also follow the progress of those close to him with much interest and often others will look to him for advice. The Ox is always very much at the centre of domestic life and his role will certainly be appreciated.

However, as with any year, problems will sometimes raise their head. Sometimes these will result from tiredness, or from misunderstandings or a lack of communication. When such problems occur, the Ox should try to talk them through rather than let them linger and possibly escalate or sour what can be a promising year. And when he finds himself with a lot to do, he should not hesitate to ask for assistance. Similarly, when others are under pressure, the help and support he can give will be welcome.

The Ox's social life is well aspected, and while he may be more selective than some signs in the social events he attends, he will often greatly enjoy them. Also, as a result of changes in his work or new interests, he is likely to strike up some new and important friendships over the year.

For the unattached Ox or those enjoying newfound romance, the year is splendidly aspected. Existing romances will often grow stronger, with many Oxen marrying or settling down together, while many unattached Oxen will meet someone who will become special. Romance will certainly beckon, with many currently unattached Oxen seeing their life transformed as a result. For socializing, April to June and the last quarter of the year can be especially promising.

Overall, the Rooster year is a positive one for the Ox. In his work the prospects are especially encouraging, with many Oxen being able to make better use of their strengths and make the progress that they want. Personally, too, the Ox will value the support and love of

THE OX

his family and, for the unattached, romance can bring much happiness. The one area which requires care is finance, and here the Ox needs to be his vigilant and thorough self. Generally, though, this will be a fulfilling year and one which offers the Ox considerable scope and potential.

The Metal Ox

This will be an important and far-reaching year for the Metal Ox. With his determined nature and desire to make the most of his abilities, he will be looking to build on his present position and make further advances, and over the year his industry and application *will* be rewarded.

At work the aspects are especially encouraging and will allow the Metal Ox to put his strengths and talents to good use. He will already have much experience behind him and will be able to build on this over the year. Many Metal Oxen, by virtue of their reputation and knowledge, will find themselves well placed to put in for promotion or singled out for further responsibilities or new initiatives. By taking advantage of chances that arise, the Metal Ox can make important advances in his career.

For those Metal Oxen who feel they are drifting or not making the most of their strengths, as well as for those seeking work, the Rooster year can bring some excellent opportunities. However, to secure the position they feel is right for them, these Metal Oxen will need to remain persistent as well as prepare well when called for interview. This includes finding out more about the position and company to which they are applying as well as stressing what they could bring to the role. By making an effort and showing initiative, these Metal Oxen will often be able to tip the scales in their favour, and once in a new position, will make much of the challenge and opportunity given them. As so many will find, events in 2005 will give them the chance they have been wanting and will help set their career on a more promising path. For work developments, the months from March to early June and October are well aspected.

The Metal Ox should also make full use of any training opportunities that may be available to him, especially if taking on a new position, as these may not only be helpful for him now, but could also alert him to possibilities worth investigating in the future.

The Metal Ox should also aim to make much of his personal interests over the year, particularly those which allow him to draw on his ideas and more creative talents, as they will bring him pleasure as well as often do him good. Again, this is very much a year when the Metal Ox should make the most of his talents.

Financial matters are, however, more awkwardly aspected, and throughout 2005 the Metal Ox will need to be vigilant, particularly if he becomes involved in any transaction concerning his home or property. To avoid problems he does need to study the small print of any agreement he may be considering entering into and seek professional advice when appropriate. This is not a time for risks. The Rooster year can spring some nasty traps for the unwary or careless. Metal Oxen, take note. Also, where possible, the Metal Ox would find it helpful to set some money aside to carry out his plans over the year and, if he

THE OX

is able, consider adding to his longer-term savings. Care and control with money matters *will* make a difference.

The Rooster year will be quite an eventful one for personal matters, with changes indicated in the Metal Ox's home life. Some Metal Oxen could see relations moving for the purposes of education, work or marriage, and some will decide there could be some advantage in moving themselves. As a result, some parts of the year will see much activity. As always, the Metal Ox will play a pivotal role in organizing and overseeing what needs to be done as well as in encouraging others. So much activity will bring times of pressure, but the Metal Oxen's methodical nature will ensure that a great deal is accomplished and that his plans work out well.

Despite the often high level of activity over the year, the Metal Ox's home life will mean a great deal to him and the year will see some especially happy and memorable occasions, including good cause for a family celebration. The Metal Ox will greatly value the support and assistance of his loved ones.

The Metal Ox's social life is also favourably aspected and he will have the opportunity to forge some valuable friendships over the year. For those who are unattached or have let their social life lapse, someone they meet this year could become special. In this respect, too, the Rooster year can be a significant one for the Metal Ox.

In so many ways the Rooster year will bring the Metal Ox the opportunities he has been wanting for so long. However, to benefit, he does need to make the most of the opportunities that arise or that he creates. With determination and resolve – two qualities the Metal Ox certainly possesses – he can make this a special and successful year.

TIP FOR THE YEAR
Make the most of your strengths and talents, particularly in the areas which most interest you. This can lead to some impressive results.

The Water Ox

This will be a significant year for the Water Ox, allowing him to make substantial progress as well as develop both his skills and ideas. It is a year for action and seizing the initiative, and with the right support, much will go in his favour.

As the year starts, though, the Water Ox would do well to consider what he would like to accomplish over the next 12 months. He could find it helpful to discuss his ideas with loved ones and should listen carefully to their views and advice. In some cases they will sense whether the ideas he is considering are right for him and can sometimes suggest other possibilities and approaches. Much can come from discussions held early in the year and once the Water Ox has decided on particular aims, he will find himself better able to direct his attention and energies. His plans can relate to almost any aspect of his life, from domestic projects to developing interests, realizing a personal ambition or furthering his work. With the aspects as they are and a willingness to take positive action, much *is* possible during the year.

At work this is a time for progress, with the Water Ox being able to advance his position over the year. Openings will sometimes arise in unexpected ways as colleagues leave, new positions are created or initiatives launched, and with the experience he has behind him, the Water Ox will often be well placed to benefit. Similarly, if there is a position or type of work he would like to take on, he can again find events moving in his favour. However, when an opportunity does arise, he needs to act quickly and show both his enthusiasm and commitment to any new role. For work opportunities the months from March to early June and October are favoured, but in general this is very much a year when the Water Ox can advance his career.

This also applies to those Water Oxen who feel that prospects are limited in their current position or who are seeking work. By actively looking for new positions, they will often find themselves benefiting from chance developments. Again, once they see an opportunity, they should act quickly and make the most of the situation. Also, once they do secure a new position, many will find the work they are given will allow them to make more of their skills and, as a result, their output and sense of fulfilment will be that much greater. For those Water Oxen who may start the year disillusioned with their situation, this *is* a time to draw a line under the past and start afresh. With determination and a willingness to move forward, they will find events can at last start to turn their way.

The Water Ox will also find this a good year for his own personal interests and despite the many demands on his time, he should not only set a regular time aside for these but consider taking them further. Whether his interests are practical, creative or involve the outdoors in some way, they can bring him much satisfaction. Also, if he is able to meet fellow enthusiasts, this can encourage him and add to his knowledge.

As far as his domestic life is concerned, this will be a busy but often rewarding year for the Water Ox. As always, he will take a keen interest in the activities and progress of his loved ones and give much support. However, he should remember that this is very much a year for dialogue and for doing and planning things together. If he can do so, the understanding and rapport he shares will be that much greater and the year will give rise to many fine occasions, including family holidays and trips and appreciating home improvements.

The Water Ox will also do much to assist more senior relations in 2005 and the time, support and advice he gives will often mean far more than he may realize.

Although the Water Ox will have a lot to occupy his time, it is also important he does not let his social life suffer. Throughout the year he should make sure he keeps in contact with friends as well as going to any events that appeal to him. His social life can provide a valuable balance to his lifestyle. And for any Water Oxen who may have experienced personal difficulties of late, the Rooster year will offer the chance to move forward. By going out more often and involving themselves in new activities and social groups, these Water Oxen will not only give their lives new meaning but also build up a new social circle, and some will meet someone who will quickly become special. Again, if the Water Ox is prepared to take action, the Rooster year will help.

The Water Ox will, though, need to be careful in financial matters over the year and when conducting important transactions, should check the terms and implications. He should also avoid any risky undertakings. Fortunately his usually cautious nature will help, but to avoid problems, he should take care and manage his money well. Water Oxen, take note.

Overall, the Rooster year holds much promise for the Water Ox. It is a time for following up ideas and plans and making the most of talents. With determination and the good fortune and opportunities the year will bring, this can be a significant and successful time.

TIP FOR THE YEAR
Seize the initiative and look to advance. With your talents, ideas and self-belief, a great deal is possible. Go forward and aim for what you want.

The Wood Ox

This will be an exciting year for the Wood Ox, with a great deal happening in several different areas of his life. It will be a busy but often exhilarating time, with the Wood Ox making important headway.

One area which is especially well aspected is his personal life, with the affairs of the heart meaning a great deal. Many existing romances will continue to flourish, with quite a few Wood Oxen deciding to settle down with their partner. And for those who have had a romance turn sour or who are seeking someone special, the Rooster year will bring an upturn in fortune, with many opportunities to meet someone who will quickly become important. Such is the nature of the year that such a meeting could come about in a chance way, but with destiny playing its part. For affairs of the heart, the Rooster year is a splendid time.

The Wood Ox will also value his social life over the year, although this too could see some changes. New interests and changed circumstances could result in the Wood Ox meeting many new people, some of whom will become close friends. There will also be plenty of opportunities for him to go out and enjoy himself, and he will find himself in demand. The months from April to June and the last quarter of the year could see particularly important developments in both the Wood Ox's personal and social life.

The Wood Ox will also take much pleasure from his personal interests, and whether these are of a sporting and outdoor nature or more creative or practical, by spending time on them and developing them further, he will find them bringing him a great deal of satisfaction. Those Wood Oxen who have thought of turning an interest into a vocation can also can make important strides over the year by learning more and becoming more proficient at what they do. Also, all Wood Oxen should take advantage of any facilities available, whether these are clubs and societies in their area, courses or projects that they can do on their own. Expanding their interests can be another rewarding and beneficial aspect of the year.

For those Wood Oxen in education, this will be a significant year, with the Wood Ox's work often having an important bearing on his future. For this reason, he should set about his studies carefully, allowing plenty of time to prepare for exams or complete course work. Fortunately his methodical and organized approach will help, but in

2005 these Wood Oxen will need to remain disciplined and focused. As a result, though, many will find their efforts well rewarded.

For those Wood Oxen in work, again the year will see important developments. Some, having demonstrated their commitment and willingness to learn, will take on greater responsibilities and secure well-deserved promotion in their current organization. Others will decide to look elsewhere. Either way the Wood Ox will be gaining experience as well as discovering more about his strengths. One important feature of the year will be the chance it gives him to determine the direction of his career. Work-wise, this can be a positive time, with late February to early June and October seeing important developments.

Similarly, those Wood Oxen seeking work need to remain active in their quest and not become discouraged, even if certain applications do not go their way. With persistence and effort, many will secure a position which will not only give them valuable experience but also provide an important platform on which to build. Again, the significance of what the Wood Ox achieves in the Rooster year should not be underestimated.

One area which does, though, require care is finance. Although the Wood Ox is usually careful with his money, he should be wary about taking risks or allowing himself to be misled by false promises or claims. He needs to be especially vigilant where accommodation matters are concerned. If he has any doubts it really would be worth seeking guidance as well as checking the terms and implications of any contracts. However, provided the Wood Ox is careful and manages his resources well, he will find that he will be able to do a great deal. Sometimes limited funds will certainly not lessen his enjoyment of the year.

Overall, the Rooster year holds great prospects for the Wood Ox. He has the personality, the strengths and gifts to go far in life and what he does this year will help him to establish an important platform for the future. And friendship and love will make the year all the more special.

TIP FOR THE YEAR
Although much will go in your favour in 2005, do not be discouraged if problems arise. It is by meeting and overcoming them that you will ultimately gain so much. Have faith.

The Fire Ox

This will be a satisfying year for the Fire Ox, particularly as it will allow him to further so many of his plans and activities.

The Fire Ox does tend to have specific areas of interest and as a result will have built up a great deal of specialist knowledge. In 2005 he will be able to make good use of this, not only immersing himself in various personal projects but also sometimes sharing his knowledge with others. His existing interests will bring him much satisfaction, although many Fire Oxen will also be keen to extend their knowledge and skills in other areas, for instance adding to their computer knowledge or finding out about subjects that have aroused their curiosity. By following these up and making the most of the opportunities available, the Fire Ox will find his interests bringing him considerable pleasure during the Rooster year.

THE OX

The Fire Ox will also enjoy any travelling he undertakes over the year and if he sees a break or holiday advertised which appeals to him, he should follow this up. Visits to family and friends living some distance away can also lead to some enjoyable occasions. Travel-wise, there will certainly be some excellent opportunities for the Fire Ox and he should take advantage of them.

As far as his home life is concerned, this will be a full and interesting year. Again the Fire Ox's eager and practical nature will be to the fore and he will often set about projects which will add to the style and comfort of his home. He will also greatly enjoy the activities and interests he can share with his loved ones, with some Fire Oxen deciding to enrol on a course with their partner or devoting more time to a mutual interest. By carrying out activities together, as well as sharing plans and ideas, the Fire Ox will find his home and family life will be all the more meaningful. He will also follow the activities of younger relations with interest and, when he can, will be glad to offer advice or practical support. This will often mean a great deal.

This will also be a positive year as far as his social life is concerned. Although the Fire Ox does tend to have a select group of friends, he will find that by meeting those who share similar interests and by going to events that appeal to him, he will get to meet many new people over the year and will add to his circle of acquaintances. Fire Oxen who keep themselves to themselves and do not tend to go out much too should consider joining a local interest group. They will not only find themselves welcome, but will also enjoy some convivial occasions. Fire Oxen who may be lonely or wish to meet others would do well to give this careful consideration. It really can make the year all the more rewarding.

While the Rooster year holds such encouraging prospects, no year is ever free from its problems and, if any difficult matter does arise, the Fire Ox should be open about it and seek the advice of others. If necessary, talking to experts could be especially helpful. And, as with others of his sign, he must also be careful when dealing with financial matters, particularly if entering into agreements or completing financially related forms. If he has any doubts, it is essential that he obtains proper advice. This is a year for thoroughness and care. Fire Oxen, take note.

Overall, though, this *is* a positively aspected year for the Fire Ox and by spending time on activities and projects that appeal to him, he will enjoy a great deal of satisfaction, as well as be encouraged by the support of others.

TIP FOR THE YEAR
Look to further your interests, either existing ones or new ones which appeal to you. This can add something extra to this already promising year.

The Earth Ox

The Earth Ox is tenacious. When he has set himself a goal or objective he will work steadily towards it, even if it sometimes takes many years to attain. And in 2005, his commitment and patience will be well rewarded. This is a year for progress, for realizing long-term aims and for enjoyment. Much is possible and the aspects are firmly on the Earth Ox's side.

THE OX

As far as his work is concerned, this will be a significant year. In view of his years of experience, the Earth Ox will find himself in an excellent position to make further progress and will be well placed for any promotion opportunities that arise. Also over the year he will be able to make more of his expertise and this too will bring him a greater satisfaction.

Similarly, for those Earth Oxen who have been wanting to switch to another type of work or who are seeking work, the Rooster year will give rise to some excellent opportunities. By putting themselves forward and emphasizing their experience and the ways in which they could contribute, many Earth Oxen will be successful in gaining an interesting position which suits their talents well. The months from March to early June and October could see promising developments.

The progress that the Earth Ox makes in his work will lead to an increase in income and some Earth Oxen could also benefit from an additional sum of money over the year, perhaps the fruition of a policy, an investment or gift. However, while his earning abilities may be good, the Earth Ox does still need to manage his resources carefully. When entering into important agreements, especially if related to accommodation, he must be thorough and check the details and implications fully. Without such vigilance, there is a risk that he could be disadvantaged. He would also find it helpful to set funds aside for forthcoming plans and requirements as well as, if possible, reducing his borrowings. By managing his finances carefully, he will fare better and often find himself able to do more. This is a year for care and thoroughness.

Recreational pursuits are more favourably aspected, and whether developing existing interests, taking up something new or perhaps travelling, the Earth Ox will enjoy his leisure time. He should also give some consideration to what *he* would like to do. If there are particular places he would like to visit or holiday destinations that appeal to him, he should follow them up. Not only will he benefit from the change of scene but the Rooster year could also help him to realize some long-held aims.

As far as his domestic life is concerned, this will be a satisfying year. Although everyone in the Earth Ox's household will be busy with their own activities and concerns, by spending time together and being forthcoming over plans and ideas, all will benefit. At busy times, the Earth Ox's ability to organize will prove a useful asset and those around him will often be thankful for his solid and dependable nature.

In addition to the projects and general household activities the Earth Ox will tackle over the year, he can look forward to some fine family occasions, perhaps celebrating a graduation, a wedding, the birth of a grandchild or the progress of a loved one. The activities and achievements of those close to him will always mean a great deal. Family bonds *are* very precious to the Earth Ox.

As he is often so busy, he does tend to be quite selective in attending social events, but it is important that he does not neglect his social life and he would do well to go out regularly over the Rooster year. Any Earth Ox who may feel lonely or have had some recent personal difficulties will find the Rooster year can bring the gift of an important friendship, and for some, romance too. To benefit, though, the Earth Ox should give himself the opportunity to meet and get to know others. His social life will also bring an important balance to his lifestyle.

Overall, the Rooster year is a highly favourable one for the Earth Ox and by making the most of his strengths and the chances that arise, he will find this a successful and fulfilling year.

TIP FOR THE YEAR
Do make sure your lifestyle has balance and in spite of everything you may have to do, spend time enjoying and appreciating the rewards you have worked so hard for.

FAMOUS OXEN

King Abdullah of Jordan, Robert Altman, Hans Christian Andersen, Johann Sebastian Bach, Warren Beatty, Kate Beckinsale, David Blaine, Napoleon Bonaparte, Rory Bremner, Albert Camus, Jim Carrey, Johnny Carson, Charlie Chaplin, Melanie Chisholm (Mel C), George Clooney, Jean Cocteau, Natalie Cole, Bill Cosby, Tom Courtenay, Tony Curtis, Diana, Princess of Wales, Marlene Dietrich, Walt Disney, Patrick Duffy, Harry Enfield, Jane Fonda, Gerald Ford, Edward Fox, Michael J. Fox, Peter Gabriel, Richard Gere, Ricky Gervais, Handel, King Harald V of Norway, Adolf Hitler, Dustin Hoffman, Anthony Hopkins, Saddam Hussein, Billy Joel, King Juan Carlos of Spain, B. B. King, Mark Knopfler, Burt Lancaster, Jessica Lange, Kate Moss, Alison Moyet, Eddie Murphy, Paul Newman, Jack Nicholson, Leslie Nielsen, Gwyneth

Paltrow, Oscar Peterson, Colin Powell, Paula Radcliffe, Robert Redford, Lionel Richie, Tim Roth, Rubens, Greg Rusedski, Meg Ryan, Jean Sibelius, Sissy Spacek, Bruce Springsteen, Meryl Streep, Lady Thatcher, Alan Titchmarsh, Scott F. Turow, Vincent van Gogh, Gore Vidal, Minette Walters, Zoë Wanamaker, Sigourney Weaver, the Duke of Wellington, Barbara Windsor, W. B. Yeats.

26 JANUARY 1914 ~ 13 FEBRUARY 1915	*Wood Tiger*
13 FEBRUARY 1926 ~ 1 FEBRUARY 1927	*Fire Tiger*
31 JANUARY 1938 ~ 18 FEBRUARY 1939	*Earth Tiger*
17 FEBRUARY 1950 ~ 5 FEBRUARY 1951	*Metal Tiger*
5 FEBRUARY 1962 ~ 24 JANUARY 1963	*Water Tiger*
23 JANUARY 1974 ~ 10 FEBRUARY 1975	*Wood Tiger*
9 FEBRUARY 1986 ~ 28 JANUARY 1987	*Fire Tiger*
28 JANUARY 1998 ~ 15 FEBRUARY 1999	*Earth Tiger*

THE
TIGER

THE PERSONALITY OF THE TIGER

> I'm sure you have a theme: the theme of life. You can embellish it or desecrate it, but it's your theme, and as long as you follow it, you will experience harmony and peace of mind.
>
> *Agatha Christie, a Tiger*

The Tiger is born under the sign of courage. He is a charismatic figure and usually holds very firm views. He is strong-willed and determined, and sets about most of his activities with tremendous energy and enthusiasm. He is very alert and quick-witted and his mind is forever active. He is a highly original thinker and is nearly always brimming with new ideas or full of enthusiasm for some new project or scheme.

The Tiger adores challenges and loves to get involved in anything which he thinks has an exciting future or which catches his imagination. He is prepared to take risks and does not like to be bound either by convention or the dictates of others. He likes to be free to act as he chooses and at least once during his life he will throw caution to the wind and go off and do the things he wants to do.

The Tiger does, however, have a somewhat restless nature. Even though he is often prepared to throw himself wholeheartedly into a project, his initial enthusiasm can soon wane if he sees something more appealing. He can also be rather impulsive and there will be occasions in his life when he acts in a manner he later regrets. If the Tiger were to think things through or be prepared to persevere in his various activities, he would almost certainly enjoy a greater degree of success.

Fortunately the Tiger is lucky in most of his enterprises, but should things not work out as he hoped, he is liable to suffer from severe bouts of depression and it will often take him a long time to recover. His life often consists of a series of ups and downs.

The Tiger is, however, very adaptable. He has an adventurous spirit and rarely stays in the same place for long. In the early stages of his life he is likely to try his hand at several different jobs and he will also change his residence fairly frequently.

The Tiger is very honest and open in his dealings with others. He hates any sort of hypocrisy or falsehood. He is also well known for being blunt and forthright and has no hesitation in speaking his mind. He can be rebellious at times, particularly against any form of petty authority, and while this can lead him into conflict with others, he is never one to shrink from an argument or avoid standing up for what he believes is right.

The Tiger is a natural leader and can invariably rise to the top of his chosen profession. He does not, however, care for anything too bureaucratic or detailed and he does not like to obey orders. He can be stubborn and obstinate and throughout his life he likes to retain a certain amount of independence in his actions and be responsible to no one but himself. He likes to consider that all his achievements are due to his own efforts and he will not ask for support from others if he can avoid it.

Ironically, despite his self-confidence and leadership qualities, the Tiger can be indecisive and will often delay making a major decision until the very last moment. He can also be sensitive to criticism.

Although the Tiger is capable of earning large sums of money, he is rather a spendthrift and does not always put his money to its best use. He can also be most generous and will often shower lavish gifts on friends and relations.

The Tiger cares very much for his reputation and the image that he tries to project. He carries himself with an air of dignity and authority and enjoys being the centre of attention. He is very adept at attracting publicity, both for himself and for the causes he supports.

The Tiger often marries young and he will find himself best suited to those born under the signs of the Pig, Dog, Horse and Goat. He can also get on well with the Rat, Rabbit and Rooster, but will find the Ox and Snake a bit too quiet and serious for his liking, and he will be highly irritated by the Monkey's rather mischievous and inquisitive ways. He will also find it difficult to get on with another Tiger or a Dragon – both partners will want to dominate the relationship and could find it difficult to compromise on even the smallest of matters.

The Tigress is lively, witty and a marvellous hostess at parties. She takes great care over her appearance and is usually most attractive. She can be a very doting mother and while she believes in letting her children have their freedom, she makes an excellent teacher and will ensure that her children are well brought up and want for nothing. Like her male counterpart, she has numerous interests and likes to have sufficient independence and freedom to go off and do the things she wants to do. She has a most caring and generous nature.

The Tiger has many commendable qualities. He is honest, courageous and often a source of inspiration to others. Providing he can curb the wilder excesses of his restless nature, he is almost certain to lead a fulfilling and satisfying life.

THE FIVE DIFFERENT TYPES OF TIGER

In addition to the 12 signs of the Chinese zodiac there are five elements, and these have a strengthening or moderating influence on the sign. The effects of the five elements on the Tiger are described below, together with the years in which the elements were exercising their influence. Therefore those Tigers born in 1950 are Metal Tigers, those born in 1962 are Water Tigers, and so on.

Metal Tiger: 1950

The Metal Tiger has an assertive and outgoing personality. He is very ambitious and while his aims may change from time to time, he will work relentlessly until he has obtained what he wants. He can, however, be impatient for results and become highly strung if things do not work out as he would like. He is distinctive in his appearance and is admired and respected by many.

Water Tiger: 1962

This Tiger has a wide variety of interests and is always eager to experiment with new ideas or satisfy his adventurous nature by going off to explore distant lands. He is versatile, shrewd and has a kindly nature. He tends to remain calm in a crisis, although he can be annoyingly indecisive at times. He communicates well with others and through his many capabilities and persuasive nature usually achieves what he wants in life. He is also highly imaginative and is often a gifted orator or writer.

Wood Tiger: 1914, 1974

The Wood Tiger has a friendly and pleasant personality. He is less independent than some of the other types of Tiger and is more prepared to work with others to secure a desired objective. However, he does have a tendency to jump from one thing to another and can easily become distracted. He is usually very popular, has a large circle of friends and invariably leads a busy and enjoyable social life. He also has a good sense of humour.

Fire Tiger: 1926, 1986

The Fire Tiger sets about everything he does with great verve and enthusiasm. He loves action and is always ready to throw himself wholeheartedly into anything which catches his imagination. He has many leadership qualities and is capable of communicating his ideas and enthusiasm to others. He is very much an optimist and can be most generous. He has a likeable nature and can be a witty and persuasive speaker.

Earth Tiger: 1938, 1998

This Tiger is responsible and level-headed. He studies everything objectively and tries to be scrupulously fair in all his dealings. Unlike other Tigers, he is prepared to specialize in certain areas rather than get distracted by other matters, but he can become so involved with what he is doing that he does not always take into account the opinions of those around him. He has good business sense and is usually very successful in later life. He has a large circle of friends and pays great attention to both his appearance and his reputation.

PROSPECTS FOR THE TIGER IN 2005

The Chinese New Year starts on 9 February 2005. Until then, the old year, the Year of the Monkey, is still making its presence felt.

The Year of the Monkey (22 January 2004 to 8 February 2005) will have been a reasonable one for the Tiger and while he will enjoy the remaining months, he will need to remain careful as he sets about his various activities. This is not a time for risks or too much independent-mindedness.

In his work the Tiger will fare best by liaising closely with others and acting as a team member rather than trying to do too much on his own. With the support of others, he will not only be in a stronger position now but will also help his prospects in the more favourable Rooster year that follows. Also, any additional experience he can acquire at this time can prove useful in the year ahead.

The Tiger's personal life will get busier as the Monkey year draws to a close, with opportunities to go out and meet others and plenty to do and arrange. However, while he will often revel in all this activity, he does need to be mindful of those around him. To be inflexible when making plans or not listen closely to others could lead to some awkward situations. Should he be involved in any difference of opinion, again he needs to deal with the situation carefully and tactfully. Both his domestic and social life can be rewarding, but care and consideration *are* needed.

The closing months of the year can also bring opportunities for travel and if the Tiger wants to have a break or receives invitations to visit others, he should follow these up. Times away in the last quarter will often be enjoyable and will do him good.

The Year of the Rooster starts on 9 February and will be an important one for the Tiger. During the year there will be some excellent chances for him to improve on his present position and his personal life will see much activity. However, to benefit, the Tiger will need to make the most of the prevailing situations rather than adopt too independent (or wayward) an approach. This is another year which calls for care and keeping a check on his sometimes impulsive nature.

THE TIGER

At work the Tiger's prospects are encouraging and by making the most of his strengths, he can look forward to making good headway. However, his best results will come from concentrating on the areas in which he already has expertise rather than venturing into anything different. Also, to benefit from the opportunities the year will bring, he will need to be fairly flexible in his attitude. If, for instance, new methods and schemes are introduced, he should be prepared to make the most of them rather than appear resistant to change. As many Tigers will find, new initiatives and proposals can sometimes lead to the creation of new posts which could benefit them. Similarly, as colleagues leave, more senior positions may become vacant which the Tiger will be well placed to apply for. It is for this reason that he has to be careful not to undermine his reputation by digging his heels in. March, May, July and November could see some interesting work developments and the chance to take on more interesting and fulfilling duties.

Those Tigers who are seeking work or who feel their present prospects are limited will also find that by following up interesting openings and remaining persistent, they will often be successful in obtaining a new position, and importantly, one with potential. When taking on any new role, the Tiger should show himself willing to learn. With the right attitude he can quickly make a favourable impression and do his prospects much good.

Another positive feature of the year will be the way it allows the Tiger to get to know others in his line of work. With his outgoing nature, he will impress many and this again will be to his advantage both in this and following years.

The progress the Tiger makes in his work will lead to a welcome increase in his income, and as far as financial matters are concerned, this will be a positive year. Some Tigers may also be able to supplement their earnings with some additional or freelance work and could be blessed with a certain amount of luck, receiving a gift or bonus or even enjoying a competition win. However, to benefit from any financial upturn, the Tiger should use his money carefully, planning his major purchases in advance and setting funds aside for specific requirements, including, if possible, adding to his savings.

The Tiger will enjoy the travel opportunities that will arise over the year and should give some thought to the places he would like to visit. With the aspects as they are, he could see some impressive sights in 2005 and enjoy his times away.

The Tiger's personal life also promises to be active. Domestically, some parts of the year will be especially busy. One reason for this will be the plans the Tiger will be keen to carry out, with his practical and active nature being to the fore this year. Some Tigers will decide to redecorate and alter certain rooms, some will mount an efficiency drive and rid themselves of accumulated items and some will decide to move to more suitable accommodation. Whatever the Tiger does, it will involve time, effort and disruption, but despite the pressures and occasional fraught moment, the end result will be worth it.

Throughout any practical undertaking the Tiger should, though, make every effort to liaise with others and listen to their thoughts and suggestions. This way problems and differences of opinion can be averted and the often considerable tasks will be easier to accomplish. While the Tiger's domestic life will often be busy, the year will nevertheless contain some very rewarding occasions and the Tiger will enjoy the time spent in sharing interests and enjoying the company of his loved ones.

The Tiger's social life will also see much activity, with the changes in his work leading to him meeting many new people and increasing his social circle. On a social level this can be a pleasing year, but if at any time a difference of opinion should arise, the Tiger should tread carefully. Although he may not feel the issue is that important, to be too dismissive or ignore the feelings of others could seriously undermine a friendship. In awkward situations, the Tiger does need to be tactful, careful and understanding. Tigers, take note. March, June, October and December could see much social activity and be good times for meeting others. Any Tiger who is keen to build up his social life or would welcome romance will find the Rooster year certainly holds encouraging prospects. By taking the action to bring about what he wants – and for new friendships, this often means going out more and joining in with group activities – he can achieve a great deal.

In 2005 the Tiger will certainly have much in his favour but it is a case of making the most of the situations and opportunities that arise. The Tiger may have his own ideas, but this is a year for realism and for being practical. With care, however, this can be a prosperous and pleasurable time.

The Metal Tiger

This year holds considerable potential for the Metal Tiger, although just how he fares is very much in his own hands. The year will contain many fine opportunities, but to benefit the Metal Tiger will need to show some flexibility in his outlook. Also, whenever he has ideas he wishes to pursue, no matter what area of his life they may concern, he does need to talk to others and consider the advice and feedback he is given. This is not a year for being too independent in attitude or acting without support.

In his work the prospects are especially encouraging and will give the Metal Tiger the chance to put his skills and knowledge to more effective use. As a result of his experience, others will often look to him for guidance, advice and sometimes training too. In the Rooster year the Metal Tiger's experience will certainly be in demand. Although there will be opportunities for promotion over the year and offers of additional responsibilities, some Metal Tigers will decide to remain where they are, feeling fulfilled in their present role and satisfied in the way they are able to use their skills. Some even may reduce their hours in order to give themselves time for other activities. However, for those who would welcome a new career challenge, the Rooster year will contain some excellent opportunities. When these appear, the Metal Tiger should be swift in following them up. By demonstrating his desire to move ahead, he will often be successful in securing the responsibilities he seeks.

Similarly, those Metal Tigers seeking work should remain persistent. While sometimes competition for certain posts will be considerable, by showing initiative and stressing their skills and what they could bring to the position, many will be given the chance they have sought for so long. March, May, July and November could see some particularly interesting possibilities.

Another positive area will concern the Metal Tiger's personal development. The Metal Tiger possesses a keen and inquisitive nature and if he should be offered training or see a course that appeals to him, even if it is one he has to pursue in his own time, he should follow it up. Again, much can happen as a result of his initiative.

The Rooster year is also favourably aspected for travel and the Metal Tiger should aim to go away at some time over the year. By choosing his destinations carefully as well as following up any invitations he receives, he will enjoy himself as well as benefit from the rest and change a holiday can bring. Many Metal Tigers could also be tempted by some short bargain breaks or go away on a whim. Travel-wise, this can be an interesting and positive year.

The Metal Tiger's financial prospects also indicate an improvement, with many Metal Tigers increasing their income over the year as well as receiving funds from another source. However, while this upturn will be welcome, the Metal Tiger should keep tabs on his spending and would be wise not to let any surplus funds lead him into too many impulsive or extravagant buys. By planning his purchases well, he will be pleased with many of his acquisitions as well as the various activities he is able to carry out. In addition, for those Metal Tigers who enjoy collecting or appreciate more aesthetic items, there could be some excellent finds and acquisitions over the year.

In so much of what he does the Metal Tiger will be well supported. However, to benefit, he does need to listen carefully to the views of others and be prepared to amend his ideas in the light of what he is told. This is not a year for inflexibility or too much single-mindedness. In his home life in particular, he should be forthcoming with his thoughts and ideas. Whether these concern domestic projects, any worries or pressures he may have or plans he is considering, if he lets others know what is on his mind he will find himself being helped and encouraged more. Also, such openness will be good for general understanding and rapport.

The Metal Tiger will also enjoy time spent on family activities and home projects over the year, and with travel well aspected, he would do well to give thought to a family holiday that everyone could enjoy. Domestically, this can be a busy but rewarding year.

With his outgoing nature the Metal Tiger also sets much store by his social life and he will enjoy socializing over the year, with late February, March, June and December seeing much activity. In view of everything the Metal Tiger will get involved with over the year, he will find his circle of friends and acquaintances set to grow, and any Metal Tiger who may be lonely will find that a new friendship made after an almost fortuitous encounter could become very special.

In so many respects the aspects are firmly on the Metal Tiger's side, but to benefit he does need to be mindful of the prevailing situations and the attitudes of others and be prepared to adapt accordingly. By doing so, he can make this a personally satisfying *and* successful year.

TIP FOR THE YEAR
Although you may have your own ideas and plans, do consult others. This is not a year for acting alone or for being too independent in outlook, especially if you are to benefit from the fine aspects that prevail.

The Water Tiger

This year holds encouraging prospects for the Water Tiger, with most areas of his life going well.

In his work there will be excellent opportunities for him to build on his present position and throughout the year he should positively consider any promotion opportunities, chances to transfer to other duties and any training that may be offered. By making the most of these, he will not only add to his experience but also make good headway.

For those Water Tigers seeking work, the year will also contain some good opportunities, with March, May, July and November seeing some good possibilities. However, the Water Tiger will generally be successful by going after positions in the areas in which he is most skilled rather than looking for anything too different. Once in a position, however, by demonstrating his keenness to master his work, he will be quick to impress and will mark himself out for further responsibilities in the future. This is a good year to make progress, but the Water Tiger does need to show willing, use his skills well and concentrate his efforts on the types of work he is most familiar with and best suited for.

Also, with the Water Tiger's effectiveness as a communicator, if his work or his personal interests involve him in writing, speaking or giving presentations, or place him in the public eye, he should make the most of his talents. By doing so he can make quite an impression and can look forward to some well-deserved successes.

This also applies to his hobbies and interests. By setting time aside for these and looking to develop them further, the Water Tiger will find them bringing him both pleasure and satisfaction. Whether his interests are creative, practical or purely recreational, they will often be a welcome contrast to his usual activities as well as help him relax and unwind.

Travel, too, is favourably aspected and the Water Tiger should aim to go away at some time over the year. If there is a particular destination that appeals to him or he is tempted away for a short break, he should follow this up. He will benefit from the rest and change of scene that his travels will bring as well as often enjoy himself a great deal.

As far as finance is concerned, the progress the Water Tiger makes in his work will often lead to an increase in his income and some Water Tigers could find they are able to supplement this by putting an interest or skill to profitable use. The Water Tiger's earning ability will certainly be in good form in the Rooster year, with his commitment and enterprise being well rewarded. To benefit from the positive trends the Water Tiger should, though, manage his finances well and plan ahead rather than proceed in too much of an ad hoc way. With care and consideration, he will be able to do and enjoy a great deal as well as improve his general financial position.

Domestically, this will be a busy year. With all the Water Tiger's own activities as well as those of his loved

THE TIGER

ones, there will nearly always be something happening. It is for this reason that the Water Tiger needs to regularly consult those around him and liaise over various activities. Also, he should try to ensure that some time is set aside for spending together rather than for each family member to become preoccupied with their own concerns. This can make a real difference to family life.

In addition, the Water Tiger will do much to help others over the year, with both younger and more senior relatives being grateful for his support and assistance. Some Water Tigers could see a family member leave home, perhaps for the purposes of education, work or marriage, and again the Water Tiger's help and advice can make what can be a big transition run more smoothly. In 2005 his thoughtfulness will be valued by many.

The Water Tiger's social life will also see much activity and his personal interests and travelling will often lead to him making new friends. Over the year, his circle of friends and acquaintances is set to grow appreciably, and for those Water Tigers who would welcome a new friendship or even romance, the year holds excellent prospects. With his warm and genial nature, the Water Tiger will certainly find his social life going well.

So much can go in the Water Tiger's favour in the Rooster year, but it is a case of making the most of his strengths and qualities rather than for striking off at new tangents or being too independent in attitude or outlook. If he bears this in mind and makes the most of the opportunities that arise, then this can be a highly successful year for him.

TIP FOR THE YEAR
Look to further your skills and personal interests, as they will not only bring you much satisfaction but can often have other benefits too.

The Wood Tiger

The Wood Tiger is set to make good progress in the Rooster year, although the level of his success is very much in his own hands. He possesses many fine qualities, including the ability to get on well with many people, but he does have a tendency to spread his energies widely and despite his good intentions, does not always finish what he starts. This is something he must watch in the Rooster year. To make the most of his potential he needs to decide upon his priorities and concentrate on them. This is a year when focus and determined effort really can lead to some impressive results.

At work in particular, many Wood Tigers will have gained much experience and seen considerable change in recent years and the Rooster year will give them the chance to build on this. In many cases, the Wood Tiger's experience will lead to him being given greater responsibilities and the chance to put his ideas into practice. For those with their sights set high, significant promotion opportunities could beckon. However, in the Rooster year, the Wood Tiger should concentrate his attention in the areas he knows well and focus on his best skills.

With his genial and assured manner, he will certainly impress many and throughout the year he should aim to add to his circle of contacts and get to meet others in similar lines of work. By becoming better known, he will not only find himself benefiting from the advice and support he is given but also helping his future prospects.

For those Wood Tigers seeking work or feeling in a rut, again the year can offer some important opportunities. Admittedly, competition for some positions will be keen and not all applications may go the Wood Tiger's way, but by keeping faith with himself and concentrating on openings which suit his skills and experience, he may well be successful in securing what can be a significant new post. Pleasingly, too, such a position will not only offer a new incentive but also be a base from which to progress.

As with any year, problems and pressures will sometimes arise, but by showing his tenacious qualities and dealing effectively with the situations before him, the Wood Tiger will learn a great deal and enhance his reputation. For work opportunities, late February, March, May, July and November are the most favourable months.

The headway the Wood Tiger makes in his work will lead to an increase in income and financially this will be a positive year. However, with his many obligations as well as some of his accommodation and travel plans, the Wood Tiger would do well to manage his finances carefully. Also, if he has large borrowings, he should consider reducing these as well as reviewing his financial position. In some cases he could find he has funds that could be moved to higher-yielding accounts or subscriptions and outgoings that are no longer necessary. By looking at his current situation and taking better control of his finances, he can improve his overall position.

With travel favourably aspected, the Wood Tiger would also do well to go away for a holiday or break over the year. A change of scene will not only do him good but he will often enjoy his time away and satisfy his adventurous Tiger nature.

He will also obtain much pleasure from his personal interests and despite the many other pressures on his time should make sure he sets a regular time aside for recreational activities and pursuits. Also, those Wood Tigers who have creative interests should aim to promote what they do, as they could be considerably encouraged by feedback given. This is a year when the Wood Tiger's strengths and talents will be appreciated.

As far as the Wood Tiger's domestic life is concerned, this will be a full and busy year. By making time for his loved ones and sharing interests and plans, however, he will enjoy many special occasions. In addition, he will give much valuable encouragement and advice to those around him and his interest and support will count for a great deal. Domestically, this can be a rewarding year.

The Wood Tiger's social life is also pleasingly aspected and he will have the chance to attend to a wide range of occasions and gatherings. For those Wood Tigers who would welcome new friends and a more active social life, the Rooster year can bring some wonderful opportunities and very often the chance to meet someone who will become important. For socializing, March, June, October and December could be especially active.

Generally, the Rooster year holds encouraging prospects for the Wood Tiger, but it is very much a case of making the most of his experience and skills and the prevailing situations. With a willing attitude and good use of his time and strengths, though, he can make this a significant and successful year.

TIP FOR THE YEAR
Organize your time well and concentrate on your priorities. This way your results will not only be more substantial but can also help reduce some of the pressure you may be under.

The Fire Tiger

The Rooster year holds excellent prospects for the Fire Tiger and during it he will make important progress as well as enjoy himself a great deal.

His personal life is particularly well aspected and with his genial and outgoing nature, he will find himself in great demand. In addition, as many Fire Tigers will move or change their circumstances in some way over the year, they will find themselves meeting new people and widening their circle of friends and acquaintances. For socializing, March, June and the months from October to December are especially favourable, but such is the nature of the year that the Fire Tiger will almost always have something to look forward to.

This can also be a good year for romance and while the path of love rarely runs smoothly, many Fire Tigers will meet someone who will become special as the year develops, and for some, true love will blossom. In this respect, too, the Rooster year can be a significant one.

Over the year the Fire Tiger will value the support given by close friends and whenever he has uncertainties or feels under pressure, he should not hesitate to tell others about his concerns. Sometimes someone else can provide the reassurance he needs or the advice he is given can lead to new possibilities and approaches. This year the Fire Tiger should not hesitate to draw on his friends' advice if necessary. This is, after all, another important aspect of friendship.

The Fire Tiger will take pleasure from his interests over the year and will derive much satisfaction from adding to his knowledge and taking his interests further. For those Fire Tigers keen on sport, travel and the outdoors, the year will certainly bring some memorable times, and throughout the year they should actively follow up their ideas and spend time in ways they enjoy. With travel well aspected, the Fire Tiger should also make the most of any opportunities and offers that arise. Many Fire Tigers could travel considerable distances over the year, sometimes to interesting and impressive destinations.

This will also be an important year both academically and professionally. For those Fire Tigers in education, there will be exams to be prepared for and much material to be covered. With his results often having a significant bearing on his future, the Fire Tiger would do well to tackle his work steadily and thoroughly rather than leave too much to the last moment. Indeed, one important feature of the Rooster year is that good organization does pay off and this will certainly be true for those currently involved in study.

For those Fire Tigers in employment or seeking work, the year can also bring important developments. With his keen and ambitious nature the Fire Tiger may have visions of his future career, but in the Rooster year it is very much a case of making the most of current conditions. Sometimes the type of work the Fire Tiger desires may not be easy to obtain, but he should not lose heart. By making the most of any opening he is given, he will be adding to his experience in some way as well as having a base from which to develop. And even though sometimes his work may be uninspiring or routine, by showing commitment he will mark himself out as someone with potential. He is, after all, at the start of his working life and the Rooster year will provide him with the chance to get some excellent experience. For work developments March, May, July and November are favourable months, but by being prepared to adapt and make the most of the prevailing situations throughout the year, the Fire Tiger can make this a productive and important time.

As far as finance is concerned, the Fire Tiger's resourceful nature will be to his advantage this year and whether in work or studying, he will find he is able to do a great deal with the money he has. However, he does need to manage his money well and take particular care when entering into agreements. This includes reading the small print and seeking clarification or advice about any uncertainties. Although this is a reasonable year for money matters, it is not one for risks or carelessness.

Also, while the Fire Tiger may like to retain a certain independence in his actions, he should not hesitate to talk over his ideas, plans and activities with family members, especially more senior ones. By being forthcoming he will not only benefit from the advice he receives but could also be given further assistance and encouragement, sometimes in ways he may not have anticipated. His close relations do think highly of him and in 2005 he will have good reason to value their support and affection.

Overall, this will be an important year for the Fire Tiger with the progress he makes and the experience and qualifications he gains helping his future progress. His interests, social life and good friendships will also help make this a special time.

TIP FOR THE YEAR
Be flexible in outlook and make the most of the chances that are available, even though they may not fit in entirely with what you had in mind. Each positive step you take *will* be a step to build on.

The Earth Tiger

The Rooster year holds good prospects for the Earth Tiger, particularly as it will give him the chance to follow through many of his plans and ideas as well as further his interests. Also, he will be well supported in most of his activities.

One area which will be especially satisfying will be his personal interests, and by spending time on them and setting himself some projects to do, he will find them bringing him pleasure and often being an absorbing use of his time. Also, with his keen and inquisitive nature, he could be tempted to follow up new subjects that have caught his interest. For some Earth Tigers, this could involve adding to their computer knowledge or learning a

THE TIGER

new skill, but whatever he does, by making the most of his ideas and the opportunities available to him, the Earth Tiger will be pleased with what he is able to accomplish.

Where possible he should also try to involve his loved ones in his interests, as he will find pursuits and projects that can be carried out together can often be all the more satisfying. Some Earth Tigers might even decide to take up a new interest or enrol on a course with a partner or friend. Again, they will find that doing this together can make it more fun and purposeful.

This also applies to any household or garden projects the Earth Tiger may have in mind. Not only will he benefit from a pooling of ideas and talents, but he will also find that carrying them out with others can often make them easier to accomplish. This is one of the key messages for the Earth Tiger in 2005: so much more will be gained by involving others.

Over the year the Earth Tiger will follow the activities of family members with fond interest and will do much to help and advise those dear to him. His good judgement and ability to empathize will be greatly appreciated. Also, he can look forward to some pleasing family developments, including the successes enjoyed by younger relations, some of which will give rise to a possible family celebration.

However, while the Earth Tiger's family life can go well and mean a great deal to him, no year is without its problems and the Rooster year will be no exception. If any difference of opinion or disagreement should arise, the Earth Tiger should try to deal with it quickly and in a way that is satisfactory to everyone involved. As he will find, it is better to sort out difficulties early rather than let them escalate or linger in the background. Also, should any matter arise which causes the Earth Tiger concern, especially involving paperwork, bureaucracy or some financial transaction, he should seek the advice from a helpline or competent adviser rather than deal with the matter single-handedly. With awkward problems, he should remember that help is at hand should he need it.

The Rooster year is, though, a positive one for financial matters and many Earth Tigers can look forward to receiving some extra funds over the year. However, to make the most of his finances, the Earth Tiger should plan his more substantial purchases carefully, taking the time to consider the different ranges, options and prices. This way he will often obtain items that are more suitable as well as better value. With travel favourably aspected, he should also set funds aside for going away at some time over the year and if there is any particular destination he is keen to visit, he should make enquiries and see what is possible. He could also benefit from some strokes of luck and if he sees a competition which interests him or draws on his skills or knowledge, he would do well to enter it.

The Earth Tiger will also value going out over the year, whether to social events that appeal to him or to meet up with friends, and he should follow up his ideas and any invitations he receives. Those Earth Tigers who would welcome more company will find that joining an interest group or becoming more involved in local activities or even charity work will often lead to a fuller and more rewarding social life.

Overall, the Rooster year holds much promise for the Earth Tiger, particularly in the way that it will allow him to follow through his ideas and further his interests. And by joining with others and making the most of the opportunities that arise, he will find this a satisfying and personally rewarding year.

TIP FOR THE YEAR
Take advantage of the positive nature of the year and act upon your ideas and plans. With the support of others and the pleasure that many of your activities will bring, this is very much a year for action – and for enjoyment.

FAMOUS TIGERS

Debbie Allen, Kofi Annan, Sir David Attenborough, Queen Beatrix of the Netherlands, Victoria Beckham, Beethoven, Tony Bennett, Tom Berenger, Chuck Berry, Jon Bon Jovi, Sir Richard Branson, Emily Brontë, Garth Brooks, Mel Brooks, Isambard Kingdom Brunel, Agatha Christie, Charlotte Church, Phil Collins, Robbie Coltrane, Sheryl Crow, Tom Cruise, Penelope Cruz, Charles de Gaulle, Leonardo DiCaprio, Emily Dickinson, David Dimbleby, Dwight Eisenhower, Queen Elizabeth II, Enya, Roberta Flack, E. M. Forster, Frederick Forsyth, Jodie Foster, Crystal Gayle, Elliott Gould, Buddy Greco, Alan Greenspan, Germaine Greer, Ed Harris, Hugh Hefner, Tim Henman, William Hurt, Jewel, Ray Kroc, Stan Laurel, Jay Leno, Paul Martin, Groucho Marx, Karl Marx, Marilyn Monroe, Demi Moore, Eric Morecambe, Alanis Morissette, Jeremy Paxman, Marco Polo, Beatrix Potter, John Prescott, the Princess Royal, Renoir, Kenny Rogers, Dame Joan

Sutherland, Dylan Thomas, Liv Ullman, Jon Voight, Julie Walters, H. G. Wells, Oscar Wilde, Robbie Williams, Dr Rowan Williams, Tennessee Williams, Terry Wogan, Stevie Wonder, William Wordsworth.

29 JANUARY 1903 ~ 15 FEBRUARY 1904	*Water Rabbit*
14 FEBRUARY 1915 ~ 2 FEBRUARY 1916	*Wood Rabbit*
2 FEBRUARY 1927 ~ 22 JANUARY 1928	*Fire Rabbit*
19 FEBRUARY 1939 ~ 7 FEBRUARY 1940	*Earth Rabbit*
6 FEBRUARY 1951 ~ 26 JANUARY 1952	*Metal Rabbit*
25 JANUARY 1963 ~ 12 FEBRUARY 1964	*Water Rabbit*
11 FEBRUARY 1975 ~ 30 JANUARY 1976	*Wood Rabbit*
29 JANUARY 1987 ~ 16 FEBRUARY 1988	*Fire Rabbit*
16 FEBRUARY 1999 ~ 4 FEBRUARY 2000	*Earth Rabbit*

THE
RABBIT

THE PERSONALITY OF THE RABBIT

> The talent of success is nothing more than doing what you can do well, and doing well whatever you do.
> *Henry Wadsworth Longfellow, a Rabbit*

The Rabbit is born under the signs of virtue and prudence. He is intelligent, well-mannered and prefers a quiet and peaceful existence. He dislikes any sort of unpleasantness and will try to steer clear of arguments and disputes. He is very much a pacifist and tends to have a calming influence on those around him. He has wide interests and usually a good appreciation of the arts and the finer things in life. He also knows how to enjoy himself and will often gravitate to the best restaurants and nightspots in town.

The Rabbit is a witty and intelligent speaker and loves being involved in a good discussion. His views and advice are often sought by others and he can be relied upon to be discreet and diplomatic. He will rarely raise his voice in anger and will even turn a blind eye to matters which displease him just to preserve the peace. He likes to remain on good terms with everyone, but he can be rather sensitive and takes any form of criticism very badly. He will also be the first to get out of the way if he sees any form of trouble brewing.

The Rabbit is a quiet and efficient worker and has an extremely good memory. He is very astute in business and financial matters, but his degree of success often depends on the conditions that prevail. He hates being in a situation which is fraught with tension or where he has to make sudden decisions. Wherever possible he will plan his various activities with the utmost care and a good deal of caution. He does not like to take risks and does not take kindly to change. Basically, he seeks a secure, calm and stable environment, and when conditions are right he is more than happy to leave things as they are.

The Rabbit is conscientious and because of his methodical and ever-watchful nature he can often do well in his chosen profession. He makes a good diplomat, lawyer, shopkeeper, administrator or priest, and he excels in any job where he can use his superb skills as a communicator. He tends to be loyal to his employers and is respected for his integrity and honesty, but if he ever finds himself in a position of great power he can become rather intransigent and authoritarian.

The Rabbit attaches great importance to his home and will often spend a lot of time and money maintaining and furnishing it and fitting it with all the latest comforts – the Rabbit is very much a creature of comfort! He is also something of a collector and there are many Rabbits who derive much pleasure from collecting antiques, stamps, coins, *objets d'art* or anything else which catches their eye or particularly interests them.

The female Rabbit has a friendly, caring and considerate nature, and will do all in her power to give her home a happy and loving atmosphere. She is also very sociable and enjoys holding parties and entertaining. She has a great ability to make the maximum use of her time and although she involves herself in numerous activities, she always manages to find time to sit back and enjoy a good read or a chat. She has a great sense of humour, is very artistic and is often a talented gardener.

The Rabbit takes considerable care over his appearance and is usually smart and well turned out. He also attaches great importance to his relations with others and matters of the heart are particularly important to him. He will rarely be short of admirers and will often have several serious romances before he settles down. The Rabbit is not the most faithful of signs, but he will find that he is especially well suited to those born under the signs of the Goat, Snake, Pig and Ox. Due to his sociable and easy-going manner he can also get on well with the Tiger, Dragon, Horse, Monkey, Dog and another Rabbit, but he will feel ill at ease with the Rat and Rooster as both these signs tend to speak their mind and be critical in their comments, and the Rabbit just loathes any form of criticism or unpleasantness.

The Rabbit is usually lucky in life and often has the happy knack of being in the right place at the right time. He is talented and quick-witted, but he does sometimes put pleasure before work, and wherever possible will tend to opt for the easy life. He can at times be a little reserved and suspicious of the motives of others, but generally will lead a long and contented life and one which – as far as possible – will be free of strife and discord.

THE RABBIT

THE FIVE DIFFERENT TYPES OF RABBIT

In addition to the 12 signs of the Chinese zodiac there are five elements and these have a strengthening or moderating influence on the sign. The effects of the five elements on the Rabbit are described below, together with the years in which the elements were exercising their influence. Therefore those Rabbits born in 1951 are Metal Rabbits, those born in 1963 are Water Rabbits, and so on.

Metal Rabbit: 1951
This Rabbit is capable, ambitious and has very definite views on what he wants to achieve in life. He can occasionally appear reserved and aloof, but this is mainly because he likes to keep his thoughts to himself. He has a quick and alert mind and is particularly shrewd in business matters. He can also be very cunning in his actions. The Metal Rabbit has a good appreciation of the arts and likes to mix in the best circles. He usually has a small but very loyal group of friends.

Water Rabbit: 1963
The Water Rabbit is popular, intuitive and keenly aware of the feelings of those around him. He can, however, be rather sensitive and tends to take things too much to heart. He is very precise and thorough in everything he does and has an exceedingly good memory. He tends to be

quiet and at times rather withdrawn, but he expresses his ideas well and is highly regarded by his family, friends and colleagues.

Wood Rabbit: 1915, 1975

The Wood Rabbit is likeable, easy-going and very adaptable. He prefers to work in a group rather than on his own and likes to have the support and encouragement of others. He can, however, be rather reticent in expressing his views and it would be in his own interests to become a little more open and let others know how he feels on certain matters. He usually has many friends, enjoys an active social life and is noted for his generosity.

Fire Rabbit: 1927, 1987

The Fire Rabbit has a friendly, outgoing personality. He likes socializing and being on good terms with everyone. He is discreet and diplomatic and has a very good understanding of human nature. He is also strong-willed and provided he has the necessary backing he can go far in life. He does, not, however, suffer adversity well and can become moody and depressed when things are not working out as he would like. He has a particularly good manner with children, is very intuitive and there are some Fire Rabbits who are even noted for their psychic ability.

THE RABBIT

Earth Rabbit: 1939, 1999

The Earth Rabbit is a quiet individual, but he is nevertheless very astute. He is realistic in his aims and is prepared to work long and hard in order to achieve his objectives. He has good business sense and is invariably lucky in financial matters. He also has a most persuasive manner and usually experiences little difficulty in getting others to fall in with his plans. He is held in high esteem by his friends and colleagues and his views are often sought and highly valued.

PROSPECTS FOR THE RABBIT IN 2005

The Chinese New Year starts on 9 February 2005. Until then, the old year, the Year of the Monkey, is still making its presence felt.

The Year of the Monkey (22 January 2004 to 8 February 2005) will have been a variable one for the Rabbit and in the closing months, he will need to remain careful. This especially applies to money matters, and with the last months of the year being an expensive time, the Rabbit would do well to watch his spending and avoid unnecessary risks. This is a time for vigilance and thoroughness.

For those Rabbits looking to make headway in their work or seeking a position, October and November could bring some interesting opportunities.

The Rabbit can also look forward to a full and active personal life at this time. In his home life there will often be a lot to do and he will also do much to help others. Here his ability to organize as well as relate so effectively with others will be much appreciated.

The Rabbit's social life also promises much activity, with the months from August to October and December bringing many opportunities to go out and add to his social circle. And for the unattached, the Monkey year does favour affairs of the heart. For some Rabbits, the last quarter of the year can be a romantic and exciting time.

The closing months will certainly bring their pleasures, but such is the nature of the Monkey year that the Rabbit will need to remain careful in his undertakings, especially where money matters are concerned.

The Year of the Rooster begins on 9 February and contains mixed fortunes for the Rabbit. Over the year he could find progress difficult and he will also need to be careful when dealing with some of his activities. However, despite the variable aspects, the Rooster year *will* be a significant one, with what the Rabbit achieves now preparing him for the considerable success he will enjoy in following years. Neither the preceding year nor the present one may be the smoothest for the Rabbit, but they can leave a significant legacy.

In the Rabbit's work this will be an important year, especially in the way that it will allow him to build on his skills and experience. And by taking advantage of any training opportunities or chances to become involved in other duties, he will be doing his prospects much good. This is very much a year for the Rabbit to add to his experience.

THE RABBIT

In addition to any training that may be available through his work, the Rabbit should consider other ways in which he can further himself, and whether enrolling on courses in his own time or studying by himself, he will find that what he is able to learn now can do his future prospects much good. Also, throughout the year, he should work closely with others rather than be too independent in approach. This way his contribution is likely to be much more valued and his reputation enhanced. In addition, with the Rooster year bringing its pressures and challenging moments, by working closely with others the Rabbit will find some of the situations he faces easier to deal with. And while there may be times when he will despair about his workload, he will find what he does achieve will add to his experience and can be of considerable value to him in the future.

For those Rabbits who are keen to move on from their present position or are seeking work, March and June could see some interesting opportunities. Also, the Rabbit will find that his prospects will steadily improve during the last quarter of the year.

The Rooster year can prove an expensive one, however, with the Rabbit spending a great deal on accommodation, travel and transport as well as his other commitments. In view of this, he would do well to keep a close watch on his outgoings and make provision for forthcoming expenses. Fortunately he is usually adept in dealing with money matters, but this is very much a year for careful management and control. Also, should problems arise or he have uncertainties over any forms and paperwork he has to complete, he should seek guidance. In some cases a helpline could provide the answers he needs. With difficult or complex matters, the Rabbit should remember that help is available and *can* make a difference.

In spite of the challenges of the year, the Rabbit will appreciate the time he spends on his interests. Some Rabbits will enjoy setting themselves an interesting project or personal challenge, while others could be tempted to take up something new. Whatever the Rabbit does, by setting time aside for activities and pursuits that appeal to him, he can find this a pleasurable and often beneficial aspect of the year.

Also, many Rabbits will spend time on home alterations during the year and here the Rabbit's sense of style will be to the fore. Whether he is redecorating certain rooms or altering the layout of his home, his ability to gauge what looks good will lead to some impressive results. And any Rabbit who enjoys collecting and has a penchant for antiques, *objets d'art* or more aesthetic items, will find his fine taste leading to some splendid purchases.

In both his interests and home projects, the Rabbit will be well supported by those around him, although where more practical projects are concerned, he does need to allow plenty of time for their completion. He may be eager for results, but some undertakings could take longer and be more disruptive than initially envisaged.

The Rabbit should also be forthcoming if he has any concerns or feels under pressure at any time. That way others will be better placed to understand and help. And during times of pressure, he should also be careful not to take his irritations out on others. In some cases just talking or giving himself time to unwind will do him – and others – much good. However, while the Rabbit's home life will often be busy, there will be a lot for him to value. This includes the progress of loved ones, interests and projects that can be shared and any outings, family treats or holidays that take place over the year.

The Rabbit's social life will also see much activity and while this will mostly go well, in certain situations he will need to tread carefully. Sometimes a difference of opinion could place him in an awkward position or a certain friendship could run into difficulty. The Rabbit, who so hates discord, will feel this deeply. However, he *is* adept in handling his relations with others and with dialogue and understanding will often be able to rectify any problem. For socializing, March, July, November and December are particularly favourable months.

Although the Rooster year will contain its challenges and demand much from the Rabbit, by doing his best, being careful and liaising closely with others, he will emerge from it with much to his credit. And his achievements and the experience he gains will often prove instrumental in the successes that await in 2006, the much more favourable Year of the Dog.

The Metal Rabbit

This will be an interesting year for the Metal Rabbit and while it will not be without its challenges and more awkward moments, the Metal Rabbit is blessed with a redoubtable nature and this will help him deal effectively with many of the situations that arise. Also, what he accomplishes and learns over the year will often have a significant bearing on following years.

One area which requires particular care is finance and if taking on new commitments, the Metal Rabbit should check the small print carefully. Similarly, when completing tax or other financially related forms, he needs to be thorough and seek advice on any aspect which may be unclear. Without such care, he could find himself at a disadvantage or having to contend with some extra and burdensome correspondence. He should also keep receipts, guarantees and important documents safely. Again, if problems arise, he will be glad to have kept these secure and accessible. The year could be quite expensive, particularly with family and accommodation costs, and whenever the Metal Rabbit knows of forthcoming expenses, he would do well to make early provision for them. The better he can manage his finances, the better his overall position will be.

This need for care also extends to the Metal Rabbit's work. During the Rooster year he could find himself in some challenging situations. Sometimes his workload could be heavy or he could have misgivings about certain schemes that are being introduced. The Metal Rabbit is conscientious and just likes to get on with his own activities, and he could be troubled by such developments. However, in the Rooster year, it is very much a case of adapting to the situations that arise and focusing on what needs to be done. Also, despite his concerns, the Metal Rabbit could find that some of the situations that occur will give him the chance to use his skills in new ways and this can be to his future benefit.

However, while the Rooster year will contain its pressures and irritations, it will not be without its chances to progress, and as openings become available, the Metal Rabbit could find himself with the right experience and contacts to benefit. Mid-February to the end of March, June and the last quarter of the year could see some interesting opportunities.

Similarly those Metal Rabbits seeking work or feeling in a rut will find that by actively pursuing any opportunities that come their way, they may well be successful in securing a position with future potential. Again what is accomplished in 2005 can have important long-term benefits.

Although the Metal Rabbit will have many demands on his time, he should also make sure he sets time aside for his own interests. Not only will these be a good way for him to relax and enjoy himself but they will also be a welcome break from his usual concerns. Carrying them out with others can also add to his enjoyment.

The year will see much activity domestically and for many Metal Rabbits there will be good cause for a family celebration, with a wedding, the birth of a grandchild or other pleasing family developments. And the Metal Rabbit, who follows the activities of his loved ones with such fond interest, will be particularly proud of the successes of those who mean so much to him. He will also give much support and encouragement to those close to him and his ability to relate so effectively will be greatly appreciated. If, at any time, though, he himself feels under pressure or has concerns, it is important that he is forthcoming and allows others to help him.

The Metal Rabbit will also appreciate his social life over the year, especially the chances to go out. However, such is the nature of the year that he would be wise to remain his discreet and tactful self. Sometimes a comment or gesture could be misconstrued and cause problems, and he would do well to watch this.

Although the Metal Rabbit could find parts of the year challenging, by dealing with situations as best he can and seeking the support of others, he will learn a great deal. And despite the pressures, the Rooster year will certainly contain its pleasurable and rewarding times, with the Metal Rabbit's domestic life and interests meaning a great deal to him.

TIP FOR THE YEAR
Do allow time for personal interests and recreational pursuits, and if there is one you want to develop further or something new that appeals to you, follow it up. Your personal interests can bring you much pleasure and do you good.

The Water Rabbit

This will be an important year for the Water Rabbit and while it will not be without its pressures or challenging situations, it can still be a constructive time.

At work the prospects are encouraging, with many Water Rabbits being able to build on their present position and skills. Sometimes, others will look to the Water Rabbit to play a greater role and he could find himself with the chance to take on more responsibilities or promotion. However, while the Water Rabbit will be able to make progress, he could also find himself facing some daunting tasks. And, as one who likes to be on top of his situation and maintain high standards, there will be times when he will feel under pressure or concerned about developments. The Rooster year, while bringing opportunities, will not always be an easy one.

However, when the Water Rabbit is under pressure, he will find his methodical nature will serve him well and by concentrating upon his priorities and making good use of his skills, he will get a lot done. Also, the developments of the year will teach him a great deal and whether he is learning new skills, handling a different type of work or overseeing more junior colleagues, he will gain valuable experience.

For those Water Rabbits who are anxious to move from their present position or are seeking work, the Rooster year will also contain some important developments. Although it may take these Water Rabbits several attempts to secure a position, once they do so they will often find it will allow them to add to their skills as well as discover new strengths. For work opportunities, March, June and closing months of the year are particularly favourable times.

Although the progress the Water Rabbit makes will lead to an increase in income, he will still need to handle financial matters with care. Over the year he will face many expenses, especially related to family, accommodation and transport, and in order to meet these, he will need to budget carefully. If he does not already do so, he will find it helpful to maintain a set of accounts so he can keep better track of his position and outgoings. Also, with the aspects as they are, he should be wary of taking risks or committing himself to ventures or agreements he has not properly checked out. This is very much a year for care and watchfulness. The Water Rabbit should also be thorough when dealing with financially related forms and other important paperwork. Without care he could find himself involved in additional expense or protracted correspondence. Water Rabbits, take note.

With the pressures of the year, it is also important that the Water Rabbit allows time for his own interests and recreational pursuits. Not only will these give him a break from his usual concerns but they can also get him out of doors and give him the chance to get additional exercise as well as meet others. Any Water Rabbits who may have let their interests lapse should aim to address this over the year.

The Water Rabbit should also not allow his social life to suffer through other demands on his time. By going out to events that appeal to him and meeting his friends, he will be able to relax and enjoy himself. Any Water Rabbits who may have let their social life fall away in recent years should aim to go out more over the Rooster year. By taking positive action, they will find they are able to bring something special back into their life and can forge some new and important friendships. For socializing, March, July, November and December are particularly favourable times.

As far as the Water Rabbit's domestic life is concerned, it will be another active year. Again, the Water Rabbit's ability to organize and oversee a great deal will be appreciated, especially with a possible family celebration or get-together to arrange. However, while the Water Rabbit will enjoy playing such a full role, he needs to ensure that everyone in his household does their share and that he is not taking on too much single-handed. At busy times, he should not hesitate to ask others for assistance. Also, if embarking on any practical projects, he should allow plenty of time for them rather than act in haste. As he will find, the more care and consideration he can give to his plans, the better the outcome will be.

The Rooster year may be a busy and sometimes demanding one for the Water Rabbit, but it will certainly not be without its more positive aspects. His family, social life and interests can all bring much pleasure, while what he learns and accomplishes in his work will stand him in good stead for the favourable times that await next year.

TIP FOR THE YEAR
Manage your time well. Decide on your priorities and stick with them. To try to do too much or take on too many commitments could lead to feeling overwhelmed and achieving less satisfying results. If pressures mount, ask others for assistance.

The Wood Rabbit

This marks the Wood Rabbit's thirtieth year and it will be significant one for him. As they enter a new decade in their lives, many Wood Rabbits will decide the time has come to move their situation forward and pursue some of their aims and aspirations more determinedly. And while their actual progress in 2005 may be modest, what they initiate now will often be far-reaching.

One area which will see important developments will be the Wood Rabbit's work. Over the year many Wood Rabbits will be keen to make advances in their career, particularly in ways that will allow them to make more effective use of their strengths. However, while the Wood Rabbit may have his own ideas, his progress will not always be straightforward. There could be few openings available to him, competition could be particularly keen or he could be lacking the experience to advance in the way he wants. However, while there may be moments when the Wood Rabbit will despair about his lack of progress, it is important he does not lose heart. With each position he puts in for, he will be learning more about what employers are expecting as well as strengthening his interview technique. The difficulties that some Wood Rabbits will face over the year will teach them a great deal, and by persisting, many will eventually get the chance to move their career forward. It may be a long haul to get this opportunity, but the significance of what the Wood Rabbit is able to accomplish this year should *not* be underestimated. For work matters, mid-February to the end of March, June and the last quarter of the year will see some important opportunities.

The Wood Rabbit should also make the most of any training opportunities that become available during the year. By developing his skills he will be helping both his present position and his future prospects. And, in view of some of his objectives, anything he can do to strengthen his chances will be to his advantage.

Those Wood Rabbits seeking work, either as the year starts or during it, will again need to remain persistent as well as consider new ways in which they can draw on their skills and experience. As many will find, to obtain a position in 2005 will require a great deal of effort, but it is possible to set their career off on a positive new track.

The Wood Rabbit will also need to be careful when dealing with financial matters. Over the year he could face some large expenses, especially involving accommodation and transport, and with these and other commitments, he will need to keep a close watch on his spending. Fortunately the Wood Rabbit is usually careful in money matters, but this is not a year to relax his vigilance or be less than thorough when conducting important transactions or entering into agreements. He too could find it helpful to carry out a review of his financial position. In some cases, a few modifications, particularly in cutting back on non-essentials, could make a noticeable difference. This is a time for prudence and thoroughness.

The year is more encouraging as far as the Wood Rabbit's personal interests are concerned, and whether he prefers creative, practical or outdoor activities, he will find they will do him good as well as bring him much pleasure. He will also often be able to gain a great deal of enjoyment by joining other enthusiasts.

The Wood Rabbit should also make sure he takes a proper holiday during the year. The change of scene and break from his usual routine will do him good as well as be enjoyable. If he sees any travel offers that appeal to him or receives invitations to visit friends or relatives living some distance away, he should follow these up.

As far as the Wood Rabbit's domestic life is concerned, the Rooster year will bring some very special times. Over the year the Wood Rabbit will do much to encourage and support those dear to him, with his attentiveness and consideration being greatly appreciated. Also, he will take much satisfaction in some of the projects he tackles with others, particularly those which add to his home or garden in some way. Again, his input and ideas will be well received. However, while the year will generally go well domestically, if pressures mount, any differences of opinion arise or the Wood Rabbit has anything troubling him, he should be forthcoming rather than keep his concerns to himself. Without a certain openness, there is a danger that minor issues could become inflamed and undermine the usually good rapport he enjoys with those around him. Wood Rabbits, do take note.

The Wood Rabbit also sets much store by his social life and although this may not be such an active year as some, by going to events that appeal to him and keeping in regular contact with friends, he will enjoy some pleasurable times. In addition, he could benefit from some advice he receives from close friends, and if troubled by any matter, he would do well to listen closely to their words.

Although the Wood Rabbit will need to work hard and put a lot of effort into his activities over the year, what he accomplishes can be far-reaching. With his talents and abilities, he does have a great future ahead of him and in 2005 he will do much to prepare for his future success.

And despite the year's more awkward aspects, he will enjoy spending time on his interests and value the love and support of those who mean so much to him.

TIP FOR THE YEAR
Regard this as a year for personal development and do give yourself time to learn, extend your skills and acquire new ones. What you accomplish now can open up important possibilities in the near future.

The Fire Rabbit

This will be a demanding year for the Fire Rabbit and while he will need to work hard to make progress, it will leave a powerful legacy which will shape his life for the next few years.

For the many Fire Rabbits involved in study this will be an important year and with the approach of examinations, they should work steadily and consistently rather than leave a lot to the last moment. Fortunately the Fire Rabbit's methodical nature will help, but with a lot depending on his results, it really is worth him making that extra effort. Academically, the Rooster year is encouragingly aspected and the Fire Rabbit's achievements during it can have an important bearing on the next few years. Those Fire Rabbits who are training for a vocational skill or are under apprenticeship should also make the most of their present situation, with the skills they acquire now having great future value.

For those Fire Rabbits in work or seeking it, this will also be an important year, but to benefit they will need to be flexible in their outlook and make the most of the opportunities available to them, even if these may not always be ideal. By showing commitment and proving their reliability they will not only be helping their reputation (and any references they may be given), but also adding to their experience and learning more about the world of work. Again, the Rooster year is an important one for learning, and the effort the Fire Rabbit can put in and the skills he can acquire will prove useful in following years.

The Fire Rabbit will also be helped by his ability to get on with others and over the year he will meet and impress many. Fire Rabbits who are in work will find that by building up contacts and becoming better known, they will make connections that will serve them well in the future. Also if at any time the Fire Rabbit feels under pressure or has any uncertainties, he should speak to others about them. Often family, friends or colleagues will be glad to help and can ease some of the worries he may have.

Another area which requires care is finance. In the Rooster year the Fire Rabbit will find his resources stretched and will need to be careful if he has to borrow or enter into any other financial commitments. At all times he needs to be aware of the obligations involved and if he has any uncertainties, he should seek advice. This is not a year for risks. Also, if having to borrow, it would be worth him spending time comparing the terms offered by various companies and the options available to him. Money matters do need careful attention over the year. In addition, some Fire Rabbits may be tempted by 'get rich quick' schemes or undertakings they know little about. If considering such schemes, they do need to be cautious. This is a time for vigilance and avoiding risks. Fire Rabbits, do take note.

Quite a few Fire Rabbits will be tempted to travel over the year and while this can lead to some memorable experiences, these Fire Rabbits would also find it helpful to plan their requirements and itinerary carefully before leaving. The better prepared they are, the more enjoyable and rewarding their time away will be.

With his friendly and sociable nature the Fire Rabbit can, though, look forward to some great times with his friends over the year as well as in being able to add to his social circle. Affairs of the heart will also bring him much happiness, with an existing romance becoming more meaningful or someone new entering his life. In his personal life this will be an active year, with March, July and the closing months being particularly busy. However, while the Fire Rabbit will enjoy himself, he does need to remain mindful of the views of others, and if he finds himself in any awkward situation, he should watch his words. The Rooster year could spring some awkward and embarrassing traps for the unguarded.

Also, throughout the year, the Fire Rabbit should draw on the support of family members, particularly in view of some of the decisions he may have to take or the pressures he may have. His family are often willing to help and the Fire Rabbit should be open with them and receptive to what they can offer. He does, after all, mean a great deal to them.

Generally, the Rooster year will demand a lot of the Fire Rabbit and whether in study or employment, he will need to work hard and give his best. What he accomplishes now will benefit him in the future. Financially, this will be a year for care, but his personal life will bring him much pleasure, with the prospects of socializing and new friendships adding an especially enjoyable element to the year.

TIP FOR THE YEAR
Sometimes you tend to keep things to yourself, but in the Rooster year it really would be helpful to share your concerns, hopes and ideas with others. By doing so you will not only get more support and advice but also improve your rapport with others.

The Earth Rabbit

This will be a reasonable year for the Earth Rabbit and provided he sets about his various activities in his usual careful and measured way, he will fare well. This is, though, not a time for risks or for being too independent.

One area requiring particular care concerns paperwork, especially forms related to finance. With these the Earth Rabbit does need to be thorough and prompt, otherwise a delayed response, missed detail or wrongly completed section could be to his disadvantage. Should he have any uncertainties over what is required, he should contact a helpline or adviser. He should also be careful if he enters into any important new agreement and should check the terms and small print thoroughly. This is not a year for making assumptions or being careless where his financial interests are concerned.

THE RABBIT

This need for care also extends to any practical activities that the Earth Rabbit may tackle over the year, particularly in the home or garden. If anything strenuous or complicated is involved, he should seek assistance rather than take risks.

More positively aspected, though, are the Earth Rabbit's personal interests and by devoting time to them he will be pleased with how they develop over the year. Also, with his keen and inquisitive nature, he could be tempted to follow up other subjects that appeal to him and by reading, joining a group or enrolling on a course, he will take much satisfaction from what he learns. The Earth Rabbit has always been one to use his spare time effectively and the Rooster year will be no exception.

The Earth Rabbit will also be grateful for the support he receives over the year and by discussing his ideas with those around him and encouraging others to join in with his plans, he will be able to add to the pleasure of his activities. In some cases learning a skill or tackling a project with a partner or close friend will work out particularly well.

The Earth Rabbit will also follow the activities of family members with fond interest and will be glad to help those who may be under pressure. However, with the aspects as they are, it is important that the help and support he is prepared to give is reciprocated, and whenever he has any problems or uncertainties of his own, he should not hold back from asking for assistance. Often those dear to him will be glad to have the chance to give something in return for all his past kindnesses.

There will also be some good chances for the Earth Rabbit to travel over the year and if he sees a holiday or offer which appeals to him or receives an invitation to visit family or friends living some distance away, he should follow it up. Some of his travelling this year can surpass expectations.

The Earth Rabbit will also value his social life over the year and will enjoy keeping in contact with his close group of friends. Personal interests that have a social element can be especially satisfying, and for those Earth Rabbits who may welcome more companionship, joining a local club could be an excellent way to meet others and make new friends. March, July and the last quarter of the year could be interesting and active months socially.

In many respects this will be a pleasant year for the Earth Rabbit and by spending time on his interests and playing a full role in family and social activities, there will be a lot for him to appreciate. However, with the aspects as they are, if there is any matter which concerns him, it is important that he seeks help rather than keeps his worries to himself. Also, he needs to be his usual careful self when dealing with finances and important paperwork. Provided he bears this in mind, this can be a fine and often rewarding year.

TIP FOR THE YEAR

Put your talents and interests to good use. If you are creative, set yourself some interesting projects to do, or if there are skills or subjects you wish to learn, follow these up. Over the year your personal interests and recreational pursuits can be fulfilling and pleasurable.

FAMOUS RABBITS

Bertie Ahern, Margaret Atwood, Drew Barrymore, David Beckham, Harry Belafonte, Ingrid Bergman, St Bernadette, Gordon Brown, James Caan, Nicolas Cage, Lewis Carroll, Fidel Castro, John Cleese, Confucius, Marie Curie, Johnny Depp, Albert Einstein, George Eliot, W. C. Fields, James Fox, Sir David Frost, James Galway, Cary Grant, Edvard Grieg, Oliver Hardy, Seamus Heaney, Tommy Hilfiger, John Howard, Bob Hope, Whitney Houston, Helen Hunt, John Hurt, Olivia Hussey, Anjelica Huston, Chrissie Hynde, Enrique Inglesias, Clive James, Henry James, David Jason, Angelina Jolie, Michael Jordan, Michael Keaton, John Keats, Judith Krantz, Danny La Rue, Cheryl Ladd, Patrick Lichfield, Gina Lollobrigida, George Michael, Arthur Miller, Colin Montgomerie, Sir Roger Moore, Mike Myers, Brigitte Nielsen, Graham Norton, Jamie Oliver, George Orwell, John Peel, Edith Piaf, Sidney Poitier, Romano Prodi, Ken Russell, Mort Sahl, Elisabeth Schwarzkopf, Neil Sedaka, Jane Seymour, Neil Simon, Frank Sinatra, Sting, Quentin Tarantino, J. R. R. Tolkien, Arturo Toscanini, Tina Turner, Luther Vandross, Queen Victoria, Muddy Waters, Orson Welles, Walt Whitman, Robin Williams, Kate Winslet, Tiger Woods. Jet Li

16 FEBRUARY 1904 ～ 3 FEBRUARY 1905	*Wood Dragon*
3 FEBRUARY 1916 ～ 22 JANUARY 1917	*Fire Dragon*
23 JANUARY 1928 ～ 9 FEBRUARY 1929	*Earth Dragon*
8 FEBRUARY 1940 ～ 26 JANUARY 1941	*Metal Dragon*
27 JANUARY 1952 ～ 13 FEBRUARY 1953	*Water Dragon*
13 FEBRUARY 1964 ～ 1 FEBRUARY 1965	*Wood Dragon*
31 JANUARY 1976 ～ 17 FEBRUARY 1977	*Fire Dragon*
17 FEBRUARY 1988 ～ 5 FEBRUARY 1989	*Earth Dragon*
5 FEBRUARY 2000 ～ 23 JANUARY 2001	*Metal Dragon*

THE DRAGON

THE PERSONALITY OF THE DRAGON

I will prepare and some day my chance will come.
                                Abraham Lincoln, a Dragon

The Dragon is born under the sign of luck. He is a proud and lively character and has a tremendous amount of self-confidence. He is also highly intelligent and very quick to take advantage of any opportunities. He is ambitious and determined and will do well in practically anything he attempts. He is also something of a perfectionist and will always try to maintain the high standards he sets himself.

The Dragon does not suffer fools gladly and will be quick to criticize anyone or anything that displeases him. He can be blunt and forthright in his views and is certainly not renowned for being either tactful or diplomatic. He does, however, often take people at their word and can occasionally be rather gullible. If he ever feels that his trust has been abused or his dignity wounded, he can sometimes become very bitter and it will take him a long time to forgive and forget.

The Dragon is usually very outgoing and is particularly adept at attracting attention and publicity. He enjoys being in the limelight and is often at his best when he is confronted by a difficult problem or tense situation. In some respects he is a showman and he rarely lacks an audience. His views are highly valued and he invariably has something interesting – and sometimes controversial – to say.

He has considerable energy and is often prepared to work long and unsocial hours in order to achieve what he wants. He can, however, be rather impulsive and does not always consider the consequences of his actions. He also has a tendency to live for the moment and there is nothing that riles him more than to be kept waiting. The Dragon hates delay and can get extremely impatient and irritable over even the smallest of hold-ups.

The Dragon has an enormous faith in his abilities, but he does run the risk of becoming over-confident and unless he is careful he can sometimes make grave errors of judgement. While this may prove disastrous at the time, he does have the tenacity and ability to bounce back and pick up the pieces again.

The Dragon has such an assertive personality, so much willpower and such a desire to succeed that he will often reach the top of his chosen profession. He has considerable leadership qualities and will do well in positions where he can put his own ideas and policies into practice. He is usually successful in politics, show business, as the manager of his own department or business, and in any job which brings him into contact with the media.

The Dragon relies a tremendous amount on his own judgement and can be scornful of other people's advice. He likes to feel self-sufficient and there are many Dragons who cherish their independence to such a degree that they prefer to remain single throughout their lives. However, the Dragon will often have numerous admirers and many will be attracted by his flamboyant personality and striking looks. If he does marry, he will usually marry young, and will find himself particularly well suited to those born under the signs of the Snake, Rat, Monkey and Rooster. He will also find that the Rabbit, Pig, Horse and Goat make ideal companions and will readily join in with many of his escapades. Two Dragons will also get on well together, as they understand each other, but the Dragon may not find things so easy with the Ox and Dog, as both will be critical of his impulsive and somewhat extrovert manner. He will also find it difficult to form an alliance with the Tiger, for the Tiger, like the Dragon, tends to speak his mind, is very strong-willed and likes to take the lead.

The female Dragon knows what she wants in life and sets about everything she does in a determined and positive manner. No job is too small for her and she is often prepared to work extremely hard until she has secured her objective. She is immensely practical and somewhat liberated. She hates being bound by routine and petty restrictions and likes to have sufficient freedom to be able to go off and do what she wants to do. She will keep her house tidy, but is not one for spending hours on housework – there are far too many other things that she prefers to do. Like her male counterpart, she has a tendency to speak her mind.

The Dragon usually has many interests and enjoys sport and other outdoor activities. He also likes to travel and often prefers to visit places that are off the beaten track rather than head for popular tourist attractions. He has a very adventurous streak in him and providing his financial circumstances permit – and the Dragon is usually sensible with his money – he will travel considerable distances during his lifetime.

The Dragon is a very flamboyant character and while he can be demanding of others and in his early years rather precocious, he will have many friends and will nearly always be the centre of attention. He has charisma and so much confidence that he can often become a source of inspiration to others. In China he is the leader of the carnival and he is also blessed with an inordinate share of luck.

THE FIVE DIFFERENT TYPES OF DRAGON

In addition to the 12 signs of the Chinese zodiac there are five elements and these have a strengthening or moderating influence on the sign. The effects of the five elements on the Dragon are described below, together with the years in which the elements were exercising their influence. Therefore those Dragons born in 1940 and 2000 are Metal Dragons, those born in 1952 are Water Dragons, and so on.

Metal Dragon: 1940, 2000
This Dragon is very strong-willed and has a particularly forceful personality. He is energetic, ambitious and tries to be scrupulous in his dealings with others. He can also be blunt and to the point and usually has no hesitation in speaking his mind. If people disagree with him or are not prepared to co-operate, he is more than happy to go his own way. The Metal Dragon usually has very high moral values and is held in great esteem by his friends and colleagues.

Water Dragon: 1952

This Dragon is friendly, easy-going and intelligent. He is quick-witted and rarely lets an opportunity slip by. However, he is not as impatient as some of the other types of Dragon and is prepared to wait for results rather than expect everything to happen at once. He has an understanding nature and is prepared to share his ideas and co-operate with others. His main failing is a tendency to jump from one thing to another rather than concentrate on the job in hand. He has a good sense of humour and is an effective speaker.

Wood Dragon: 1904, 1964

The Wood Dragon is practical, imaginative and inquisitive. He loves delving into all manner of subjects and can quite often come up with some highly original ideas. He is a thinker and a doer and he has the drive and commitment to put many of his ideas into practice. He is more diplomatic than some of the other types of Dragon and has a good sense of humour. He is very astute in business matters and can also be most generous.

Fire Dragon: 1916, 1976

This Dragon is ambitious, articulate and has a tremendous desire to succeed. He is a hard and conscientious worker and is often admired for his integrity and forthright nature. He is very strong-willed and has considerable leadership qualities. He can, however, rely a bit too much on his own judgement and not take into account the views and feelings of others. He can also be rather aloof and it would certainly be in his own interests to let others join in more with his various activities. The Fire Dragon usually enjoys music, literature and the arts.

Earth Dragon: 1928, 1988
The Earth Dragon tends to be quieter and more reflective than some of the other types of Dragon. He has a wide variety of interests and is keenly aware of what is going on around him. He also has clear objectives and usually has no problems in obtaining support and backing for any of his ventures. He is very astute in financial matters and is often able to accumulate considerable wealth. He is a good organizer, although he can at times be rather bureaucratic and fussy. He mixes well with others and has a large circle of friends.

PROSPECTS FOR THE DRAGON IN 2005

The Chinese New Year starts on 9 February 2005. Until then, the old year, the Year of the Monkey, is still making its presence felt.

The Year of the Monkey (22 January 2004 to 8 February 2005) will have been a generally favourable one for the Dragon and the closing months hold encouraging aspects.

One feature of the Monkey year is that it allows the Dragon to make good use of his strengths and in the remaining months he should take advantage of any opportunities to further himself and his ideas. The Monkey year is all for enterprise and initiative and the Dragon can be a major beneficiary of this. Late August to October can be a particularly positive time work-wise, with new opportunities to pursue and pleasing results coming from the Dragon's efforts.

The Dragon does, though, need be careful in money matters at this time. Without some watchfulness, his spending could creep up and be greater than he anticipated. This is also not a time for financial risks.

On a personal level the Dragon will find himself in great demand, with many invitations and chances to go out. September and December could be especially active both domestically and socially. However, with so much happening, it is important that the Dragon stays organized and regularly consults others. As the year draws to a close, he will have good reason to value the help and support he is given.

The Year of the Rooster starts on 9 February and holds excellent prospects for the Dragon. This is a year of opportunity, progress and considerable good fortune.

The Dragon's work prospects are especially encouraging and during the year he can look forward to making significant advances. This is very much a year when he can benefit from his experience and put his skills to effective use.

Almost all Dragons will have the opportunity to improve on their position over the year and those who feel in a rut or are dissatisfied with their present position will

THE DRAGON

find this an excellent time to rectify this. However, to benefit from the prevailing aspects, these Dragons *will* need to take the action to bring about the changes they desire. By actively looking for suitable openings and making enquiries, they will soon obtain results, with many being offered an exciting new challenge. Some could also find close colleagues or friends particularly helpful in their quest for a position.

Similarly, those Dragons seeking work, either as the year starts or during it, should follow up any openings that will allow them to draw on their strengths and experience. Even though they may face a few disappointments, their persistence as well as their fine reputation (and references) will lead to many securing a position that will suit them well.

Those Dragons already established in a career can also look forward to making important strides. In recognition of their commitment and knowledge, many will find themselves being offered an increased role, singled out for new initiatives or strongly placed for promotion. This is very much a year to advance, with the months from March to May and November seeing some particularly good opportunities.

The Dragon will also be helped by his ability to get on well with others and he should again make the most of any chances to meet colleagues and to build up contacts. With his outgoing and confident manner he will not only impress many but also find a lot of goodwill (and good fortune) will flow in his direction as a result. Once again, his skills and personable nature will serve him well.

The progress the Dragon makes in his work will lead to an increase in income, and financially, his prospects will be considerably brighter during the year. However, to benefit, he should manage his finances well. By setting funds aside for known commitments and saving towards more expensive purchases he will find he is often able to do more as a result. In addition, with travel favourably aspected, he should set funds aside for a holiday during the year. By choosing his destination carefully, he can find his travels working out well and doing him a lot of good.

The Dragon should also give time to his interests over the year. With his enquiring mind and eager nature, he is rarely at a loss for things to do and spending time on activities that bring him pleasure will be another satisfying aspect of the year.

His social life will also see much activity, with many chances to go out and meet friends. With his outgoing nature, the Dragon will find himself in great demand, with his social circle widening as the year develops. For the unattached or those who would welcome more companionship, the prospects are promising and by regularly going out as well as involving themselves in activities and interests they enjoy, they will get to meet others and form some good friendships. April, July to September could be active and interesting months socially, with good opportunities to meet others.

The Dragon will also appreciate the support he is given by family members, and by being forthcoming and discussing his activities with those close to him, he will often benefit from the advice he receives. He will also derive much satisfaction from some of the domestic projects he tackles over the year, especially those that enhance his home. Again, the Dragon will regard this very much as a doing year and he certainly will do plenty. However, with the many demands on his time, he should be wary of starting too much all at once and should allow plenty of time for projects to be completed. Despite his willingness, it would be wise to keep his sometimes zealous nature in check. Here again, good liaison with those around him can often prevent problems arising as well as lead to more assistance being given.

Overall, the Rooster year holds excellent prospects for the Dragon and by making the most of his strengths and following through his ideas, he will reap many rewards. This is a year for commitment, enterprise and progress.

The Metal Dragon

The Metal Dragon will enjoy the active nature of the Rooster year, with many of his activities going well.

With this marking their sixty-fifth year, some Metal Dragons will retire, and those who do will make much of the extra time and the opportunity to follow through some of their ideas. These could include travel – perhaps a special holiday – or spending more time on interests they have not had the chance to properly pursue. Some will also mark their retirement by taking up something completely different, but whatever these Metal Dragons decide, they will certainly make good use of the additional time they now have.

Those Metal Dragons who have already retired will also keep themselves busy with a myriad of activities, and whether they prefer creative pursuits, practical ones or a combination of both, by developing their interests they will find them bringing much pleasure. If there are any new subjects or skills that appeal to the Metal Dragon, he should aim follow these up over the year. And if he can persuade his partner or a close friend to join him, he will find this can give added meaning to his activities.

In addition to his interests and personal development, the Metal Dragon could also find it helpful to give some consideration to his general lifestyle, particularly reviewing whether he has sufficient exercise or eats a healthy and balanced diet. If he feels there is room for improvement, he could find it helpful to obtain medical guidance on the best way to proceed. To do all that he wants to do, he does need to look after himself and keep himself on good form. Metal Dragons, take note.

There will be chances too for the Metal Dragon to travel over the year and if there is a particular destination he is keen to visit, he should make enquiries and see what is possible. This is an excellent year for following through ideas.

The Metal Dragon will also fare well in money matters, with many Metal Dragons receiving a bonus or benefiting from a maturing policy. While anything extra he receives will be welcome, the Metal Dragon should plan what he is going to do with his money rather than be tempted to spend it too readily. Carefully considering his purchases and setting funds aside for forthcoming activities, including travel, will be of benefit to him.

However, while this can be a positive year financially, the Metal Dragon does need to deal with important paperwork carefully, especially if relating to tax, benefits or pensions. Should he have any uncertainties or questions, he should raise these rather than jump to conclusions or take risks. To delay or make a mistake could be to his detriment. Also, he should be thorough with other important paperwork he receives, including any policies due for renewal. Despite the favourable aspects, this is not a time to be lax on matters that can have important implications. Metal Dragons, take note.

As far as his relations with others are concerned, this will be a pleasing year for the Metal Dragon. He will value the love and affection of those around him and also enjoy carrying out practical projects and interests he can share. There will be many meaningful occasions, including travel, holidays and family get-togethers, and also good cause for a family celebration, with a possible wedding or the birth of a great grandchild. In keeping with the positive nature of the year, the Metal Dragon's family life will contain moments he will long treasure.

He will also find this an active year socially and will have many opportunities to go out to various events as well as to meet friends. Any Metal Dragons who may have recently moved or changed their circumstances in other ways and are keen to build up their social life will find that by becoming more involved in local activities, groups or societies, some important new friendships will be born. Some Metal Dragons could also decide to give time to charity work or to helping others and this will be another enriching aspect of their life.

In many respects, this will be an excellent year for the Metal Dragon and will give him the chance to enjoy his interests and activities and take them further. With his outgoing nature and wide interests, he will find this a very rewarding time.

TIP FOR THE YEAR
This already fine year can be made all the more interesting by trying something new. Whatever you decide upon, it will often lead to much personal satisfaction.

The Water Dragon

This year holds great prospects for the Water Dragon and with his experience and the support of others, as well as his own determined nature, he is set to do particularly well. This is a year for progress and finding greater satisfaction in what he does.

Work prospects are especially encouraging and although many Water Dragons will have seen a lot happen in recent years, the changes are not over yet. In previous years the Water Dragon will have added greatly to his experience and impressed many around him, and as a consequence, he will find himself strongly placed when opportunities arise. These could include being offered greater duties, becoming involved in projects more related to his area of specialization or securing promotion. March to May and November could see important developments, but opportunities could arise at almost any time and when they do, the Water Dragon should act quickly.

Those Water Dragons who are seeking work or anxious to change their position will also find the year offering some good opportunities. Whenever they see an opening that appeals to them, these Water Dragons should waste no time in putting themselves forward. Their eagerness, together with their experience and reputation, will often create a favourable impression and lead to many of them securing a position which not only offers promising prospects but in some cases a new start. Even if certain applications do not go his way, the Water Dragon should not lose heart. With persistence, his efforts *will* be rewarded, and often in a significant way.

Another pleasingly aspected area concerns the Water Dragon's personal interests and over the year he should not only set time aside for these but also look to develop them in some way. If he enjoys creative activities, setting himself a new project or mastering a certain skill or technique could bring him especial pleasure, while those Water Dragons who prefer more practical or outdoor pursuits will again find what they do fulfilling and enjoyable. The Water Dragon's interests can also give his lifestyle a greater balance as well as offer him the chance to relax and unwind.

The Water Dragon should also make sure he takes a holiday over the year, as the change of scene will do him good. By choosing his holiday destination well and following up any other travel opportunities or invitations that appeal to him, he will find his travelling will be another enjoyable aspect of the year. In some cases, he could form an important new friendship while away.

The progress the Water Dragon makes at work will also lead to an increase in income. As a result, he will often be tempted to spend money on his home, his interests and his loved ones. His spending will often bring pleasure both to him and others, but he would also find it helpful to set aside funds for the longer term or reduce any borrowings he may have. By managing his money well, he will find his overall position improving over the year.

With his genial nature, the Water Dragon is invariably held in high regard by others and over the year his social life holds fine prospects. His work, interests and social circle can all lead to him being invited to various occasions. And for those Water Dragons who may be feeling lonely or who have had recent personal problems, the year holds excellent prospects for meeting others and building up some significant friendships.

This will also be a busy year domestically and the Water Dragon will do much to help others, especially those under pressure or with important decisions to take. While he may sometimes worry about his loved ones and some of the situations they face, there will certainly be much which will delight him, including news of progress being made and a possible wedding or the birth of a grandchild. The Water Dragon's family does mean much to him and as always he will play a caring and important role. Also, others in his household will be thankful for the way he is able to organize and oversee so much. Domestically, this will be an active but often rewarding year.

In many respects this is a special year for the Water Dragon, giving him the chance to develop his talents and follow through many of his ideas and plans. He has much in his favour and by making the most of his position and the opportunities that arise, he will benefit and prosper.

TIP FOR THE YEAR
This is a time to follow up your ideas. Whether they concern activities to try, places to visit or ambitions to reach, *now* is the time for action. With a determined

approach and the support and goodwill of others, much will be possible in 2005.

The Wood Dragon

The Rooster year will suit the Wood Dragon well, allowing him to make good and effective use of his ideas and talents.

At work the aspects are especially promising and for those Wood Dragons looking to advance their career, there will be some excellent opportunities to pursue. This really is a year when the Wood Dragon can build on his position and good standing. The months from March to May and late October and November could bring some interesting opportunities, but given the nature of the Rooster year, the Wood Dragon could find himself being asked to take on a greater role or see some excellent chances to pursue at any time. By making the most of such opportunities, even if they are only temporary, such as covering for absent colleagues or doing extra work at busy times, he will be adding to his experience and helping his future prospects.

The aspects are also encouraging for those Wood Dragons who are seeking work or perhaps feeling they have accomplished all they can in their present role and are considering a change. By following up openings that appeal to them and stressing their experience and the contribution they feel they can make, many will secure a position that will often represent an interesting new start and one which, with their determined nature, they can make much of.

The Wood Dragon too is a gifted thinker and can often come up with ideas which have not yet occurred to others but which could make a difference. This year he should put his ideas forward, particularly any related to his work. With the favourable aspects that prevail, his input and initiative will be appreciated and often well rewarded.

This is also a good year for the Wood Dragon's personal development and whether he is adding to his vocational skills or furthering his personal interests, he will gain much from the way he is able to extend his knowledge and abilities. His interests will also bring him much pleasure and whether they take him out of doors, have a social element or allow him to draw on his more creative talents, they will often do him good as well as help him to lead a more balanced lifestyle.

The Wood Dragon will also enjoy the travel opportunities the year will bring and whether following up invitations to visit family or friends living some distance away or taking a holiday in an area he has long wanted to see, he will appreciate the chances to go away and enjoy the places he visits. Once again this is a year to make the most of his ideas and opportunities.

The progress that the Wood Dragon makes in his work will also lead to an increase in his income and some Wood Dragons could also put a skill or interest to use in supplementing this further. However, while the Wood Dragon's earning abilities will be strong, he does still need to be careful in money matters and should manage his resources well. While money may flow into his accounts, it can also flow out. In the Rooster year the Wood Dragon really would be helped by keeping accounts, monitoring his outgoings and setting funds aside for specific requirements. Despite the generally favourable financial aspects, this is not a year for carelessness.

The Wood Dragon's domestic life will bring him considerable pleasure over the year, and if he is a parent, he will do much to encourage the progress of his children. With his sense of fun and wide interests, there will be many moments that everyone will appreciate and treasure. The Wood Dragon will also value the love and support of his partner or those close to him, although to fully benefit he does need to be forthcoming and speak of any concerns, anxieties and pressures he might have, so that others are better able to understand and help. Should he at any time feel tired or tense, he should also be careful not to take his vexations out on others. Although he is usually considerate and even-tempered, too many snappy responses or moments when he is preoccupied with other concerns could undermine the rapport he has with his loved ones. This is something he should watch. But with thoughtfulness and quality time spent with those who are dear to him, the Wood Dragon's domestic life will be pleasurable and bring much contentment.

Socially, too, the Rooster year holds fine prospects and the Wood Dragon will often have the chance to meet up with others and go to events that appeal. Also, as he becomes involved in different activities or meets others through changes in his work or circumstances, he will find his social circle widening. For unattached Wood Dragons, particularly those looking to put some personal difficulties behind them, this is very much a year for moving forward. By joining interest groups and meeting those they have something in common with, they can see quite a transformation in their personal lives over the year. April and July to mid-October will be particularly active for social matters.

In so many respects this is a highly promising year for the Wood Dragon, but to benefit he does need to put himself forward and make the most of his talents and the opportunities the year will bring. With determination – and the Wood Dragon *is* determined – this can be a rewarding and successful time.

TIP FOR THE YEAR
In spite of the activity the year will bring, do make sure you spend time enjoying the company of those who are important to you. These are precious times and with the love and full-hearted support of those who mean so much, the year can be all the more special and successful.

The Fire Dragon

The Fire Dragon has a keen and ambitious nature and in the Rooster year he is set to make impressive progress. With his talents and ideas, backed by his drive, this is very much a year for progress.

Already many Fire Dragons will have seen considerable changes in their work in recent years and the experience they have gained and contacts and reputation they have built up will lead to further progress being made over the year. In many cases their in-house knowledge will place them in a strong position when vacancies and promotion opportunities arise, and by putting themselves forward, many will be successful in gaining a more senior role in their current organization.

Those who feel there may be better prospects elsewhere, who desire a change or are seeking work should also actively pursue any positions that appeal to them. As these Fire Dragons recognize, in order to make the progress they desire, it does rest with them to take the initiative. During the Rooster year their determination and self-belief will often lead to them securing an important new position.

Another feature of the year will be the chance it gives many Fire Dragons to take on different types of duties and so widen their experience. By making the most of such chances the Fire Dragon will again take an important step in his onward development. For work opportunities, March to May and November are particularly well aspected, but in general this is a year for looking to advance.

The progress that the Fire Dragon makes in his work will lead to a welcome increase in income, but he does still need to manage his resources carefully. Without care he could find his spending levels greater than they need be and over the year he should avoid succumbing to too many impulsive buys. Also, if he can make early provision for some of his more expensive purchases, including travel and possible equipment for his home, he would find this helpful. He should also be careful when dealing with any important paperwork and financial forms. Again, vigilance and prompt attention are of the essence.

The Fire Dragon also needs to manage his time well over the year. Although he is committed to his work, it is important that his lifestyle has balance and his personal interests are not neglected. Not only can these be a great source of pleasure, but they are also a good way for him to unwind and have a break from more everyday concerns. And if the Fire Dragon is sedentary for much of the day, activities that take him out of doors or provide him with additional exercise would be particularly beneficial. To keep himself in good form, it is important that he gives some consideration to his lifestyle and well-being.

The Fire Dragon will particularly appreciate his domestic life over the year and especially the love and affection shown by those around him. The year can be marked by a notable personal celebration, including a possible addition to his family or the achievement of someone special. The Fire Dragon will also enjoy many of the activities he carries out with his loved ones, including projects in the home and garden as well as time spent on shared interests.

As with any year, however, problems will sometimes raise their head and whenever the Fire Dragon feels under pressure or has matters concerning him, he should be open and forthcoming rather than allow tensions to brew. Also, at busy times, he should make sure that quality time with his loved ones does not suffer. If he is mindful of this and allows others to help, he will have good reason to value the richness of his home and family life.

The Fire Dragon's social life can go well over the year and by meeting friends and going to social events that appeal to him, he will often enjoy himself. Many Fire Dragons will find changes in their work and interests will bring them into contact with new people, some of whom they will strike up a good friendship with. For those seeking romance, there will also be chances to meet others, but the Fire Dragon would be wise to let any new relationship develop in its own time rather than be too hasty. To build up high expectations in the early stages could put undue pressure on the relationship and lead to disappointment. Fire Dragons, do take heed. Affairs of the heart can go well and mean a great deal, but do not be over-hasty.

In so many respects, this will be a year of opportunity for the Fire Dragon, especially in the way that it will allow him to develop his career. However, with much demanded of him and his own eagerness to do well, he does need to manage his time carefully and make sure his progress at work does not make too many incursions into other areas of his life. In the Rooster year he should really strive for a balanced lifestyle. By doing so, he can make this a satisfying and pleasing year.

TIP FOR THE YEAR
Take full advantage of the chances to develop yourself, your skills and your interests. What you can achieve now can bring satisfaction as well as be to your long-term good.

The Earth Dragon

This is a year of fine opportunity for the Earth Dragon, although to benefit he will need to act well upon chances that arise. But with a positive and willing attitude, a great deal is possible.

For the Earth Dragon involved in study this will be an important year and as examinations approach, he should set about his revision in an organized and thorough manner. Also, to keep himself motivated, he should bear in mind the opportunities that will open up as a result of him doing well, whether these are entry into further education or into a certain type of work. The efforts the Earth

Dragon makes over the year will certainly have important implications.

The Earth Dragon too will benefit from the support of those around him and if at any time he has uncertainties over certain subject areas or would welcome advice about his future, he should not hesitate to talk to his tutors or those in a position to advise. He will be both helped and encouraged as a result.

During the year some Earth Dragons will decide to enter the world of work rather than continue with their education, and for these Earth Dragons this can prove a significant year. Although some of the work they are offered will be routine, by making an effort and showing a willingness to learn, they will quickly make an impression and mark themselves out for future progress. In some cases they could find themselves improving on their position or moving to greater responsibilities within just a few months, such are the favourable aspects of the year. Also, these Earth Dragons should make the most of any training they may be offered. Any skills they can learn and additional qualifications they can gain will be to their benefit. For work opportunities, the months from March to May and October and November are particularly favourable.

As far as the Earth Dragon's finances are concerned, he will certainly be glad of his earnings and with an often active social life as well as all the things he will want to do and buy, he will enjoy the fruits of his labours. Those Earth Dragons still involved in education will also often be able to help their financial position by taking on a small job or assisting others. Financially, this can be a positive year, and with sensible control over his purse strings, the Earth

THE DRAGON

Dragon will be pleased with his position. However, despite the favourable aspects, he would be wise not to take unnecessary risks or become involved in schemes or agreements he has not properly checked or does not fully understand.

The Earth Dragon's social life is, however, splendidly aspected and over the year he will find himself in great demand. Also, by furthering some of his interests, he could get to meet others and in some cases some significant and sometimes lifelong friendships will be forged. April and July to September could see considerable social activity.

The Earth Dragon will also be grateful for the encouragement he is given by his family and those close to him. While there may be times when he would perhaps welcome a greater independence, or views may clash, by being willing to talk and listen, the Earth Dragon will gain much from family life. Also, by being willing to play his part and help more with certain household tasks, he will find what he does will be appreciated as well as help with the rapport he has with those close to him. And should he have any matters concerning him, including any decisions he needs to take, he should be forthcoming and raise these with family members. Despite the gap in years, he will find they can relate to his position more than he may realize, as well as offer helpful guidance.

Another important area of the year concerns the Earth Dragon's personal interests and he would do well to develop these further, perhaps by joining other enthusiasts or setting himself a new challenge. His interests can often benefit him as well as bring pleasure.

And this does sum up the nature of the Rooster year. The aspects *are* on Earth Dragon's side and by being willing and making the most of his situation and the chances available to him, he will make worthy progress as well as derive satisfaction from most of his activities.

TIP FOR THE YEAR
Build up your qualifications and skills. What you learn now will often prove very important in the long term. Make the most of the opportunities available.

FAMOUS DRAGONS

Dan Aykroyd, Clive Anderson, Maya Angelou, Jeffrey Archer, Joan Armatrading, Joan Baez, Roseanne Barr, Count Basie, Maeve Binchy, Sandra Bullock, Julie Christie, James Coburn, Courteney Cox, Randy Crawford, Bing Crosby, Russell Crowe, Roald Dahl, Salvador Dali, Charles Darwin, Lindsay Davenport, Neil Diamond, Bo Diddley, Matt Dillon, Christian Dior, Placido Domingo, Fats Domino, Kirk Douglas, Faye Dunaway, Bruce Forsyth, Sigmund Freud, Graham Greene, Che Guevara, David Hasselhoff, Sir Edward Heath, James Herriot, Paul Hogan, Joan of Arc, Tom Jones, Immanuel Kant, Martin Luther King, Eartha Kitt, John Lennon, Abraham Lincoln, Elle MacPherson, Queen Margrethe II of Denmark, Yehudi Menuhin, François Mitterrand, Andrew Motion, Hosni Mubarak, Florence Nightingale, Nick Nolte, Al Pacino, Gregory Peck, Pelé, Edgar Allan Poe, Vladimir Putin, Christopher Reeve, Keanu Reeves, Sir Cliff Richard, Harold Robbins, Ronaldo, George Bernard Shaw, Martin Sheen, Alicia Silverstone, Ringo Starr, Princess Stephanie of Monaco, Dave Stewart, Karlheinz Stockhausen, Shirley Temple, Maria von Trapp, Andy Warhol, Johnny Weissmüller, Raquel Welch, The Earl of Wessex, Mae West, Frank Zappa.

4 FEBRUARY 1905 ~ 24 JANUARY 1906   Wood Snake

23 JANUARY 1917 ~ 10 FEBRUARY 1918   Fire Snake

10 FEBRUARY 1929 ~ 29 JANUARY 1930   Earth Snake

27 JANUARY 1941 ~ 14 FEBRUARY 1942   Metal Snake

14 FEBRUARY 1953 ~ 2 FEBRUARY 1954   Water Snake

2 FEBRUARY 1965 ~ 20 JANUARY 1966   Wood Snake

18 FEBRUARY 1977 ~ 6 FEBRUARY 1978   Fire Snake

6 FEBRUARY 1989 ~ 26 JANUARY 1990   Earth Snake

24 JANUARY 2001 ~ 11 FEBRUARY 2002   Metal Snake

THE
SNAKE

THE PERSONALITY OF THE SNAKE

> If you want to be respected, the great thing is to respect yourself.
>
> *Fyodor Dostoevsky, a Snake*

The Snake is born under the sign of wisdom. He is highly intelligent and his mind is forever active. He is always planning and always looking for ways in which he can use his considerable skills. He is a deep thinker and likes to meditate and reflect.

Many times during his life he will shed one of his famous Snake skins and take up new interests or start a completely different job. The Snake enjoys a challenge and he rarely makes mistakes. He is a skilful organizer, has considerable business acumen and is usually lucky in money matters. Most Snakes are financially secure in their later years, provided they do not gamble – the Snake has the distinction of being the worst gambler in the whole of the Chinese zodiac!

The Snake generally has a calm and placid nature and prefers the quieter things in life. He does not like to be in a frenzied atmosphere and hates being hurried into making a quick decision. He also does not like interference in his affairs and tends to rely on his own judgement rather than listen to advice.

At times the Snake can appear solitary. He is quiet, reserved and sometimes has difficulty in communicating with others. He has little time for idle gossip and will certainly not suffer fools gladly. He does, however, have a good sense of humour and this is particularly appreciated in times of crisis.

The Snake is certainly not afraid of hard work and is thorough in all that he does. He is very determined and can occasionally be ruthless in order to achieve his aims. His confidence, willpower and quick thinking usually ensure his success, but should he fail it will often take a long time for him to recover. He cannot bear failure and is a very bad loser.

The Snake can also be evasive and does not willingly let people into his confidence. This secrecy and distrust can sometimes work against him and it is a trait which all Snakes should try to overcome.

Another characteristic of the Snake is his tendency to rest after any sudden or prolonged bout of activity. He burns up so much nervous energy that he can, if he is not careful, be susceptible to high blood pressure and nervous disorders.

It has sometimes been said that the Snake is a late starter in life and this is mainly because it often takes him a while to find a job in which he is genuinely happy. However, the Snake will usually do well in any position which involves research and writing and where he is given sufficient freedom to develop his own ideas and plans. He makes a good teacher, politician, personnel manager and social adviser.

The Snake chooses his friends carefully and while he keeps a tight control over his finances, he can be particularly generous to those he likes. He will think nothing of buying expensive gifts or treating his friends or loved ones to the best theatre seats in town. In return he demands loyalty. The Snake is very possessive and he can become extremely jealous and hurt if he finds his trust has been abused.

The Snake is also renowned for his good looks and is never short of admirers. The female Snake in particular is most alluring. She has style, grace and excellent (and usually expensive) taste in clothes. A keen socializer, she is likely to have a wide range of friends and a happy knack of impressing those who matter. She has numerous interests and her opinions are often highly valued. She is generally a calm-natured person and while she involves herself in many activities, she likes to retain a certain amount of privacy in her undertakings.

Affairs of the heart are very important to the Snake and he will often have many romances before he finally settles down. He will find that he is particularly well suited to those born under the signs of the Ox, Dragon, Rabbit and Rooster. Provided he is allowed sufficient freedom to pursue his own interests he can also build up a very satisfactory relationship with the Rat, Horse, Goat, Monkey and Dog, but he should try to steer clear of another Snake as they could very easily become jealous of each other. The Snake will also have difficulty in getting on with the honest and down-to-earth Pig, and will find the Tiger far too much of a disruptive influence on his quiet and peace-loving ways.

The Snake certainly appreciates the finer things in life. He enjoys good food and often take a keen interest in the arts. He also enjoys reading and is invariably drawn to subjects such as philosophy, political thought, religion or the occult. He is fascinated by the unknown and his enquiring mind is always looking for answers. Some of the world's most original thinkers have been Snakes, and although he may not readily admit it, the Snake is often psychic and relies a lot on intuition.

The Snake is certainly not the most energetic member of the Chinese zodiac. He prefers to proceed at his own pace and to do what he wants. He is very much his own master and throughout his life he will try his hand at many things. He is something of a dabbler, but at some time – usually when he least expects it – his hard work and efforts will be recognized and he will invariably meet with the success and the financial security which he so desires.

THE FIVE DIFFERENT TYPES OF SNAKE

In addition to the 12 signs of the Chinese zodiac there are five elements, and these have a strengthening or moderating influence on the sign. The effects of the five elements on the Snake are described below, together with the years in which the elements were exercising their influence. Therefore those Snakes born in 1941 and 2001 are Metal Snakes, those born in 1953 are Water Snakes, and so on.

Metal Snake: 1941, 2001

This Snake is quiet, confident and fiercely independent. He often prefers to work on his own and will only let a privileged few into his confidence. He is quick to spot opportunities and will set about achieving his objectives with an awesome determination. He is astute in financial matters and will often invest his money well. He also has a liking for the finer things in life and a good appreciation of the arts, literature, music and good food. He usually has a small group of extremely good friends and can be generous to his loved ones.

Water Snake: 1953

This Snake has a wide variety of interests. He enjoys studying all manner of subjects and is capable of undertaking quite detailed research and becoming a specialist in his chosen area. He is highly intelligent, has a good memory and is particularly astute when dealing with business and financial matters. He tends to be quietly spoken and a little reserved, but he does have sufficient strength of character to make his views known and attain his ambitions. He is very loyal to his family and friends.

Wood Snake: 1905, 1965

The Wood Snake has a friendly temperament and a good understanding of human nature. He is able to communicate well and often has many friends and admirers. He is witty, intelligent and ambitious. He has numerous interests and prefers to live in a quiet, stable environment where he can work without too much interference. He enjoys the arts and usually derives much pleasure from collecting paintings and antiques. His advice is often highly valued, particularly on social and domestic matters.

THE SNAKE

Fire Snake: 1917, 1977

The Fire Snake tends to be more forceful, outgoing and energetic than some of the other types of Snake. He is ambitious, confident and never slow in voicing his opinions – and he can be very abrasive to those he does not like. He does, however, have many leadership qualities and can win the respect and support of many with his firm and resolute manner. He usually has a good sense of humour, a wide circle of friends and a very active social life. He is also a keen traveller.

Earth Snake: 1929, 1989

The Earth Snake is charming, amusing and has a very amiable manner. He is conscientious and reliable in his work and approaches everything he does in a level-headed and sensible way. He can, however, tend to err on the cautious side and never likes to be hassled into making a decision. He is adept in dealing with financial matters and is a shrewd investor. He has many friends and is very supportive towards the members of his family.

PROSPECTS FOR THE SNAKE IN 2005

The Chinese New Year starts on 9 February 2005. Until then, the old year, the Year of the Monkey, is still making its presence felt.

The Year of the Monkey (22 January 2004 to 8 February 2005) will have been a reasonable one for the Snake, with the closing months being an active time.

In his work the Snake can make useful progress, but he should aim to work closely with others and show himself a good team member. This is not a time for him to be too independent either in attitude or approach. For those Snakes seeking work or keen to progress, September and October 2004 could bring some interesting opportunities.

The Snake also needs to be his thorough self when dealing with financial matters in the closing months of the Monkey year, and with many outgoings at this time, he would do well to keep track of his spending and avoid unnecessary risks.

He will, though, particularly value his domestic and social life and by being forthcoming and discussing any ideas and concerns he may have, he will be encouraged by the advice and support he receives. Also, while the Snake may not be such an active socializer as some, he should follow up any invitations he receives and make the most of any opportunities to go out. Not only will he enjoy himself but he could also meet people who will prove helpful to him over the next year.

The holiday period at the end of the year will also go well and as the Monkey year draws to a close, the Snake will feel his prospects are on the turn and will be more determined than ever to make the most of the forthcoming year.

The Year of the Rooster starts on 9 February and will be a significant one for the Snake. Always keen to use his talents and ideas, he will enjoy some excellent opportunities which will enable him to make progress and reap considerable rewards. And, on a personal level, the year holds considerable promise.

Almost as soon as the Rooster year begins, the Snake will sense that this is a year which holds special promise and he will start to consider ways to improve on his position. At work, some Snakes will decide to remain with their present employer but take advantage of in-house opportunities and chances to make more of their expertise. With the knowledge and contacts that they have, these Snakes will often find themselves excellently placed to progress. Also, they could find events moving in fortuitous ways, with some unexpected offers which will move their career forward.

Some Snakes will, however, feel they will gain more by moving to a different organization and so broadening their experience. While finding a suitable position will often take some time, by remaining determined, many Snakes will be successful in their quest and will secure a position which will not only allow them to extend their skills but also have good potential for the future.

Those Snakes seeking work should also actively pursue any openings that appeal to them. Even though some applications may not go their way, they should not allow themselves to become too disheartened. This *is* a year of opportunity and some disappointments could even turn out to be blessings in disguise, as better opportunities arise in their wake. As the Snake will find, opportunities could appear quickly and at almost any time during the year, but February, April, July and October could see particularly interesting developments.

In view of the positive nature of the year, the Snake should also make the most of any opportunities that come his way, and whether these involve training, covering for colleagues or having the chance to do something extra, by showing willing he will not only be adding to his experience but also helping his prospects and reputation. The Rooster year does reward the keen and industrious.

This is also a positive year for financial matters, with some Snakes being able to supplement their income with occasional freelance work or by furthering an idea they have. However, while the Snake may enjoy a rise in income, this could be an expensive year for him. Family activities, accommodation, travel and personal interests could all involve a great deal of outlay and it would be to the Snake's advantage to keep a close watch on his outgoings and make allowance for his obligations. In some instances making early provision for expensive purchases or activities will help. Also, while the Snake usually possesses good judgement in financial matters, he must not allow his vigilance to slip and should be especially careful if considering anything of a more speculative nature. This is a year for careful management and control, not risks.

The Snake will, however, derive much satisfaction from his interests over the year and should aim to set a regular time aside for them. For the more creative Snakes, interests which allow them to express themselves and develop their talents will be especially fulfilling. And if the Snake sees an interest or hobby that intrigues him or there is a particular skill he would like to develop, he would do well to follow it up. His interests will not only bring him much pleasure over the year but can also be an absorbing and rewarding use of his time.

The Snake's domestic life is also excellently aspected and he will not only draw much encouragement from the love and support of those dear to him but also enjoy many of the family activities that take place. These may include projects and interests that can be carried out together, as well as trips out and any holidays and breaks. The Snake will play a full part in what goes on and often instigate a great deal of it. Also, the year could be marked by an important family celebration and whether this is a graduation, engagement, wedding, addition to his family or the success enjoyed by a loved one, it will be very special to the Snake.

Throughout the year the Snake will also be helped by listening closely to his loved ones and, should he have any problems, concerns or important decisions to take, he himself should be prepared to talk the matter over. This is not a year for him to keep his thoughts to himself, especially when he can gain so much from advice and support that others can give.

His social life will, though, need care. Quite a few Snakes do like to keep themselves to themselves and, due to their own commitments and personal activities, will decide to keep their social life low-key this year. While they may like it that way, these Snakes should still try to avoid becoming too solitary or remote, as they could be missing out on an enriching aspect of their life. In this promising year, these Snakes do need to bear this in mind and allow time for a certain amount of socializing.

For other Snakes, though, including the unattached or those enjoying the early stages of romance, the year will give rise to some pleasant social occasions, although the Snake does need to be attentive and aware of the viewpoints of other people. With this being such a successful year, it will be worth giving extra care and attention to friendships and social situations. The best months for socializing are from April to June and December.

Generally, the Rooster year holds excellent prospects for the Snake and by taking positive steps to improve his situation and taking advantage of any opportunities that come his way, he will make progress and prosper as well as enjoy himself.

The Metal Snake

The Rooster year holds much potential for the Metal Snake and by following through his ideas and making the most of chances that arise, he will be satisfied with how it develops.

The Metal Snake's domestic life is particularly well aspected and he will take much pleasure in carrying out projects on his home and garden. Not only will he delight in watching his ideas unfold and the improvements that result, but by involving his loved ones, he will also find his projects taking on a greater meaning as well as leading to greater understanding and rapport. This is very much a year for going ahead with plans for domestic projects and then enjoying the results.

The Metal Snake will also take a keen interest in family activities over the year and those close to him will often look to him for advice. With his considerable experience and level-headed outlook, the Metal Snake will find his views and judgement will be well regarded. In addition, he will have good cause for a family celebration during the year and if any arrangements need making, he will play an active part and help to ensure that all goes well. Again, his willingness to be involved will be much appreciated.

The year will also bring some good opportunities for the Metal Snake to travel. In addition to receiving invitations to visit family and friends living some distance away he could be tempted by a short break he sees advertised or decide to visit an area he has wanted to see for a long time. By following up the opportunities that arise, he will find that travel is another positive aspect of the year.

This is also an encouraging year for the Metal Snake's personal interests and he should set aside time for activities he enjoys. These may involve learning a new skill, taking up some sort of personal challenge or following up subjects that interest him, but whatever he does, by acting upon his ideas he will enjoy some rewarding times.

However, while so much is in the Metal Snake's favour during the year, there are certain areas which require care. One of these relates to social situations. During the year, the Metal Snake does need to remain aware of the views of friends as well as keep a close watch over his tongue. An inadvertent comment or a moment's inattention could lead to some difficulty and possibly undermine a friendship. When he is with others on a social basis, the Metal Snake does need to watch his words. Also, while he may have strong convictions, he must accept that not everyone will share his views and in some instances a certain discretion could help matters. However, the Metal Snake will still enjoy many of the social occasions of the year, with the months from late March to June and December seeing much social activity.

Another area that requires care concerns the Metal Snake's finances. This could prove an expensive year, particularly with family activities and accommodation plans as well as travel to take into account. While he will not begrudge his spending and the considerable pleasure it will bring, the Metal Snake should still keep a close watch on his financial situation. By doing so, he could find it possible to cut back on certain non-essentials and so leave more for other activities. By being watchful, he will fare that much better.

For those Metal Snakes in work this will be a satisfying year, especially in the way that it allows them to put their experience to effective use. By making the most of their strengths and, in some cases, training and advising others, these Metal Snakes will find this a productive and fulfilling year.

Overall, this is the type of year that suits the Metal Snake. With his earnest nature and many ideas, he will enjoy the activity of the year and be highly satisfied with the way that many of his plans develop.

TIP FOR THE YEAR
Do look to further yourself and your interests over the year, either by learning a new skill or setting yourself an interesting challenge or project. With good and purposeful use of your spare time, you will find the activities you tackle bringing pleasure and often much benefit.

The Water Snake

This will be a significant year for the Water Snake, allowing him to make substantial progress as well as enjoy a rich and often rewarding personal life. However, while the aspects may be favourable, much does depend upon the Water Snake himself. Unfortunately there are some Water Snakes who do not always make the progress they could, due to their rather reserved and reticent nature. In the Rooster year the Water Snake really should keep faith with himself and *seize the initiative*. For the determined, the rewards of the year can be substantial.

As far as the Water Snake's work is concerned, the aspects are especially promising. With his considerable experience, ideas and reliability, the Water Snake will often find others looking to him to play a greater role or take on more specialist duties. He may also be ideally placed for promotion. By making the most of the opportunities that arise, he will not only be able to move his career forward but also make better use of his talents and strengths. For the many Water Snakes who are keen to advance their career, February, April, July and October could see some fine opportunities.

For those Water Snakes seeking work or considering a career change, the Rooster year also holds encouraging prospects. However, to benefit, these Water Snakes will need to remain persistent. Even though certain applications may not go their way, they should not lose heart. The aspects *are* on their side and their persistence will, in the end, be rewarded, with many securing a position which will not only allow them to extend their skills but will also open up other possibilities for the future. The Rooster year *is* one of opportunity and important developments.

This will also be an excellent year for the Water Snake's own personal development and he will gain a great deal by following up any training offered by his employers as well as any courses he may be able to take himself. Whether these relate to his work, interests or well-being or are purely for recreation, they can bring many benefits as well as reinforce the constructive nature of the year.

The Water Snake also possesses a strong creative streak and with the aspects as they are, he should make the most of it. If he has ideas which may be helpful in his work, he should put them forward, while if he has interests which allow him to draw on his more creative talents, he should spend time developing and promoting them. This is not a year to be reticent – there is potentially much to be gained.

As far as financial matters are concerned, this will be a generally positive year, with many Water Snakes enjoying an increase in income as well as sometimes benefiting from funds from another source. However, while this may be an encouraging time, it will also be an expensive one, with many demands on the Water Snake's resources. This could be due to family expenses as well as accommodation costs and other plans. With so much possible outlay, the Water Snake does need to manage his finances carefully and would find it helpful to keep a regular check on his position. The more care he can take, the better he will fare.

This is, however, a pleasingly aspected year as far as the Water Snake's family life is concerned and he will play a full and active part in the many family activities that will take place. Whether carrying out more practical projects, sharing interests or helping others, he will find the time he gives to his home life will be appreciated as well as make it all the more rewarding. The Water Snake does have a tendency to keep his thoughts to himself, but by being willing to discuss ideas and any concerns he may have, he will find himself being encouraged by the advice and support of those around him.

He should also not neglect his social life over the year, as it will do him good as well as lead to some interesting times. In addition, some of the people he meets in connection with his work or interests could prove especially helpful to him. However, to benefit, the Water Snake does need to make the most of social situations and, in common with all Snakes in 2005, remain attentive and mindful of the views of others.

Overall, the Rooster year is an encouraging one for the Water Snake, particularly as it will give him the chance to develop his strengths, talents and ideas. By making the most of his opportunities, he will be able to make good progress at work as well as enjoy greater fulfilment. In addition, his family life and personal interests will bring him much pleasure.

TIP FOR THE YEAR

Your talents and often original approach can lead to a great deal of progress over the year, but to benefit you do need to put yourself forward. Remember, *Nothing ventured, nothing gained.* In 2005, venture.

The Wood Snake

This year marks the Wood Snake's fortieth year and it will be a significant one for him. As they enter a new decade of their life, many Wood Snakes will decide that the time has come to move forward. And with their determination to make things happen, they are set to make considerable progress.

At work this is a year of important developments. Although many Wood Snakes will have accomplished a great deal in recent years, there will be quite a few who feel stale or unchallenged and who would welcome the chance for further development. As a result, almost as soon as the Rooster year begins, many Wood Snakes will start to look for openings which would advance their career. Whenever they see a suitable opportunity, they should act quickly and put themselves forward. Although it could take several attempts to secure a new position, once they do succeed, they will revel in their new responsibilities. For so many Wood Snakes, the Rooster year will give them the chance to progress.

This also applies to those Wood Snakes seeking work. By persisting in their quest and stressing to prospective employers their experience and what they feel they can bring to any new role, many will be able to secure a position which will suit them well and be one they can build on. February, April, July and October could see some interesting work opportunities.

The Wood Snake's progress at work will also lead to an increase in his income and some Wood Snakes may be able to supplement this over the year by possible freelance work or putting one of their skills or interests to profitable use. However, as with all Snakes, the Wood Snake will find this an expensive year and he will need to keep a close watch on his outgoings. Without vigilance these could exceed what he expected or budgeted for. Also, should he take on any new financial commitment, he should be thorough in checking the terms and implications. Where money matters are concerned, this is a year for careful management and control.

The Rooster year will, though, bring some fine travel opportunities. Some Wood Snakes will choose to mark their fortieth year by taking a special holiday, perhaps visiting somewhere they have wanted to see for a long time. However, by following up their ideas as well as taking advantage of any invitations they receive, the Wood Snakes' travels can bring them considerable pleasure. Also, many Wood Snakes could take an almost spur of the moment decision to go away and the spontaneity will lead to some particularly enjoyable occasions.

The Wood Snake's domestic life is also favourably aspected, and by planning and carrying out home projects with loved ones, as well as sharing interests, encouragement and support, he will find it meaning a great deal. Also, throughout the year, the Wood Snake will do much to help more senior as well as younger relations and in both cases his caring but attentive manner will be appreciated. Similarly, when he himself has important decisions to take or feels under pressure, he should be forthcoming and allow others to help and advise. And if at any time a difference of opinion should arise, he would find it helpful to talk it over and aim to resolve it quickly and amicably rather than let it cast a shadow on what can be such an agreeable year.

Although the Wood Snake will have many demands on his time, it is also important that he does not allow his social life to suffer as a result. By meeting up with friends and going to events that appeal to him, he will not only enjoy himself but also benefit from the chance to relax and unwind. Also, through meeting colleagues socially, he will find himself being helped and encouraged as well as establishing some important new contacts. However, as with all Snakes in 2005, the Wood Snake does need to be attentive to others and aware of their views. Without care, a *faux pas* could cause embarrassment. Wood Snakes, take note.

Overall, this will be an encouraging year for the Wood Snake and with his experience and personal strengths, his efforts can help make this, his fortieth year, a significant and successful one.

TIP FOR THE YEAR
Have faith in yourself and look to move forward. This is a year for positive action and to further your aims and ambitions.

The Fire Snake

The Fire Snake possesses a keen and determined nature and in the Rooster year he will be able to make much of his talents as well as find himself excellently placed to benefit from the opportunities that arise. This is a year for some well-deserved success.

At work the aspects are especially favourable and over the year the Fire Snake will be able make good use of his experience and to build on his present position. He will also be helped by his contacts and those who know of his skills and capabilities. As he will find, he *will* have much in his favour over the year.

In view of their expertise, many Fire Snakes will find themselves being singled out to play a greater role and be given more specific responsibilities. The Fire Snake will often revel in the chance this gives him to make more of his skills. Often he will find the extra responsibilities will bring promotion and increased remuneration, but if not and he decides to look elsewhere, he should actively follow up any suitable openings he sees. As he recognizes, his progress does depend on his own efforts and over the year his determination and persistence will be rewarded. February, April, July and October could see positive work developments, but given the favourable aspects of the year, whenever the Fire Snake sees an opening he should act swiftly.

This also applies to those Fire Snakes seeking work, either as the Rooster year starts or during it. When applying for a position, they could find it helpful to make further enquiries about the company and the post they are putting in for. In this way their informed comments at interview will impress. Again, the Rooster year does look favourably on those who are prepared to make the effort.

Also, the Fire Snake should aim to follow through his ideas over the year. If they are related to his work, he should put them forward, as he will often find his initiative welcomed. In addition, he would do well to consider his own development, and by adding to his knowledge and skills, whether through training offered through his work or study he can do himself, he will not only find what he learns helpful but that it will reinforce the positive nature of the year. This really is a time to move forward.

As far as financial matters are concerned, almost all Fire Snakes will enjoy an increase in income over the year and some could also receive a gift or bonus. However, the Fire Snake's outgoings are also likely to increase and he would do well to keep watch on his situation over the year and, where possible, make early provision for his various commitments. With careful management and control, he will fare well, but equally if he is too carefree or lax, problems could loom and economies be called for. Also, many Fire Snakes will be involved in considerable costs relating to their accommodation over the year and, if they have to increase their borrowings or enter into a new agreement, they would do well to check the terms and implications carefully and resolve any queries beforehand. Fortunately the Fire Snake is usually thorough in such matters, but with many demands on his resources, this is not a time to let his vigilance slip.

One of the most encouraging areas of the year will be the Fire Snake's domestic life, and for those with a partner, shared activities will mean a great deal. By talking over his plans and hopes, as well as discussing any concerns he may have, the Fire Snake really will benefit from the support he receives. There could also be good cause for celebration over the year as a result of some pleasing family news.

Many Fire Snakes will also have good reason to value the support of more senior relations, appreciating not only the time and help they are able to give but also the advice offered. While there will often be a considerable gap of years, others are often able to understand the Fire Snake's position much better than he may realize and he will be glad of all they can do for him.

THE SNAKE

Although this will be a busy year for the Fire Snake, he should make sure his social life does not suffer due to his various commitments. By meeting friends and going to social occasions that appeal to him, he will not only enjoy himself but also gain a great deal. In some cases, significant friendships and contacts can result. The months from late March to June and December could be especially busy socially.

The Fire Snake should also make sure his personal interests and recreational pursuits do not suffer due to the activity of the year, and by regularly setting time aside for them and developing them further, he will again find them benefiting him and bringing him pleasure. Those Fire Snakes with creative interests should also consider promoting what they do. With the aspects as they are, they could be encouraged by the response to their efforts.

Overall, this is a very positive year for the Fire Snake and by making the most of his talents and the opportunities that arise, he can look forward to making good progress. Also, he will be well supported, and the love of another and some pleasing personal or family news can help make the year all the more special.

TIP FOR THE YEAR

Be prepared to act upon your ideas, particularly any related to your work and personal interests. These would be worth taking further.

The Earth Snake

This will be a significant year for the Earth Snake, with what he achieves now having an important bearing on the next few years.

For many Earth Snakes there will be important examinations to prepare for, and with these and the other work he has to do, the Earth Snake could find some of the year demanding. However he is blessed with a conscientious nature and while he may feel daunted by all he has to learn, by working steadily and consistently he will acquit himself well. Also, with so much hinging on his results, it really would be worth him putting in the extra effort and making the most of the challenge and opportunity before him.

The Earth Snake will also be well supported by those around him and if he feels he needs extra guidance in certain areas, he should not hesitate to ask. Sometimes just an additional explanation can make something much clearer and lead to better grades. To benefit, though, the Earth Snake does need to be forthcoming and ask.

The work that the Earth Snake does now will also have an important bearing on his development and future education, particularly in indicating what he should do next. Many Earth Snakes will be keen to focus more on their favourite subjects and they should make sure their preferences are known. Even if the Earth Snake is not yet sure which subject areas to concentrate on, he should be prepared to talk through his options rather than being persuaded into making decisions he does not feel comfortable with. In the Rooster year he does need to be open and frank rather than let others make decisions for him. And, while so many Earth Snakes will do well over the year, if certain results are disappointing, the Earth Snake should not allow himself to get too discouraged. There is plenty of time for him to improve, and with everything he has in his favour, his prospects are certainly encouraging.

The Earth Snake should also take advantage of the opportunities and facilities available to him, especially recreational ones. By developing his skills he will add to the pleasure his interests bring. Some Earth Snakes will enjoy being involved in youth groups, clubs and other out-of-school activities, and by taking advantage of what is available and joining friends in various activities, the Earth Snake can look forward to some great times. Also, as he becomes involved in new activities, he will find himself making new friends as the year develops. However, while his social life holds good prospects, he does need to be careful in certain situations and should not let himself be persuaded into doing anything he may have misgivings about. At certain times, he would be wise to stand his ground.

As far as his finances are concerned, the Earth Snake's resourcefulness will be useful over the year, with many Earth Snakes being able to earn something extra by helping others or taking on a small job. However, there will often be a great deal that the Earth Snake will want to do and buy, and he would find it helpful to plan ahead and save towards his various purchases. He should also be wary of making too many impulsive buys or being tempted by risky or dubious schemes. As far as his money is concerned, this is a year for careful control and good planning.

Those Earth Snakes who decide to leave school over the year and take on a job will be required to make some significant adjustments, particularly in adapting to new journeys, schedules and requirements. While the first few days of any new situation will be demanding, with a positive attitude, the Earth Snake will quickly settle into his new routine and make a favourable impression. With the aspects being so favourable, he could find that his first job will quickly pave the way to something more interesting and responsible.

As far as the Earth Snake's domestic life is concerned, those around him will be keen to support and advise him, but to benefit he does need to be prepared to talk over any decisions he has to make or any concerns he may have. While he may sometimes like to keep his thoughts to himself (a typical Snake trait), he will find a more open attitude will be to his advantage. And, despite a gap in years, those around him often understand and can empathize more than he may realize. The Earth Snake himself can also help ensure he enjoys a good rapport with those around him by offering to help more with household activities and chores. What he can do *will* be appreciated.

Overall, the Rooster year holds considerable potential for the Earth Snake and by making the most of his abilities and opportunities, he will not only learn a great deal but also sow some particularly important seeds for the future.

TIP FOR THE YEAR
Take full advantage of the opportunities to learn and add to your skills. This is a superb year for development. Also, by

furthering your personal interests you will find they can become more satisfying and purposeful.

FAMOUS SNAKES

Muhammad Ali, Tim Allen, Ann-Margret, Yasser Arafat, Lord Baden-Powell, Kim Basinger, Björk, Tony Blair, Michael Bloomberg, Heinrich Böll, Michael Bolton, Brahms, Pierce Brosnan, Casanova, Chubby Checker, Dick Cheney, Jackie Collins, Tom Conti, Jim Davidson, Cecil B. de Mille, Fyodor Dostoevsky, Bob Dylan, Elgar, Sir Alex Ferguson, Sir Alexander Fleming, Henry Fonda, Mahatma Gandhi, Greta Garbo, Art Garfunkel, J. Paul Getty, Dizzy Gillespie, W. E. Gladstone, Johann Wolfgang von Goethe, Princess Grace of Monaco, Stephen Hawking, Audrey Hepburn, Jack Higgins, Michael Howard, Howard Hughes, Tom Hulce, Elizabeth Hurley, James Joyce, Stacy Keach, Ronan Keating, Howard Keel, J. F. Kennedy, Carole King, Cyndi Lauper, Courtney Love, Dame Vera Lynn, Mao Tse-tung, Henri Matisse, Robert Mitchum, Nasser, Alfred Nobel, Mike Oldfield, Aristotle Onassis, Jacqueline Onassis, Pablo Picasso, Mary Pickford, Brad Pitt, Daniel Radcliffe, Franklin D. Roosevelt, Mickey Rourke, J. K. Rowling, Jean-Paul Sartre, Franz Schubert, Charlie Sheen, Brooke Shields, Paul Simon, Delia Smith, Paul Theroux, Madame Tussaud, Shania Twain, Dionne Warwick, Charlie Watts, Ruby Wax, Oprah Winfrey, Victoria Wood, Virginia Woolf.

25 JANUARY 1906 ~ 12 FEBRUARY 1907   *Fire Horse*

11 FEBRUARY 1918 ~ 31 JANUARY 1919   *Earth Horse*

30 JANUARY 1930 ~ 16 FEBRUARY 1931   *Metal Horse*

15 FEBRUARY 1942 ~ 4 FEBRUARY 1943   *Water Horse*

3 FEBRUARY 1954 ~ 23 JANUARY 1955   *Wood Horse*

21 JANUARY 1966 ~ 8 FEBRUARY 1967   *Fire Horse*

7 FEBRUARY 1978 ~ 27 JANUARY 1979   *Earth Horse*

27 JANUARY 1990 ~ 14 FEBRUARY 1991   *Metal Horse*

12 FEBRUARY 2002 ~ 31 JANUARY 2003   *Water Horse*

THE
HORSE

THE PERSONALITY OF THE HORSE

Your success depends on what you do yourself, with your own means.

P. T. Barnum, a Horse

The Horse is born under the signs of elegance and ardour. He has a most engaging and charming manner and is usually very popular. He loves meeting people and likes attending parties and other large social gatherings.

The Horse is a lively character and enjoys being the centre of attention. He has considerable leadership qualities and is much admired for his honest and straightforward manner. He is an eloquent and persuasive speaker and has a great love of discussion and debate. He also has a particularly agile mind and can assimilate facts remarkably quickly.

He does, however, have a fiery temper and although his outbursts are usually short-lived, he can often say things which he will later regret. He is also not particularly good at keeping secrets.

The Horse has many interests and involves himself in a wide variety of activities. He can, however, get involved in so much that he can often waste his energies on projects which he never has time to complete. He also has a tendency to change his interests rather frequently and will often get caught up with the latest craze or 'in thing' until something better or more exciting turns up.

The Horse also likes to have a certain amount of freedom and independence. He hates being bound by petty rules and regulations and as far as possible likes to feel that he is answerable to no one but himself. But despite this spirit of freedom, he still likes to have the support and encouragement of others in his various enterprises.

Due to his many talents and likeable nature, the Horse will often go far in life. He enjoys challenges and is a methodical and tireless worker. However, should things work against him and he fail in any of his enterprises, it will take a long time for him to recover and pick up the pieces again. Success to the Horse means everything. To fail is a disaster and a humiliation.

The Horse likes to have variety in his life and he will try his hand at many different things before he settles down to one particular job. Even then, he will probably remain alert to see whether there are any better opportunities for him to take up. He has a restless nature and can easily get bored. He does, however, excel in any position which allows him sufficient freedom to act on his own initiative or which brings him into contact with a lot of people.

Although the Horse is not particularly bothered about accumulating great wealth, he handles his finances with care and will rarely experience any serious financial problems.

The Horse also enjoys travel and loves visiting new and faraway places. At some stage during his life he will be tempted to live abroad for a short period of time and due to his adaptable nature he will find that he will fit in well wherever he goes.

The Horse pays a great deal of attention to his appearance and usually likes to wear smart, colourful and rather distinctive clothes. He is very attractive to others and will often have many romances before he settles down. He is loyal and protective to his partner, but despite his family commitments he still likes to retain a certain measure of independence and have the freedom to carry on with his own interests and hobbies. He will find that he is especially well suited to those born under the signs of the Tiger, Goat, Rooster and Dog. He can also get on well with the Rabbit, Dragon, Snake, Pig and another Horse, but he will find the Ox too serious and intolerant for his liking. The Horse will also have difficulty in getting on with the Monkey and the Rat – the Monkey is very inquisitive and the Rat seeks security, and both will resent the Horse's rather independent ways.

The female Horse is usually most attractive and has a friendly, outgoing personality. She is highly intelligent, has many interests and is alert to everything that is going on around her. She particularly enjoys outdoor pursuits and often likes to take part in sport and keep-fit activities. She also enjoys travel, literature and the arts, and is a very good conversationalist.

Although the Horse can be stubborn and rather self-centred, he does have a considerate nature and is often willing to help others. He has a good sense of humour and will usually make a favourable impression wherever he goes. Provided he can curb his slightly restless nature and keep tight control over his temper, he will go through life making friends, taking part in a multitude of different activities and generally achieving many of his objectives. His life will rarely be dull.

THE FIVE DIFFERENT TYPES OF HORSE

In addition to the 12 signs of the Chinese zodiac there are five elements, and these have a strengthening or moderating influence on the sign. The effects of the five elements on the Horse are described below, together with the years in which the elements were exercising their influence. Therefore those Horses born in 1930 and 1990 are Metal Horses, those born in 1942 and 2002 are Water Horses, and so on.

Metal Horse: 1930, 1990

This Horse is bold, confident and forthright. He is ambitious and a great innovator. He loves challenges and takes great delight in sorting out complicated problems. He likes to have a certain amount of independence and resents any outside interference in his affairs. He has charm and a certain charisma, but he can also be very stubborn and rather impulsive. He usually has many friends and enjoys an active social life.

Water Horse: 1942, 2002

The Water Horse has a friendly nature and a good sense of humour and is able to talk intelligently on a wide range of topics. He is astute in business matters and is quick to take advantage of any opportunities that arise. He does, however, have a tendency to get easily distracted and can change his interests – and indeed his mind – rather frequently, and this can often work to his detriment. He is nevertheless very talented and can often go far in life. He pays a great deal of attention to his appearance and is usually smart and well turned out. He loves to travel and also enjoys sport and other outdoor activities.

Wood Horse: 1954

The Wood Horse has a most agreeable and amiable nature. He communicates well with others and is able to talk intelligently on many different subjects. He is a hard and conscientious worker and is held in high esteem by his friends and colleagues. His opinions are often sought and, given his imaginative nature, he can often come up with some very original and practical ideas. He is usually widely read and likes to lead a busy social life. He can also be most generous and often holds high moral views.

Fire Horse: 1906, 1966

The element of Fire combined with the temperament of the Horse creates one of the most powerful forces in the Chinese zodiac. The Fire Horse is destined to lead an exciting and eventful life and to make his mark in his chosen profession. He has a forceful personality and his intelligence and resolute manner bring him the support and admiration of many. He loves action and excitement and his life will rarely be quiet. He can, however, be rather blunt and forthright in his views and does not take kindly to interference in his own affairs or to obeying orders. He is a flamboyant character, has a good sense of humour and will lead a very active social life.

Earth Horse: 1918, 1978

This Horse is considerate and caring. He is more cautious than some of the other types of Horse, but he is wise, perceptive and extremely capable. Although he can be rather indecisive at times, he has considerable business acumen and is very astute in financial matters. He has a quiet, friendly nature and is well thought of by his family and friends.

PROSPECTS FOR THE HORSE IN 2005

The Chinese New Year starts on 9 February 2005. Until then, the old year, the Year of the Monkey, is still making its presence felt.

The Year of the Monkey (22 January 2004 to 8 February 2005) holds encouraging prospects for the Horse, with the closing months seeing much activity.

At work the aspects are especially favourable and the Horse should take advantage of any opportunities to further his position and add to his experience. With determination, he can achieve a great deal at this time, with October seeing some particularly positive developments.

The Horse's personal qualities will also serve him well, with his manner and style impressing many. As the year draws to a close he will have many opportunities to go out and socialize, with September and December being two especially fine months.

The Horse's domestic life will also be busy, with a lot to do and arrange. However, with the support of those around him, he will take great satisfaction in all that he is able to accomplish. A few Horses will even move before the year is out. The Horse does like activity and the Monkey year will not disappoint him.

As far as finance is concerned, the closing months will be expensive and while the Horse will not begrudge his spending, he would be wise to keep watch on his outgoings as well as avoid risky undertakings. The Monkey year may be favourable, but is not one for the Horse to become over-complacent or to push his luck too far.

The Year of the Rooster starts on 9 February and holds fine prospects for the Horse. However, he will need to work hard for results as well as watch his independent tendencies. This is a year for proceeding with care as well as being flexible in outlook.

At work the Horse's prospects are generally encouraging. However, in view of the changes of the preceding year, many Horses will decide to concentrate on their existing role and continue learning about the various aspects of their work. By immersing themselves in what they do and giving their best, these Horses will often find their work satisfying and will be able to improve on and add to their skills. While many will be content in their existing role, should the opportunity arise for them to take on other responsibilities, they should make the most of it.

THE HORSE

Not only will the additional experience be helpful now, but it will often be to their long-term advantage as well.

For those Horses who are unhappy in their present situation and keen to move on, as well as those seeking work, again the Rooster year will contain some good opportunities. However, such is the nature of the year that these Horses will need to put in the effort in order to secure something suitable. This includes preparing thoroughly for any interview as well as presenting themselves in the best possible light. As the Horse will find, he *will* need to work hard to make progress, but with commitment and determination, he may well secure what will be an interesting new position, and one with the potential for further development. March, April, June and November in particular could see some fine opportunities.

The Horse should also take advantage of any training that may be available to him. Even though he may already be proficient at what he does, he will benefit from improving his skills and keeping up to date with developments.

As far as financial matters are concerned, the Horse will need to proceed with care in the Rooster year. With the many things he would like to do and buy, he will need to plan ahead, including setting certain sums aside for more expensive purchases as well as keeping watch on his general level of spending. With care and control, he will be pleased with how he fares, but he does need to use his resources well. Also, he should be wary of entering into commitments too hurriedly and without checking the terms and implications, otherwise he could come to regret his haste. With finances, especially with large transactions, thoroughness is the key.

The Rooster year is, though, favourably aspected for travel and the Horse should aim to go away at some time during the year. By going somewhere that appeals to his adventurous Horse nature, he will often enjoy himself as well as benefit from the break. Some Horses may take advantage of travel offers at short notice or follow up invitations to visit those living some distance away. The aspects for travel are certainly encouraging.

The Horse will also derive a great deal of satisfaction from his personal interests over the year, especially those which take him out of doors or have a practical element to them. The Horse often has the knack of using his leisure time well, and with his many ideas, this can be a particularly rewarding year for him.

This also applies to his domestic life. Again, the Horse will nearly always have some activity lined up and will certainly contribute a lot to family life. In addition, he will provide much useful support to those around him and whenever a loved one needs encouragement or advice, the Horse will be there. Some of the help he is able to offer to those much younger and older than himself will mean far more than he may realize. However, while he will do much to assist others, the Horse should also listen carefully to any advice and suggestions he receives from those close to him. They do speak with his interests at heart.

The Horse's social life holds pleasing prospects over the year and he will enjoy going out and spending time with friends. In view of his often wide-ranging interests and the various activities he gets involved in, he will often meet others and widen his social circle. For those Horses who may be lonely or have had some recent personal difficulty, the Rooster year can be a more positive time, and by going out and pursuing their interests, many will see quite a transformation in their social life. For the unattached, affairs of the heart could feature prominently and will help to make the year all the more special. For socializing and meeting others, the months from February to early April and August and September are particularly well aspected.

Overall, the Rooster year holds good prospects for the Horse, but to benefit he will need to work hard and make the most of his opportunities. His accomplishments this year will often serve him well in the more auspicious Dog year that follows.

The Metal Horse

The Rooster year holds considerable promise for the Metal Horse and with a positive attitude and a willingness to make the most of the available opportunities, he can look forward to making substantial progress.

In his schoolwork, in particular, this is a year when hard work will be well rewarded, and by making an effort and working consistently, the Metal Horse will learn a great deal. What he has to study now will often lay important groundwork for exams he will be taking later on. While he will have some strong and favourite subject areas, he should not give up on those which he finds more difficult. By asking when necessary *and* making an effort, he will find he will be able to lift his overall performance as well as boost his confidence.

The Metal Horse should also aim to further his personal interests over the year. Those keen on sport should make the most of facilities at school and in their local area, while those who like music and are learning an instrument (and many Metal Horses are talented musically) will find that joining a local group, band or class can add to their knowledge as well as their pleasure. This also applies to any other skills and interests that the Metal Horse has. By making the most of the chances available to him, he can often develop his interests in an encouraging and constructive way.

The Metal Horse will also value his close circle of friends over the year and will enjoy the chance to share thoughts (and some secrets) with those he gets on with. He will also spend many enjoyable times in the company of his friends. Any Metal Horse who may feel slightly lonely, perhaps as a result of having moved to a new area or not feeling in tune with those around him, should not despair. By following up his interests, he will often get to meet those with similar outlooks and lasting friendships will be born. Socially, this *is* a well-aspected year.

The Metal Horse will, though, need to be careful in money matters. Often he will want to do a great deal, but his resources will be limited and he will need to watch his spending. Sometimes more thought before making hasty and impulsive purchases would help, as would planning ahead and saving towards more substantial purchases. Many Metal Horses will be able to supplement their means by taking on a small job or helping others in some way. But money-wise, this is a year for careful control.

The Metal Horse's home life will be important to him over the year and he will be grateful for the support and guidance given. However, to benefit, the Metal Horse does need be forthcoming with his ideas and keep his rather independent Metal Horse nature in check! Others *are* willing to help him and want to see him do well, but he does need be open and receptive. Metal Horse, take note, and do be prepared to both talk and listen.

Those Metal Horses born in 1930 will also greatly value the support given by loved ones over the year and if at any time they would welcome advice or assistance over some matter, they should not hesitate to ask. Like the younger Metal Horse, they too will derive much pleasure from their interests, especially those of a creative nature. Again, by using their skills well and following through their ideas, they can make this a most satisfying time.

Overall, the Rooster year holds encouraging prospects for the Metal Horse, although just how he fares does rest with him. If he is prepared to put in the effort and make the most of the chances available, he will do well and, for the younger Metal Horse, do much to prepare for his future success.

TIP FOR THE YEAR
Aim to develop your interests and skills. This will not only add to the pleasure but will have other benefits too, often giving rise to other opportunities.

The Water Horse

The Water Horse likes to keep himself active and as the year starts he will certainly have many thoughts about what he would like to do over the next 12 months. However, in order to make the best use of the year, he should plan what he wants to do with care and concentrate on his priorities rather than spread his energies too widely.

In his work this can be a rewarding year and by using his skills and experience well, the Water Horse can look forward to making good progress. In some cases his experience will lead to him taking on more specialist duties and he will find his work more fulfilling as a result.

There will, though, be some Water Horses who will decide to reduce their working hours this year or move to more local employment so they can spend more time with their family and on other pursuits. These Water Horses may find it takes them slightly longer to carry out their plans than they would like. However, by remaining persistent, many will be able to make the change they want and will be pleased with the difference it makes. As far as the Water Horse's work is concerned, this is very much a year when he will govern what happens, and whether increasing or decreasing his role, he can bring about some important change. Late February to April, June and November could see some interesting developments, as well as openings for those Water Horses currently looking for work.

The Water Horse needs to be disciplined in financial matters over the year. With his current obligations and the many plans he will be keen to carry out, he would do well to keep a close watch on his financial position as well as make early provision for some of the larger purchases he has in mind. By managing his money well, he will often find he is able to do more as a result. Also, he should not be careless in keeping important documents, guarantees or receipts. Should problems arise, it could be essential to refer back to these. In financial matters and paperwork, efficiency is key this year.

The Water Horse will value his personal interests over the year, especially those which have a social element. If he has not already done so, he could get much value from joining a local group or society. By meeting other enthusiasts, he will not only find his knowledge increasing but could also forge some new friendships. Similarly, if there is a subject or skill that has been intriguing him, he should aim to find out more this year and again, joining a local course or class could be a good way to do this.

Many Water Horses have a fondness for the outdoors and whether they enjoy gardening, following sport, walking or visiting different areas, by spending time on their pursuits they will be able to enjoy many rewarding occasions over the year. Travel is also favoured and the Water Horse should aim to go away for a holiday at some time as well as follow up any invitations to visit others. As he will find, by using his time well, he will be able to do a great deal in the Rooster year.

Throughout the year the Water Horse will also be encouraged by the support he receives from his loved ones, and by talking over his thoughts and plans and involving others, he will find many of his ideas moving forward as well as benefiting from the input and assistance others can give. Also, where more practical projects are concerned, the more help the Water Horse can get, the better.

The Water Horse will also take considerable pleasure in following the progress of family members over the year and there will be several family occasions and pieces of news which will mean a great deal to him. In addition, the support he is able to give to a close relation who may be under pressure or have a problem to deal with will be especially appreciated, with the Water Horse's good sense and judgement being valued.

The year is also favourably aspected for social matters, with the Water Horse enjoying meeting his friends as well as going to various events that appeal to him. Existing and new interests could also have a pleasing social element. The months from February to early April and August and September could be particularly active socially.

Overall, the Rooster year holds fine prospects for the Water Horse, but to benefit he does need to be disciplined in the way he sets about his activities. If he uses his time well and makes the most of the opportunities that arise, he can make this a pleasing and rewarding year.

TIP FOR THE YEAR

Be forthcoming about your plans and ideas. That way, not only will you benefit from the advice and support you are given, but also, in some cases, from extra assistance. The year holds great prospects, but to benefit fully, *do* involve others.

The Wood Horse

This will be a busy and sometimes demanding year for the Wood Horse, but despite the pressures, he will find this a satisfying time, particularly as it will allow him to draw on his experience and follow through many of his ideas.

At work he will often find himself with a heavy workload and a lot being expected of him. However, by tackling his duties systematically and remaining his organized self, he will not only cope well but also achieve some notable successes. Also, he will be pleased with the way he is able to draw on his skills, and despite everything he has to do, he will often find his work bringing a greater fulfilment.

Many Wood Horses will decide to remain in their existing role over the year. However, while these Wood Horses may feel settled, they should not be resistant to any opportunities that arise. If, for instance, they have the chance to take on further responsibilities, adapt their role in some way or become involved in a new project or initiative, they will find it will not only add to their experience but also be helpful to their future prospects. Also, while the Wood Horse may feel competent in his work, he should consider taking up any training he may be offered. By keeping his skills up to date as well as acquiring new ones, he will again benefit now as well as sometimes open up possibilities for later.

For those Wood Horses who are seeking work or who are particularly anxious to change their position, the Rooster year will contain some interesting opportunities. However, in view of the considerable competition there will be for certain positions, the Wood Horse will need to make an effort when making applications, including finding out more about the position he is putting in for as well as preparing well for any interview. This is not a time to undersell himself. As he will find, progress in the Rooster year will require determination on his part. However, even if certain applications do not go his way, the Wood Horse should remain resolute. He knows that he has much to offer and by continually putting himself forward, he will often be able to secure a position that will be both interesting and full of potential. Work-wise,

March, April, June and November could see some interesting opportunities.

As far as financial matters are concerned, the Wood Horse will need to be his careful self over the Rooster year. He could have some large expenses, particularly in assisting family members, possibly with wedding costs, educational costs or other outlay involving accommodation and transport. When these are known about in advance, the Wood Horse should make early provision for them as well as save regularly for other commitments and plans he has in mind. By being careful and managing his resources well, he will be pleased with how he copes in what could be quite an expensive year.

One of the most favourably aspected areas of the year concerns the Wood Horse's personal interests, and while he will often have many demands on his time, he should not neglect these, as they will bring both pleasure and benefit. With the Wood Horse's keen and enquiring nature, if there is a subject that has been intriguing him, this would be a good year to follow it up. Where the Wood Horse's interests are concerned, it can be a fulfilling time.

Travel, too, is well aspected and the Wood Horse should aim to go away at some time over the year. With his adventurous nature, he will often enjoy visiting areas new to him and will benefit from the rest and change any holiday or break will bring.

As far as his domestic life is concerned, there will be some rewarding occasions, with some family events and the progress of someone dear to him meaning a great deal. He will also value the assistance he is given in many of his activities and, particularly when setting about more practical household projects, will find that joint effort can make an appreciable difference. However, while his home life will mean a great deal over the year, it could have its more awkward moments. Particularly in view of some of the work pressures the Wood Horse may be under, there will be times when he is tired and preoccupied with his thoughts. And, while others will often be understanding, if he becomes too snappy or short-tempered, he could find this undermining an otherwise agreeable family life. Wood Horses, take note, and at busy times, do not hesitate to ask others for help. In this way, pressures can be eased considerably.

In view of the busy nature of the year, the Wood Horse will also appreciate his social life, and whether going out to meet friends or attend social events, he will enjoy the break from his everyday concerns. Late February to early April, August and September could be active months socially.

With the demands of the year, the Wood Horse should not neglect his well-being and if he feels he does not get sufficient exercise or that his diet could be improved, he should seek guidance on the best way to proceed. This will certainly help keep him in good form.

Overall, while the Rooster year will often be a busy and demanding one for the Wood Horse, it will give him the opportunity to further both his skills and interests. And as a result he will not only gain greater fulfilment from what he does but also lay the groundwork for the more encouraging Dog year that follows.

TIP FOR THE YEAR
Do be forthcoming and remember that those around you are keen to support you. In return, despite the pressures on

your time, do spend time with those important to you. The attention you give to personal relationships will be important *and* valued.

The Fire Horse

This will be an important year for the Fire Horse and although he will need to work hard for results and not everything will go as smoothly as he would like, he will still emerge from the year with some impressive gains to his credit. Also, what he achieves now will prepare the way for the greater progress he will make over the next few years. The long-term significance of the Rooster year can be considerable indeed.

At work the Rooster year will demand much of the Fire Horse. Many Fire Horses will face a heavy workload and sometimes daunting challenges. However, the Fire Horse is tenacious and his abilities and commitment will lead to him accomplishing a great deal as well as enhancing both his reputation and prospects. Also, some of the tasks given him will allow him to put his experience and training to more effective use and in the process he will discover certain strengths or areas he will be keen to take further.

With his future in mind, if he is offered any training or feels that a certain qualification or skill would be helpful, he should make the most of his chances or investigate ways in which he can follow this up. By developing his skills, even if through home study, an evening class or a course over the media, he will help his future prospects as well as increase his options.

This also applies to those Fire Horses seeking work. They too could find it helpful to take advantage of any training they may be eligible for, particularly if it allows them to refresh certain skills or acquire new ones. Again, this is a year when personal development can lead to a great deal. However, in his quest for a position, the Fire Horse will need to remain persistent and make sure he emphasizes his experience and strengths to prospective employers. With much competition likely, it could take him several attempts before he is able to secure something suitable. However, once in a new position, the Fire Horse will find it giving him the chance to re-establish his career. Progress in 2005 may not always be easy, but for those who rise to the challenge and give their best, the rewards can be considerable. March, April, June and November could see some particularly interesting work developments.

As far as money matters are concerned, this will be a reasonable year for the Fire Horse and with good management, he will be able to do a lot with his money. However, he would do well to plan his more expensive purchases carefully rather than be too hasty. By considering his requirements and the options and ranges available, he will often find himself obtaining better deals as a result. This is a year for keeping his sometimes impulsive nature in check.

Although the Fire Horse will have many demands on his time over the year, he should make sure his personal interests do not suffer as a result. They can not only benefit him by providing a break from his usual activities, but can also, in some cases, give him the chance to get out of doors, obtain additional exercise or meet others. If there is an interest or subject that has been particularly intriguing him, this would be a good time to find out more.

With travel favourably aspected too, the Fire Horse should aim to go away for a holiday at some time during the year. By choosing his destination well, he will often enjoy himself as well as visit some interesting areas.

This will also be a busy year domestically and during it the Fire Horse will play a central role in family life, offering assistance and encouragement as well as suggesting ideas for activities and projects. However, while his home life will contain many pleasures, there will be times when he will feel under pressure, tired and possibly irritable, and at such times he should be careful not to take his vexations out on others. Also, when tired, he should ask those around him if they could help more with certain household tasks or consider deferring projects to another time. At busy times the Fire Horse must be careful not to continually push himself and be on the go all the time. Fire Horses, take note, and do keep things at a steady and sensible pace.

As far as the Fire Horse's social life is concerned, although he may not go out as frequently as in some years, he will appreciate the events he does attend as well as the times spent meeting up with friends. Fire Horses who may desire more companionship or who have had some recent difficulty in their personal life will find that by involving themselves in more local activities as well as meeting those who share similar interests, they can build up some important new friendships. Late February to early April, August and September are favourable months for socializing and meeting others.

Generally, this will be a busy year for the Fire Horse, but his gains can be considerable. By developing himself and his skills he will find what he does having much long-term value. In addition his domestic life, personal interests and travel opportunities will bring him considerable pleasure and give added meaning to the year.

TIP FOR THE YEAR
Do make sure your lifestyle has balance and that your recreational pursuits do not suffer amid all the activity. It is important that you give yourself the chance to unwind and enjoy the rewards your efforts will bring.

The Earth Horse

This will be a reasonable year for the Earth Horse and while his progress may not always meet his expectations, what he does accomplish can be of great value, particularly in the longer term.

In his work this will be a challenging year, with the Earth Horse often facing a heavy workload and finding some of his activities subject to delay or niggling problems. Work-wise, this will not be an easy or straightforward year, but as has been shown so many times, a challenge does bring out the best in the Earth Horse, and by concentrating on his duties and doing his best, he will add considerably to his experience and reputation. Also, some of the problems that arise will be a good test of his skills, and as he tackles the tasks before him, he will discover strengths that will be useful to him in future years. The lessons of the Rooster year can be considerable and far-reaching.

The Earth Horse will also be helped by acting closely with colleagues and showing himself a good team member. Not only will this help when dealing with certain situations but it will also allow the Earth Horse to build up support for his ideas and future aims. He could also find it helpful to meet others in his line of work or in areas he would one day like to move to. By making contacts and becoming better known, he can do his prospects a lot of good.

For those Earth Horses who are looking to advance in their career or seeking work, March, April, June and November could see some interesting opportunities. However, such is the nature of the year that the Earth Horse will need to work hard to make progress and it could take him several attempts before he secures a suitable position.

He will, though, enjoy a modest improvement in his income over the year and some Earth Horses may be able to supplement this with freelance work or putting a skill or interest to profitable use. However, while the Earth Horse will see money flowing into his accounts, he does need to be careful if he is to make the best use of it. If he does not already do so, he could find it helpful to keep a set of accounts so he can keep better track of his position. The attention he can give to managing his money really can make a difference.

As far as his domestic life is concerned, this will be an active and often memorable year. Those Earth Horses who are parents or who become parents over the year will often delight in the progress of their babies or young children. Caring and attentive as ever, the Earth Horse will also do much to support his partner as well as more senior relations, and his efforts will certainly be appreciated.

However, with the activities and pressures the year will bring, if at any time the Earth Horse is troubled by any matter or would welcome greater assistance, he should be forthcoming and ask. Help and advice *are* available and can make a difference. Also, while he may be keen to carry out certain home improvements, including altering décor and adding new comforts, the Earth Horse should allow plenty of time for this rather than put pressure on himself by aiming to do everything in a hurry. After all, the year will be busy enough!

The Earth Horse will value his social life over the year and can look forward to going to a variety of often interesting and enjoyable social events. The months from February to April and August and September could see much social activity, and for those Earth Horses who would welcome new friends, there will be good opportunities to meet others. For the unattached, a significant romance could be born. The Earth Horse will also find that his interests and work will give rise to some pleasant social occasions as well as opportunities to meet others.

With all the activity and pressures of the year, the Earth Horse does, though, need to give some consideration to his own well-being, and if he relies a lot on convenience foods, he could find switching to a more balanced diet will give him more energy and help his general well-being. Also, if he is sedentary for much of the day, he could find it helpful to take some additional exercise. With some medical guidance on the best way to proceed, he will be able to reap the benefit.

Although the Rooster year will be a busy and demanding one for the Earth Horse, it will also be important, with the experience he gains and skills he learns during it being of value as he looks to make greater headway over the next few years. Also, his personal life will bring him considerable pleasure.

TIP FOR THE YEAR
With all the pressures the year will bring, you do need to take care of yourself as well as balance out your various activities. Time spent on recreational pursuits and additional exercise could be especially beneficial.

FAMOUS HORSES

Neil Armstrong, Rowan Atkinson, Samuel Beckett, Ingmar Bergman, Leonard Bernstein, Karen Black, Cherie Blair, Helena Bonham Carter, James Cameron, Jackie Chan, Ray Charles, Chopin, Sir Sean Connery, Billy Connolly, Catherine Cookson, Elvis Costello, Kevin Costner, Cindy Crawford, Michael Crichton, James Dean, Clint Eastwood, Thomas Alva Edison, Britt Ekland, Harrison Ford, Aretha Franklin, Bob Geldof, Samuel Goldwyn, Billy Graham, Gene Hackman, Rolf Harris, Rita Hayworth, Jimi Hendrix, John Edgar Hoover, Janet Jackson, Calvin Klein, Lenin, Annie Lennox, Desmond Lynam, Sir Paul McCartney, Nelson Mandela, Princess Margaret, Ben Murphy, Sir Isaac Newton, Louis Pasteur, Harold Pinter, Puccini, Lou Reed, Rembrandt, Ruth Rendell, Jean Renoir, Condoleezza Rice, Theodore Roosevelt, Helena Rubenstein, Peter Sissons, Lord Snowdon, Alexander Solzhenitsyn, Barbra Streisand, Kiefer Sutherland, Patrick Swayze, John Travolta, Kathleen

Turner, Mike Tyson, Vivaldi, Robert Wagner, Denzil Washington, Billy Wilder, Andy Williams, the Duke of Windsor, Boris Yeltsin, Will Young.

13 FEBRUARY 1907 ~ 1 FEBRUARY 1908	*Fire Goat*
1 FEBRUARY 1919 ~ 19 FEBRUARY 1920	*Earth Goat*
17 FEBRUARY 1931 ~ 5 FEBRUARY 1932	*Metal Goat*
5 FEBRUARY 1943 ~ 24 JANUARY 1944	*Water Goat*
24 JANUARY 1955 ~ 11 FEBRUARY 1956	*Wood Goat*
9 FEBRUARY 1967 ~ 29 JANUARY 1968	*Fire Goat*
28 JANUARY 1979 ~ 15 FEBRUARY 1980	*Earth Goat*
15 FEBRUARY 1991 ~ 3 FEBRUARY 1992	*Metal Goat*
1 FEBRUARY 2003 ~ 21 JANUARY 2004	*Water Goat*

THE
GOAT

THE PERSONALITY OF THE GOAT

> The real voyage of discovery consists not in seeking new landscapes, but in having new eyes.
>
> *Marcel Proust, a Goat*

The Goat is born under the sign of art. He is imaginative, creative and has a good appreciation of the finer things in life. He has an easy-going nature and prefers to live in a relaxed and pressure-free environment. He hates any sort of discord or unpleasantness and does not like to be bound by a strict routine or rigid timetable. The Goat is not one to be hurried against his will, but despite his seemingly relaxed approach to life, he is something of a perfectionist and when he starts work on a project he is certain to give his best.

The Goat usually prefers to work in a team rather than on his own. He likes to have the support and encouragement of others and if left to deal with matters on his own he can get very worried and tend to view things rather pessimistically. Wherever possible he will leave major decision-making to others while he concentrates on his own pursuits. If, however, he feels particularly strongly about a certain matter or has to defend his position in any way, he will act with great fortitude and precision.

The Goat has a very persuasive nature and often uses his considerable charm to get his own way. He can, however, be rather hesitant about letting his true feelings be known and if he were prepared to be more forthright he would do much better as a result.

The Goat tends to have a quiet, somewhat reserved nature but when he is in company he likes he can often become the centre of attention. He can be highly amusing, a marvellous host at parties and a superb entertainer. Whenever the spotlight falls on him, his adrenalin starts to flow and he can be assured of giving a sparkling performance, particularly if he is allowed to use his creative skills in any way.

Of all the signs in the Chinese zodiac, the Goat is probably the most gifted artistically. Whether it is in the theatre, literature, music or art, he is certain to make a lasting impression. He is a born creator and is rarely happier than when occupied in some artistic pursuit. But even in this the Goat does well to work with others rather than on his own. He needs inspiration and a guiding influence, but when he has found his true *métier*, he can often receive widespread acclaim and recognition.

In addition to his liking for the arts, the Goat is usually quite religious and often has a deep interest in nature, animals and the countryside. He is also fairly athletic and there are many Goats who have excelled in some form of sporting activity or who have a great interest in sport.

Although the Goat is not particularly materialistic or concerned about finance, he will find that he will usually be lucky in financial matters and will rarely be short of the necessary funds to tide himself over. He is, however, rather indulgent and tends to spend his money as soon as he receives it rather than make provision for the future.

The Goat usually leaves home when he is young but he will always maintain strong links with his parents and the other members of his family. He is also rather nostalgic and is well known for keeping mementos of his childhood and souvenirs of places that he has visited. His home will not be particularly tidy, but he knows where everything is and it will also be scrupulously clean.

Affairs of the heart are particularly important to the Goat and he will often have many romances before he finally settles down. Although he is fairly adaptable, he prefers to live in a secure and stable environment and he will find that he is best suited to those born under the signs of the Tiger, Horse, Monkey, Pig and Rabbit. He can also establish a good relationship with the Dragon, Snake, Rooster and another Goat, but he may find the Ox and Dog a little too serious for his liking. Neither will he care particularly for the Rat's rather thrifty ways.

The female Goat devotes all her time and energy to the needs of her family. She has excellent taste in home furnishings and often uses her considerable artistic skills to make clothes for herself and her children. She takes great care over her appearance and can be most attractive to others. Although she is not the most organized of people, her engaging manner and delightful sense of humour create a favourable impression wherever she goes. She is also a good cook and usually derives much pleasure from gardening and outdoor pursuits.

The Goat can win friends easily and people generally feel relaxed in his company. He has a kind and understanding nature and although he can occasionally be stubborn, he can, with the right support and encouragement, live a happy and very satisfying life. And the more he can use his creative skills, the happier he will be.

THE FIVE DIFFERENT TYPES OF GOAT

In addition to the 12 signs of the Chinese zodiac there are five elements and these have a strengthening or moderating influence on the sign. The effects of the five elements on the Goat are described below, together with the years in which the elements were exercising their influence. Therefore those Goats born in 1931 and 1991 are Metal Goats, those born in 1943 and 2003 are Water Goats, and so on.

Metal Goat: 1931, 1991
This Goat is thorough and conscientious in all that he does and is capable of doing very well in his chosen profession. Despite his confident manner, he can be a great worrier and he would find it helpful to discuss his concerns with others rather than keep them to himself. He is loyal to his family and employers and will have a small group of particularly close friends. He has good taste and is usually highly skilled in some aspect of the arts. He is often a collector of antiques and his home will be very tastefully furnished.

Water Goat: 1943, 2003
The Water Goat is very popular and makes friends with remarkable ease. He is good at spotting opportunities but does not always have the necessary confidence to follow

them through. He likes to have security both in his home life and at work and does not take kindly to change. He is articulate, has a good sense of humour and is usually very good with children.

Wood Goat: 1955
This Goat is generous, kind-hearted and always eager to please. He usually has a large circle of friends and involves himself in a wide variety of activities. He has a very trusting nature but he can sometimes give in to the demands of others a little too easily and it would be in his own interests if he were to stand his ground more often. He is usually lucky in financial matters and, like the Water Goat, is very good with children.

Fire Goat: 1907, 1967
This Goat usually knows what he wants in life and often uses his considerable charm and persuasive personality to achieve his aims. He can sometimes let his imagination run away with him and has a tendency to ignore matters which are not to his liking. He is rather extravagant in his spending and would do well to exercise a little more care when dealing with financial matters. He has a lively personality, many friends, and loves attending parties and social occasions.

Earth Goat: 1919, 1979
This Goat has a considerate and caring nature. He is particularly loyal to his family and friends and invariably creates

a favourable impression wherever he goes. He is reliable and conscientious in his work but sometimes finds it difficult to save and never likes to deprive himself of any little luxury he might fancy. He has numerous interests and is often very well read. He usually derives much pleasure from following the activities of the various members of his family.

PROSPECTS FOR THE GOAT IN 2005

The Chinese New Year starts on 9 February 2005. Until then, the old year, the Year of the Monkey, is still making its presence felt.

The Year of the Monkey (22 January 2004 to 8 February 2005) will have been an active one for the Goat and while he may not have always felt comfortable with the pace of it or the way certain events have developed, he will still have accomplished a great deal. And the closing months offer considerable promise.

In what remains of the Monkey year the Goat should aim to make the most of prevailing situations. Particularly in his work, if there is a chance to take on further responsibilities or add to his experience in some way, he should follow it up. The progress he makes now can serve him well in the year ahead. September and November 2004 hold particularly encouraging prospects.

As far as money matters are concerned, the last quarter of the year will be an expensive time and the Goat would do well to save towards some of the purchases and activities he has in mind. He would also find it helpful to spread more seasonal purchases out.

The Goat's domestic and social life also promises to be busy at this time. The Goat will certainly be in demand as the Monkey year draws to a close, with August and December seeing much social activity. For the lonely and unattached, there will be good opportunities to meet others.

Overall, the Monkey year will often be a demanding one for the Goat, but by making the most of his strengths and the situations that arise, he will do his prospects a considerable amount of good.

The Year of the Rooster starts on 9 February and will be a busy and generally positive one for the Goat. However, he should remember that the Rooster year favours a practical and determined approach and if he is to benefit he must put some effort into his various activities as well as watch his capricious Goat nature. This is very much a year when commitment and resolve will reap rewards.

In the Goat's work this can be a year of significant developments, with quite a few Goats looking to advance their career or switch to something different. Having made that decision to go forward, they should waste no time in making enquiries, seeking advice or putting themselves forward whenever they see a suitable opportunity. As the saying goes, *There is no time like the present*, and the Rooster year is one when determination and resolve will pay off. The period from April to June and September could see some interesting and encouraging developments.

THE GOAT

Those Goats seeking work will also find that by actively following up any positions that interest them, even if they are different from what they have done before, they may well succeed in setting their career off on a new and encouraging path.

Also, all Goats should take advantage of any training that is available to them. Keeping their skills up to date will not only help their current position but also increase their options for the future. And with this being such a fine year for personal development, the Goat should also consider furthering his personal interests in some way. With his enquiring nature, he can find his interests bringing him considerable satisfaction over the year. Those Goats who enjoy creative and expressive pursuits would also do well to promote what they do, as many will be considerably heartened by the responses they receive to their work. This is a year when the Goat should use his talents well. He will often benefit as a result, and sometimes in surprising ways.

Travel, too, is favoured over the year and the Goat should make the most of any chances to go away, including taking up invitations to visit family or friends living some distance away.

However, while the Rooster year holds encouraging prospects for the Goat, there are certain areas which require greater care, and one of these is finance. This can be a costly year for the Goat, particularly with accommodation and family expenses. In view of this, he would do well to manage his finances carefully, keeping watch on his spending as well as making provision for his obligations. He also needs to be wary of taking risks and be thorough when dealing with important paperwork. This includes making sure insurance and other policies are kept up to date as well as dealing with financially related forms promptly and thoroughly. Inattention, delay or carelessness could be to the Goat's cost. Goats, take note.

With his outgoing and sociable nature, the Goat always set much store by his relations with others and over the year these will continue to mean a lot to him. Not only will he be encouraged by the support he is given, but by talking over his plans and ideas, he will find himself helped a great deal, sometimes in unexpected ways. In 2005 family, friends and close colleagues can all serve the Goat well.

As far as his home life is concerned, this will be a busy and sometimes eventful year. As always, the Goat will do much to assist those dear to him and the support and advice he gives will be much appreciated. Over the year many Goats will embark on some major projects to their home. In setting about such projects the Goat does need to plan carefully as well as consult others – the more help and input he can get, the better. With the eventful nature of the Rooster year there will also be some Goats who will move house. While again this will be time-consuming and disruptive, these Goats will welcome the new opportunities their move will bring and will regard it as the start of a new chapter in their lives. Here again, the Rooster year can often be a significant one.

However, in view of the activity and pressures some of the year will bring, there will be occasions when tempers get frayed and disagreements arise. In the Rooster year these do need to be resolved early to avoid the risk of them escalating or undermining the good relationships the Goat so values.

Goats, do take note, and remember that in difficult situations openness and dialogue can be worth a great deal.

The Goat's social life is, however, well aspected, and the Goat is likely to make the most of his chances to go out with friends or attend social events. With his sociable nature, he too will enjoy the opportunities he has to meet and get to know others. March, May and the period from July to early September could be particularly active. The Goat could also get to meet others through his interests or a holiday he goes on and form an important new friendship as a result.

Generally, the Rooster year holds encouraging prospects for the Goat and by carrying through his plans and making the most of his talents, he will accomplish a great deal. This is very much a year for forging ahead and the Goat will be supported and encouraged throughout.

The Metal Goat

This will be an important year for the Metal Goat, although just how he fares is dependent on his attitude. Over the year there will be many opportunities for him to learn, and by showing willing, he can make significant progress. However, if he lets himself fall into a malaise and does not make the most of himself, then this could be a year of wasted opportunities. As the Chinese proverb reminds us, *Achievement comes from diligence and nothing is gained by fooling around*, and the Rooster year is no year to fool around!

In his schoolwork the Metal Goat can look forward to making important strides, although, again, attitude will be an important factor. By applying himself and setting about his studies in a keen and eager way, he will not only learn a great deal but also build an important base for more advanced work. While some Metal Goats may feel that the really significant exams are some years away, what they study now will be helpful to them later on. Also, by immersing himself in what he has to do, the Metal Goat will not only find his studies more satisfying but also that he is getting more out of school life generally.

The Metal Goat will also gain a lot by furthering his skills and interests, and should take advantage of the opportunities available to him. Sometimes joining a local interest group or taking part in an after-school activity will help. He will certainly find his interests becoming more rewarding as a result of his new knowledge and skills.

However, while the Rooster year holds much promise for the Metal Goat, it will not be free from problems. Some areas of his schoolwork may be more difficult than others and if at any time the Metal Goat feels he is struggling or does not understand something, he should tell others of his concerns. Sometimes a more patient explanation can make a considerable difference.

The Metal Goat will enjoy his social life over the year, especially parties and other social events, and will value his close friendships. However, while his social life can bring him a great deal of pleasure, if at any time he is in a situation which he has misgivings about, he needs to be careful and not involve himself in anything he may later regret. Fortunately this warning only applies to a few Metal Goats, but in awkward situations the Metal Goat does need to be on his guard.

This need for care also applies to money matters, particularly as the Metal Goat will often want to do a great deal with sometimes limited means. In view of this, he should try to be disciplined in his spending and set money aside for the things he wants rather than succumb to too much impulse buying. He should also be wary about certain claims or 'too good to be true' offers. Without care, some Metal Goats could lose money unnecessarily. This *is* a year to be wary.

As far as the Metal Goat's domestic life is concerned, by being forthcoming and willing to discuss his thoughts and activities, he will gain a lot from the assistance and support others can give. Also, by contributing to family life and being willing to help with certain household tasks, he will find his efforts being appreciated. However, while much in his home life can go well, there will be times when he will find himself at odds with others. At such times, rather than dig his heels in, he would find it helpful to discuss his viewpoint as well as listen to what others are saying. Being willing to reach an understanding over certain issues will often be far better than being inflexible. The Metal Goat should remember that others *do* have his best interests at heart and often speak with the benefit of experience. Metal Goats, do take note, and do not let certain issues spoil an otherwise agreeable year.

Those Metal Goats born in 1931 will also value the support of their loved ones and by talking openly about their ideas and concerns, they will be helped and encouraged in many different ways. Both younger and more senior Metal Goats will gain so much by being forthcoming over the year.

Overall, the Rooster year holds good prospects for the Metal Goat and by taking advantage of the opportunities available, he can make it a significant time. On a personal level, he will enjoy the year, with friendships both old and new meaning a lot to him.

TIP FOR THE YEAR
Aim to develop your personal interests by learning and practising new skills. They can add so much to the pleasure and satisfaction your interests bring.

The Water Goat

This will be a pleasant and generally constructive year for the Water Goat. However, to benefit from the prevailing aspects, he would do well to give some thought to what he wants to accomplish over the next 12 months. With some plans in mind, he will find himself making better use of his time as well as making the year that much more rewarding.

One area which the Water Goat will give attention to will be his accommodation. Many Water Goats will be keen to add new comforts as well as improve the style, look and sometimes tidiness of certain areas. By discussing his ideas and considering the various options, the Water Goat will be pleased with how his plans take shape. However, he will need to allow plenty of time to complete practical activities, as well as accept there could be disruption and some inconvenience involved. In this respect, too, good planning will count for a great deal.

In addition to the satisfaction his practical undertakings will bring, the Water Goat will follow the activities of those dear to him with fond interest. While he may not wish to be interfering, he will often value the chance to help when needed, and once again his experience and empathy will be much appreciated. As well as helping others, the Water Goat will also enjoy any activities and interests he can share with those around him. There will certainly be a lot to make his domestic life rewarding.

However, while so much will go well, as with any year, problems will sometimes occur. Whenever any disagreements arise, the Water Goat would do well to deal with them quickly, before they have a chance to escalate. Often a willingness to discuss matters and understand different viewpoints will help. Should any matter occur which could have greater implications, the Water Goat should seek guidance. In most respects the Rooster year can be a good one for him, but problems do need to be tackled promptly and with care.

This need for care also extends to money matters and over the year the Water Goat should keep a close watch on his financial position and avoid risks or succumbing to too many impulsive buys. Without some watchfulness he could find his outgoings greater than he anticipated and his money not always being spent in the best way. He also needs to be careful with paperwork and any other matters that could have important financial implications. Should he have any uncertainties or questions, he should address these rather than take risks. Financially, this is a year for vigilance and care.

For those Water Goats in work this will be a satisfying year, with many being able to use their skills and experience to good effect. Also, sometimes these Water Goats could become involved in passing on their knowledge to more junior colleagues, and this too will be rewarding.

Those Water Goats who retire this year or who may have done so over the last few years will also often be able to put certain skills to use, with some even taking up a new position involving fewer hours. Work-wise, this can be a rewarding year and one which can have interesting developments.

The Water Goat will also value his social life over the year. With his sociable nature and wide interests, he will rarely find himself at a loss for things to do, people to meet or places to go. Those Water Goats who would welcome more companionship will find that by joining in with local activities and interest groups they can soon get to meet others. In addition, some new friends can be made while travelling. For social matters, this will be an active and favourable year.

Generally, the Rooster year does hold good prospects for the Water Goat, but it is very much a case of deciding what he wants to do and then acting on his ideas. With the support of others, however, he will be able to make this a personally rewarding and enjoyable year.

TIP FOR THE YEAR
Encourage others to share in your plans and interests. With the help, support and encouragement of those around you, so much more will be possible.

The Wood Goat

This marks the Wood Goat's fiftieth year and it holds much promise for him. It is a year for action, for setting about his plans and activities in earnest.

In his work the Wood Goat will be given good chances to use his talents, especially as others will look to him to play a greater role or become involved in more specialist tasks. By making the most of his opportunities, he will not only make good progress but also find his work bringing him greater satisfaction.

Although many Wood Goats will remain with their present employer, benefiting from in-house opportunities and making progress in their current area, those who want to move to a different type of work or are seeking work should be active in making enquiries and following up any openings that appeal to them. As the Wood Goat will find, he will need to work for results in the Rooster year, but by remaining determined, he may well secure what will be a very good opportunity. With competition sometimes being keen, he could help his chances by preparing thoroughly for any interview, including carrying out background research into the company. The months from April to June and September and October could see interesting work developments, but in general this is a year for the Wood Goat to push forward and to make the most of himself. He does, after all, have much to offer.

Another important aspect of the year will be the way the Wood Goat is able to further his personal interests, either by making greater use of his knowledge and skills, setting himself an interesting project to do or joining other enthusiasts. His interests can bring him considerable satisfaction over the year. Those Wood Goats who enjoy creative pursuits should also consider promoting what they do, as many will be encouraged by the response they receive. Here too the Rooster year can reward the Wood Goat who makes the most of his talents. Similarly, any Wood Goats who may have let their interests lapse should try to rectify this over the year and aim to devote time to activities which could give their lifestyle a greater balance.

There will also be some excellent chances for the Wood Goat to travel over the year and many Wood Goats will choose to mark their fiftieth year with a trip to somewhere they have longed to see. By carefully planning his time away, the Wood Goat will find his travels can lead to some memorable times. Also, visits to family and friends living some distance away can go well. For travelling, this is a favourable year.

The Wood Goat will also enjoy many aspects of his domestic life and in addition to the marking of his own birthday, there could be other reasons to celebrate, including a possible graduation or wedding or the birth of a grandchild. As always, the Wood Goat will immerse himself in what goes on, helping to organize a great deal. However, if at any time he feels under pressure or that others should be doing more, he should not hesitate to ask for additional help. Similarly, if he has any concerns or problems, he should be forthcoming. Unfortunately, if not addressed early, problems have a habit of escalating, and the Wood Goat does need to watch this.

With his genial nature, the Wood Goat sets much store by his social life and once again he will enjoy going out and meeting up with friends. Those Wood Goats who would welcome more companionship, perhaps as a result of having moved to a new area or because of other personal changes, will find that by going out more and getting involved in interest groups and local activities their social life will become busier and far more rewarding.

One area which does require care is finance. In 2005 the Wood Goat will face some large expenses and would do well to make early provision for them whenever possible. In order to do all that he wants over the year, he does need to manage his resources well. He too could find it helpful to keep watch on his spending, particularly if tempted to go on shopping sprees. This is not a time for impulsive purchases. Neither is it a year for succumbing to risks or being dilatory over important paperwork and financial forms. Wood Goats, take note. Be thorough and manage money matters with care.

In most respects, however, the Wood Goat's prospects are encouraging and by making the most of his skills, ideas and opportunities, he will have good reason to be pleased with his progress. His fiftieth year can be a rewarding one indeed.

TIP FOR THE YEAR

Your interests and recreational pursuits can bring you considerable pleasure over the year and despite other pressures on your time, do not neglect these. By using your spare time wisely, you really can benefit in a great many ways.

The Fire Goat

This will be an important year for the Fire Goat, bringing both change and considerable opportunity. And with the Fire Goat's keen nature and desire to make the most of himself, he is set to do well. The key message is that this is a time to move forward, and, should the Fire Goat have had any recent disappointments or problems, he should aim to put these behind him and move on.

In his work the prospects are especially encouraging. Although many Fire Goats will already have accomplished a great deal in their career, there will be quite a few who feel that they could be making better use of their skills or who would welcome a new challenge. For these Fire Goats, the Rooster year can have important developments in store. By keeping alert for openings, making enquiries and talking to others (and here some of the Fire Goat's colleagues and contacts can be helpful), many will learn of new possibilities to consider. The Rooster year favours those prepared to take action and here the Fire Goat's determined nature will be a great asset. The months from April to June and September and October could see some particularly good developments, but in general this is a year to advance.

The encouraging aspects also apply to those Fire Goats seeking work, either as the Rooster year starts or during it. Although these Fire Goats will sometimes despair over their position, they should try not to let any disappointments hold them back. They do have much to offer and can set their career off on an exciting and potentially more rewarding path this year.

Also, with this being a year for change and progress, the Fire Goat should take advantage of any training he may be

THE GOAT

offered. By improving on his skills, he will be able to widen his range of options for the future. Similarly, those Fire Goats seeking work could find that courses allowing them to refresh their skills or acquire new ones will be helpful to their future prospects.

However, while this is an encouraging year for work matters, where finance is concerned it is one for care and prudence. In the Rooster year the Fire Goat could face considerable expense, especially in relation to accommodation, transport and family. In view of this he would find it helpful to keep a close watch on his financial situation and to budget for forthcoming expenses whenever possible. Also, by watching his outgoings, he will find he is sometimes able to cut back on certain outgoings, which, over time, can make a difference. This is a year for careful management and control.

Although the Fire Goat will have much to do over the year, it is also important that he allows time for his recreational pursuits. Not only will these bring him pleasure but they will also give him a break from his usual concerns and allow him to unwind. He too should not neglect his well-being over the year, especially if he is sedentary for much of the day. Sometimes some additional walking or exercise such as swimming or cycling could help. By taking medical advice on the best way to proceed, the Fire Goat will often benefit from what he does.

As far as the Fire Goat's domestic life is concerned, this will be a busy year, with both younger and more senior relations appreciating the support and advice he is able to give. His general input into family life will also be greatly valued, as will his suggestions for family activities.

However, while the Fire Goat will play such a pivotal role, if at any time he feels in need of more help or considers that others could be contributing more, he should ask. Also, should any awkward matter or disagreement arise, he should aim to deal with it as quickly and amicably as he can. Without care, certain issues could escalate and undermine the normally good relations he has with those around him. Fire Goats, do take note.

The Fire Goat will, however, value his social life over the year. Through his interests and sometimes his work, he will have many chances to go out and will often enjoy himself as well as impress many of the people he meets. For those Fire Goats who have had recent problems or disappointments in their personal life, this is a year to move forward. By becoming involved in new activities, they can do much to transform their situation.

Overall, the Rooster year does hold much promise for the Fire Goat and by acting upon his ideas and opportunities, he will find this a time of change and often significant progress.

TIP FOR THE YEAR

In view of the busy nature of the year, it is important to manage your time well. Balance your activities and make sure you spend quality time with those who are special to you as well as on interests that you enjoy. This can be a successful year, but you do need to use your time to good effect.

The Earth Goat

The Earth Goat can accomplish a great deal in the Rooster year, although, as he will soon discover, it will require much effort on his part. This is a year for dedication and hard work rather than for hoping things will just work out. The Rooster year can be a hard taskmaster, but is fair and certainly capable of rewarding the Earth Goat well.

One area which will see much activity over the year will be the Earth Goat's personal life with quite a few Earth Goats having good reason to celebrate, perhaps through a marriage or an addition to their family. Those Earth Goats with partners will often delight in the many activities they carry out together, with the year containing some special moments.

For many Earth Goats accommodation matters will figure prominently, with some moving as well as carrying out plans to improve their home. The Earth Goat's sense of style will be to the fore, and will be much appreciated. Domestically, this will be a busy and eventful year, with the Earth Goat often delighting in the activity.

The Earth Goat will certainly appreciate his social life too and in addition to keeping in regular contact with friends, he will receive many invitations to go out. He could also find that his interests and changes in his work will lead to him meeting others, and some important new friendships and contacts will be made. Any Earth Goat who has had recent problems in his personal life should regard this as a year to move forward. By getting involved in new activities and making the most of his chances to go out, he may well meet someone who will become special. For socializing, March, May and July to early September are particularly well aspected.

However, while the Earth Goat's domestic and social life holds much promise, as with any year, problems will arise from time to time and disagreements may raise their head. At such times the Earth Goat should try to deal with matters quickly and amicably. Tensions that linger in the background could be an unwelcome distraction in what is such a promising and potentially exciting year. Earth Goats, take note, and remember that dialogue and a willingness to talk will do much to resolve any difficult situation.

This is, however, an excellent year for the Earth Goat's own personal development and despite other demands on his time, he would do well to further his interests and skills, particularly if he is interested in creative pursuits. Those Earth Goats who have considered turning an interest or creative skill into a vocation will find that by continuing to develop their talents they can do much to keep their dream alive.

As far as the Earth Goat's work is concerned, this will be a demanding year, with much being expected of him. There could be pressures and deadlines to be met and sometimes certain aspects of his work, such as the more bureaucratic elements, could be tiresome. However, by rising to the challenge and maintaining his high standards, the Earth Goat will do much to help his reputation and when opportunities arise, he will be well placed to benefit. Again, this is a year when hard work and commitment will be rewarded, with many Earth Goats finding themselves promoted or being given more specialist duties as the year progresses.

For those looking for a change or seeking work, the Rooster year can give rise to some interesting developments, and for many Earth Goats it will be a year of new

THE GOAT

starts. Results in 2005 *will* need to be worked for, but the long-term rewards can be considerable. The months from April to early June and September and October could see some good opportunities to make progress.

More awkwardly aspected, though, are financial matters. With a possible move for some and high accommodation costs for many, Earth Goats will often find their resources stretched. As a result, they would do well to keep a close watch on their spending as well as make allowance for their various obligations. This is a year for control and watchfulness, and when taking on new commitments, the Earth Goat would do well to check the terms and implications involved. Financial matters do need careful attention over the year.

In many respects, however, this will be a year of opportunity for the Earth Goat and by using his skills to good effect, he will be able to make important progress. Also, in so much of what he does, he will be encouraged by the love and support of another, with his personal life being active and often special. And there may be a personal celebration to enjoy as well.

TIP FOR THE YEAR

Aim to further your interests and skills over the year. What you do now will not only be satisfying but often of long term benefit.

FAMOUS GOATS

Pamela Anderson, W. H. Auden, Jane Austen, Anne Bancroft, Daniel Bedingfield, Cilla Black, Lord Byron, Leslie Caron, Coco Chanel, Mary Higgins Clark, Nat 'King' Cole, Robert de Niro, Catherine Deneuve, John Denver, Charles Dickens, Ken Dodd, Sir Arthur Conan Doyle, Daphne du Maurier, Umberto Eco, Douglas Fairbanks, Dame Margot Fonteyn, Noel Gallagher, Bill Gates, Mel Gibson, Whoopi Goldberg, Mikhail Gorbachev, John Grisham, Larry Hagman, Oscar Hammerstein, George Harrison, Sir Edmund Hillary, John Humphrys, Billy Idol, Julio Iglesias, Sir Mick Jagger, Norah Jones, Ulrika Jonsson, John Kerry, Nicole Kidman, Sir Ben Kingsley, John le Carré, Doris Lessing, Franz Liszt, John Major, Michelangelo, Joni Mitchell, Rupert Murdoch, Mussolini, Randy Newman, Des O'Connor, Sinead O'Connor, Michael Owen, Michael Palin, Eva Peron, Marcel Proust, Keith Richards, Julia Roberts, William Shatner, Gary Sinise, Jerry Springer, Lana Turner, Mark Twain, Rudolph Valentino, Vangelis, Barbara Walters, John Wayne, Fay Weldon, Jonny Wilkinson, Bruce Willis, Debra Winger.

2 FEBRUARY 1908 ~ 21 JANUARY 1909	*Earth Monkey*
20 FEBRUARY 1920 ~ 7 FEBRUARY 1921	*Metal Monkey*
6 FEBRUARY 1932 ~ 25 JANUARY 1933	*Water Monkey*
25 JANUARY 1944 ~ 12 FEBRUARY 1945	*Wood Monkey*
12 FEBRUARY 1956 ~ 30 JANUARY 1957	*Fire Monkey*
30 JANUARY 1968 ~ 16 FEBRUARY 1969	*Earth Monkey*
16 FEBRUARY 1980 ~ 4 FEBRUARY 1981	*Metal Monkey*
4 FEBRUARY 1992 ~ 22 JANUARY 1993	*Water Monkey*
22 JANUARY 2004 ~ 8 FEBRUARY 2005	*Wood Monkey*

THE
MONKEY

THE PERSONALITY OF THE MONKEY

> Man needs for his happiness not only the enjoyment of this and that, but hope and enterprise and change.
> *Bertrand Russell, a Monkey*

The Monkey is born under the sign of fantasy. He is imaginative, inquisitive and loves to keep an eye on everything that is going on around him. He is never backward in offering advice or trying to sort out the problems of others. He likes to be helpful and his advice is invariably sensible and reliable.

The Monkey is intelligent, well read and always eager to learn. He has an extremely good memory and there are many Monkeys who have made particularly good linguists. The Monkey is also a convincing talker and enjoys taking part in discussions and debates. His friendly, self-assured manner can be very persuasive and he usually has little trouble in winning people round to his way of thinking. It is for this reason that the Monkey often excels in politics and public speaking. He is also particularly adept in PR work, teaching and any job which involves selling.

The Monkey can, however, be crafty, cunning and occasionally dishonest, and he will seize on any opportunity to make a quick gain or outsmart his opponents. He has so much charm and guile that people often don't realize what he is up to until it is too late. But despite his resourceful nature, the Monkey does run the risk of outsmarting even himself. He has so much confidence in his abilities that he rarely listens to advice or is prepared to accept help from anyone. He likes to help others but

THE MONKEY

prefers to rely on his own judgement when dealing with his own affairs.

Another characteristic of the Monkey is that he is extremely good at solving problems and has a happy knack of extricating himself (and others) from the most hopeless of positions. He is the master of self-preservation.

With so many diverse talents the Monkey is able to make considerable sums of money, but he does like to enjoy life and will think nothing of spending his money on some exotic holiday or luxury which he has had his eye on. He can, however, become very envious if someone else has what he wants.

The Monkey is an original thinker and despite his love of company, he cherishes his independence. He has to have the freedom to act as he wants and any Monkey who feels hemmed in or bound by too many restrictions can soon become unhappy. Likewise, if anything becomes too boring or monotonous, the Monkey soon loses interest and turns his attention to something else. He lacks persistence and this can often hamper his progress. He is also easily distracted, a tendency which all Monkeys should try to overcome. By concentrating on one thing at a time, the Monkey will almost certainly achieve more in the long run.

The Monkey is a good organizer and even though he may behave slightly erratically at times, he will invariably have some plan at the back of his mind. On the odd occasion when his plans do not work out, he is usually quite happy to shrug his shoulders and put it down to experience. He will rarely make the same mistake twice and throughout his life he will try his hand at many different things.

The Monkey likes to impress and is rarely without followers or admirers. Many are attracted by his good looks, his sense of humour, or simply because he instils so much confidence.

Monkeys usually marry young and for it to be a success their partner must allow them time to pursue their many interests and indulge their love of travel. The Monkey has to have variety in his life and is especially well suited to those born under the sociable and outgoing signs of the Rat, Dragon, Pig and Goat. The Ox, Rabbit, Snake and Dog will also be enchanted by the Monkey's resourceful and outgoing nature, but he is likely to exasperate the Rooster and Horse, and the Tiger will have little patience with his tricks. A relationship between two Monkeys will work well – they will understand each other and be able to assist each other in their various enterprises.

The female Monkey is intelligent, extremely observant and a shrewd judge of character. Her opinions are often highly valued and having such a persuasive nature, she invariably gets her own way. She has many interests and involves herself in a wide variety of activities. She pays great attention to her appearance, is an elegant dresser and likes to take particular care over her hair. She can be a doting parent and will have many good and loyal friends.

Provided the Monkey can curb his desire to take part in everything that is going on around him and concentrate on one thing at a time, he can usually achieve what he wants in life. Should he suffer any disappointment, he is bound to bounce back. He is a survivor and his life is usually both colourful and eventful.

THE FIVE DIFFERENT TYPES OF MONKEY

In addition to the 12 signs of the Chinese zodiac there are five elements and these have a strengthening or moderating influence on the sign. The effects of the five elements on the Monkey are described below, together with the years in which the elements were exercising their influence. Therefore those Monkeys born in 1920 and 1980 are Metal Monkeys, those born in 1932 and 1992 are Water Monkeys, and so on.

Metal Monkey: 1920, 1980
The Metal Monkey is very strong-willed. He sets about everything he does with a dogged determination and often prefers to work independently rather than with others. He is ambitious, wise and confident, and is certainly not afraid of hard work. He is very astute in financial matters and usually chooses his investments well. Despite his somewhat independent nature, he enjoys attending parties and social occasions and is particularly warm and caring towards his loved ones.

Water Monkey: 1932, 1992
The Water Monkey is versatile, determined and perceptive. He also has more discipline than some of the other Monkeys and is prepared to work towards a certain goal

rather than be distracted by something else. He is not always open about his true intentions and when questioned can be particularly evasive. He can be sensitive to criticism but also very persuasive and usually has little trouble in getting others to fall in with his plans. He has a very good understanding of human nature and relates well to others.

Wood Monkey: 1944, 2004

This Monkey is efficient, methodical and extremely conscientious. He is also highly imaginative and is always trying to capitalize on new ideas or learn new skills. Occasionally his enthusiasm can get the better of him and he can get very agitated when things do not quite work out as he had hoped. He does, however, have a very adventurous streak and is not afraid of taking risks. He also loves travel. He is usually held in great esteem by his friends and colleagues.

Fire Monkey: 1956

The Fire Monkey is intelligent, full of vitality and has no trouble in commanding the respect of others. He is imaginative and has wide interests, although sometimes these can distract him from more useful and profitable work. He is very competitive and always likes to be involved in everything that is going on. He can be stubborn if he does not get his own way and he sometimes tries to indoctrinate those who are less strong-willed than himself. He is a lively character, attractive to others and most loyal to his partner.

Earth Monkey: 1908, 1968

The Earth Monkey tends to be studious and well read, and can become quite distinguished in his chosen line of work. He is less outgoing than some of the other types of Monkey and prefers quieter and more solid pursuits. He has high principles, a very caring nature and can be most generous to those less fortunate than himself. He is usually successful in handling financial matters and can become very wealthy in old age. He has a calming influence on those around him and is respected and well liked. He is, however, especially careful about whom he lets into his confidence.

PROSPECTS FOR THE MONKEY IN 2005

The Chinese New Year starts on 9 February 2005. Until then, the old year, the Year of the Monkey, is still making its presence felt.

The Year of the Monkey (22 January 2004 to 8 February 2005) is an important one for Monkeys and in what remains of it, much is possible. The Monkey has always been a doer, ever ready to make the most of situations, and in the closing months of his own year, there will be good opportunities to make progress, while on a more personal level, his relations with others will mean a great deal to him.

At work the Monkey year will give the Monkey the chance to develop his talents, and those who are keen on furthering their career should actively follow up any openings they see. With determination and enterprise the Monkey can make good headway at this time, with November seeing some particularly interesting opportunities.

The last quarter of the year will, though, be an expensive time and whenever possible the Monkey should allow for forthcoming expenses and watch his spending.

The closing months will also be active both domestically and socially, with a lot for the Monkey to get involved with. In true Monkey style, he will enjoy many of the activities that take place as well as appreciate the chance to spend time with his loved ones. For the unattached, there will be many chances to go out and meet others, and for quite a few Monkeys, affairs of the heart will bring joy and happiness.

The Year of the Rooster begins on 9 February and is one of opportunity for the Monkey. However, to benefit, he will need to make the most of his talents and be prepared to put himself forward. This is a year which favours dedication and effort.

In his work there will some very good opportunities for the Monkey to make headway. However, he would do well to give some thought to his personal development, in particular whether there are any skills it would be useful to improve upon or acquire. By following this up, either through training offered through his work or personal study, he will find that there will be many more possibilities open to him. Also, looking to develop will give him a sense of moving forward and this will have a positive effect on both his outlook and chances to make further progress.

Many Monkeys will find there will be some good opportunities with their current employer and will find their contacts, in-house knowledge and reputation serving them well over the year. For those who feel there are better prospects elsewhere, who are considering a change of career or who are looking for work, the Rooster year can again provide some excellent openings. To benefit, these Monkeys will, however, need to remain persistent. With much competition likely, they would do well to emphasize their experience to prospective employers, as well as any recent training and study they have carried out. By presenting themselves in the best possible light, many will secure what will be an interesting position. For work matters April, June, September and October could see encouraging developments.

As far as finances are concerned, however, this is a year for care. In 2005 the Monkey will have many plans he wants to carry out and these, together with his existing commitments, will draw heavily on his resources. The Rooster year will be an expensive one for him and to prevent problems, he could find it helpful to keep a close watch on his financial position and to plan for forthcoming expenses whenever possible. Good discipline and management will help. Also, throughout the year the Monkey should be wary of risks or of becoming involved in speculation or undertakings he knows little about. This is a year when he will need to be thorough and on his guard.

More positively, the Monkey's domestic life will bring him considerable pleasure over the year. Spending time with his family, whether enjoying mutual interests, going out to special events or carrying out projects in the home or garden, can help the rapport the Monkey so values. However, as with all years, there will be times when problems and differences of opinion occur. When they do, the Monkey will find that talking them over can do much to defuse them. Once again, his ability to relate to others and to empathize will prove a great asset over the year.

The year is also favourably aspected for travel and the Monkey would do well to take a holiday with his loved ones over the year. It could turn out to be one of the most satisfying holidays he has had for some time. He should also follow up any invitations he receives to visit friends or relatives living some distance away. Again, such visits can go well.

The Rooster year is also a positive one for social matters and the Monkey, who likes to keep himself active, will often make the most of his chances to go out. There will be good opportunities for him to add to his social circle, with March, May, September and December being particularly busy months. Those Monkeys currently enjoying romance will often find their relationship growing stronger over the year, while for the unattached, the aspects are favourable for meeting someone who will quickly become special. The Rooster year is indeed a fine one for relationships.

However, while the Rooster year is favourable in so many respects, with the demands of his work and all his other activities, the Monkey does need to give some consideration to his well-being. To continually drive himself, have a succession of late nights or skimp on exercise or nutritious food could leave him lacking his usual sparkle or prone to niggling ailments. Whenever possible, the Monkey does need to conduct his life at a steadier pace and balance his activities. He must not expect to be on the go all the time and should give himself the opportunity to rest, unwind and appreciate what he has around him.

In many respects the Rooster year holds encouraging prospects for the Monkey and by making the most of his opportunities and using his talents well, he can accomplish a great deal. In his work his effort and commitment will often lead to important progress, while his domestic and social life will be active and enjoyable. Overall, a positive and personally rewarding year.

The Metal Monkey

This will be an interesting year for the Metal Monkey and one in which he will be able to put his strengths to good use and make important headway.

One positive aspect of the year will concern the Metal Monkey's relations with others. For those with a partner the year will contain some special times, including, for some, an addition to their family. And with the love and support of his partner, the Metal Monkey will find himself living life to the full, sharing interests and plans and doing much to add to the comfort of his home. Domestically, this will be an active and often rewarding year. However, where practical projects and more ambitious undertakings are concerned, the Metal Monkey should allow plenty of time and avoid rushed or hasty decisions. He may be eager for results, but care and good planning can make an important difference.

While the Metal Monkey may have independent tendencies, he will be helped by those around him over the year and would do well to be more open with his thoughts as well as any concerns and pressures he may have. As the saying goes, *A worry shared is a worry halved*, and the Metal Monkey will find great truth in this over the year.

Those Metal Monkeys who are unattached or who have had recent personal problems will also find this an important year, and often one of fresh starts. By looking forward, rather than back, they will find the Rooster year can usher in much brighter times, and by becoming involved in new activities, they will often find their social life picking up and leading to new friendships, one of which could become special. As far as personal relationships are concerned, the Rooster year is favourably aspected, with March, May, June, September and December seeing much activity.

This is also a good year for travel and the Metal Monkey should try to go away for a holiday at some time. By choosing his destination carefully and in consultation with others, he will find his travels will be enjoyable as well as often do him good. Also, if he is invited to visit family or friends living some distance away or has other opportunities to travel, he should follow them up.

As far as his work is concerned, this will be a year of important developments. Although the Metal Monkey will have accomplished a great deal in recent years, he may be eager to move on and make more of his talents. However, as he will discover, to make headway in the Rooster year will require effort. Sometimes competition will be keen and it could take quite a few attempts before he secures a suitable position, but what he does achieve now can often turn out to be an important step in his career development.

Many Metal Monkeys will, however, find their workload heavy over the year and there will be times when they will be concerned about all that is expected of them. However, by rising to the challenges, they will not only gain important experience but will also discover strengths which they will be able to build on in future years. Again, the Metal Monkey's accomplishments over the year can have long-term value. April, June, September and October could see interesting work developments.

The Metal Monkey should also take advantage of any training opportunities that may be available to him. He will find that adding to his skills will be helpful to his present position as well as his future prospects. Any Metal Monkeys who have been seeking work for some time or who are considering a career change will find that some training could open up some good possibilities.

However, while many Metal Monkeys will advance their career over the year and enjoy a rise in income, money matters do need to be handled with care. With his many commitments and plans, especially those concerning his accommodation, the Metal Monkey does need to watch his budget. And should he enter into any new agreement, he should check the terms and implications and obtain professional advice where necessary. This is not a year for risks or carelessness.

Overall, although the Metal Monkey will need to work hard in order to make progress over the year, his achievements and the experience he gains can be considerable and far-reaching. On a personal level, the year will often be special, with many Metal Monkeys enjoying romance as well as an active social life. In many respects, this is a year of considerable promise and potential.

TIP FOR THE YEAR
A bonus, for there are two tips. First, do be forthcoming and keep your independent Metal Monkey nature in check. You really will gain so much by being willing to let others help you, particularly with career aspirations. Secondly, look to develop yourself in some way. You have a great future ahead of you and time spent developing your skills will reward you well.

The Water Monkey

This will be an interesting and often enjoyable year for the Water Monkey, although to benefit he will need to put himself forward and make the most of the chances that arise. This is a year when effort and initiative will be rewarded well.

For those Water Monkeys born in 1992 this will be an important year, especially as they will now move on to more advanced schoolwork. Sometimes they may feel daunted by what is being asked of them, but by making an effort and rising to the challenge, they will find many of their initial doubts will prove unfounded. In addition, much of what the Water Monkey learns over the year will be an important basis for work he has to do later on.

The Water Monkey will also be well supported by those around him and if he does have any problem areas or becomes concerned about certain aspects of his schoolwork, he should be forthcoming. As he will find, by telling others of his concerns they will be better able to guide and advise.

The Water Monkey should also take advantage of the facilities available to him. If he has sporting, musical or other talents he wishes to further, by joining in with after-school activities or groups in his area, he will not only extend his skills but also take greater pleasure in what he is able to do. And in carrying these activities out with others, there will often be a fun element too.

The Water Monkey will also appreciate the companionship of his close group of friends, particularly the support they will offer. Often, he will discover that his friends have similar concerns to his own and as a result will feel less alone. Socially, the Rooster year is well aspected and as the Water Monkey becomes involved in new activities, he will often find his social circle widening as a result.

As far as his domestic life is concerned, he will particularly enjoy some of the family occasions that take place, including any holidays he goes on. He will also be grateful for the encouragement he is given, but to benefit fully, he does need be forthcoming and prepared to let others help. This is not a year for letting his independent and sometimes secretive tendencies get the better of him! As with any year, differences of opinion will sometimes arise and at such times the Water Monkey would find it helpful to talk and listen rather than be too inflexible. Although certain decisions may seem unfair to him, often they are made with his best interests at heart and he should try not to let any disagreements sour what can be an otherwise agreeable time. Water Monkeys, do take note.

For those Water Monkeys born in 1932, the Rooster year also holds encouraging prospects and is again a time for following up ideas and making the most of opportunities. If there are things the Water Monkey would like to do or places he would like to visit, he should put his ideas forward. Sometimes just by raising them, they can take on a momentum of their own. Also, with the year well aspected for travel, the Water Monkey should follow up invitations to visit others or go on any breaks or holidays that appeal to him. With his sociable nature, such trips could turn out to be good fun.

These more senior Water Monkeys will also take much pleasure from their interests over the year and in some cases will decide to pass on some of their knowledge and expertise, perhaps by talking to other enthusiasts or even by writing down their experiences. Over the year, there will certainly be those who admire the Water Monkey's skills and depth of knowledge and he will delight in being able to share these. Many Water Monkeys will also enjoy creative pursuits and for the artistic and imaginative, the year can be most satisfying.

Any Water Monkeys who are feeling lonely or who would welcome more companionship would do well to consider joining a local group. As with so many aspects of the Water Monkey's life in the Rooster year, positive action *will* be rewarded.

As far as money matters are concerned, however, this is a year for caution. If he is taking on any new obligations, the Water Monkey would do well to check the terms and implications. This is not a year for risks and should he have any uncertainties or questions, he should aim to resolve these before proceeding. Water Monkeys, take careful note, and do make the most of the help and advice that is available to you, particularly when dealing with costly or complicated matters.

In many respects, though, this will be a positive year for the Water Monkey and by making the most of his ideas, talents and opportunities, he will be pleased with how his efforts are rewarded. A good year indeed.

TIP FOR THE YEAR
Your personal interests can bring you considerable pleasure over the year and by setting yourself an interesting project to do or looking to develop your skills in some way, you can gain much personal satisfaction. Sometimes your interests can also have a pleasing social element and this too can add to the fun.

The Wood Monkey

This is a year of fine opportunity for the Wood Monkey, but to benefit he will need to give careful thought to what he would like to accomplish over the next 12 months. With a sense of direction he will find much of what he does working out well, but if he just waits and lets events unfold in their own way, then the year will not nearly be as satisfying or successful. This is a time for planning and for following ideas through.

For many Wood Monkeys, accommodation matters will figure prominently, with some deciding to move to somewhere more suitable for their present needs. For those who do move, the process could take up much time, both in the sorting out and planning that needs to be done as well as in finding somewhere else to live. However, while this will involve considerable time and effort, once installed in their new home, these Wood Monkeys will feel a sense of satisfaction at what has been achieved as well as enjoy what their new area has to offer.

For those who remain where they are, accommodation matters will also be prominent in their plans, with many Wood Monkeys deciding to alter the décor or layout of certain rooms and installing new comforts as well as replacing some furnishings. Again, these Wood Monkeys will be delighted at seeing their ideas take shape. Also, many Wood Monkeys, perhaps influenced by the Rooster year's sense of order, will embark on a major sort out, ridding their home of some of the clutter that has accumulated over the years. Again, these Wood Monkeys will appreciate the results of their efforts, feeling pleased at how much neater and better organized their home has become.

The Wood Monkey will also enjoy many of the activities he is able to share with his loved ones and will often be glad to assist younger relations, giving advice and support when needed as well as helping at busy times.

His social life is also favourably aspected, and with his interests and wide social circle, he will often have many opportunities to go out. Those Wood Monkeys who have moved or who are feeling lonely will find that joining in with local activities will lead to their social life picking up. For socializing, March, May, September and December could be busy and favourable months.

As far as money matters are concerned, however, the Wood Monkey will need to be careful and thorough. In particular, if entering into a new agreement or becoming involved in an expensive transaction, he would do well to check the terms and small print carefully and resolve any uncertainties before proceeding. This is not a year for risks or complacency. Similarly, when completing important forms, he needs to be prompt and thorough, and if he has any questions, he should seek advice. Wood Monkeys, take note, and do be careful when dealing with financial matters.

For those Wood Monkeys in work this will be a year of interesting opportunities. Although many will be content to remain in their present position, doing the work they know so well, there will be chances for them to take on other duties and extend their skills in some way. And by making the most of such opportunities, these Wood Monkeys will often feel more motivated than they have been for some time, as well as perhaps lifted out of a rut they may not have realized they have been in. For those Wood Monkeys looking for work, the year can also usher in a change of direction and provide an interesting new challenge. April, June, September and October could see important developments.

Travel is also well aspected and the Wood Monkey should make the most of any invitations he receives as well as follow up any ideas he has or any offers that appeal to him. His travels will often be both interesting and enjoyable.

Overall, the Rooster year holds fine prospects for the Wood Monkey, but it is very much a case of giving some thought to what he wants to do over the year and then following it through. In 2005, purposeful action *will* be rewarded.

TIP FOR THE YEAR

Your relations with others can go well and mean a great deal to you over the year. However, to make the most of them, do regularly consult those around you. By doing so you will not only benefit from their advice and assistance but will also enjoy a better rapport and understanding.

The Fire Monkey

There is a Chinese proverb which is very apt for the Fire Monkey this year. It goes: *Monkey see, Monkey do.* The Fire Monkey is both inquisitive and a doer, and these two traits will serve him well over the year.

At work many Fire Monkeys will have accomplished a great deal in recent years as well as added considerably to their experience. And in the Rooster year the Fire Monkey will be encouraged to put his knowledge and skills to greater use. Sometimes, because of his experience, he will find himself being singled out for particular responsibilities or asked to help with additional duties. Although this could add to his workload, by making the most of such chances he will advance his career and often find himself well placed for promotion.

While many Fire Monkeys will remain with their present employer, for those who are keen to advance their career elsewhere or are seeking work, again the Rooster year will give rise to some interesting opportunities. By deciding on the type of position they would like and keeping alert for suitable openings, many of these Fire Monkeys will be successful in their quest, and sometimes in fortuitous ways. A contact or friend could alert them to a suitable opening or they could hear of one following a chance enquiry, but whenever they see an opportunity, they should be quick in following it up. Again, it is a case of *Monkey see, Monkey do*, and with determination, many Fire Monkeys can set their career off on an exciting new track.

The Fire Monkey should also give some thought to his own personal development over the year. This includes taking advantage of any training offered by his employer as well as undertaking any study he can do by himself. Keeping informed of developments in his area of work and adding to his knowledge and skills can be another rewarding aspect of the year. However, the Fire Monkey's personal development need not be restricted to work activities. Furthering his interests and recreational pursuits can also bring him a great deal of pleasure.

He should also not ignore his own well-being over the year, and if he does not get much exercise during the day or relies heavily on convenience foods, he should consider ways in which he can correct this. By obtaining proper guidance on the best way to proceed, he will again be able to benefit.

Another favourably aspected area is travel and the Fire Monkey should try to make sure he goes away for a holiday over the year. By giving careful thought to his destination, he will not only enjoy the areas he visits but also benefit from the rest and change of scene.

As far as money matters are concerned, this can prove an expensive year and when certain expenses are known about in advance, the Fire Monkey would find it helpful to make early provision for them. The better he can control his situation, the better he will fare. Similarly, if he is planning a major purchase, some time spent considering the options and choices available could be worthwhile. Money matters do need care and at times it would be to the Fire Monkey's advantage to watch his more impulsive tendencies. He also needs to deal with financially related forms carefully as well as keep important documents and receipts safe. This is not a time to be lax over financial matters or important paperwork.

As far as the Fire Monkey's domestic life is concerned, this will be an active and pleasing year. The progress of a younger relation will especially delight him and while he will not wish to interfere, some advice and assistance he is able to give will be more valued than he may realize. Also, the encouragement he gives to family members will again be appreciated. The Fire Monkey will certainly play an important part in the lives of many over the year!

He will also enjoy many of the activities he is able to carry out with his loved ones, whether sharing mutual interests, undertaking home improvements or going on trips. However if, at any time, the Fire Monkey does feel under pressure or has a heavy workload, he should tell others so that they are better able to understand as well as assist with certain activities. This is a year when much will be gained by being forthcoming and drawing on the willing support of others.

The Fire Monkey's social life will also be fairly active over the year and often his work and personal interests will bring opportunities for him to go out. For some Fire Monkeys, particularly those who are unattached and starting the year feeling rather dispirited, the Rooster year can bring the gift of a rewarding friendship or romance.

March, May, September and December could be active months socially.

Overall, the Rooster year will be a favourable one for the Fire Monkey and by making the most of his strengths and ideas and acting upon the opportunities that arise, he can look forward to making good progress as well as enjoying both his domestic and social life.

TIP FOR THE YEAR
Although you will have many demands on your time, make sure your interests and recreational pursuits do not suffer and that you allow yourself time to relax and unwind. At busy times, do not forget that there are others who can give you extra support.

The Earth Monkey

This year holds good prospects for the Earth Monkey and by setting about his various activities in his usual earnest way, he will enjoy himself as well as reap some well-deserved rewards.

In his work the aspects are especially encouraging and by using his strengths and experience well, he will both impress others and do his prospects a considerable amount of good. Whenever promotion opportunities arise or there is the chance to put in for other duties, the Earth Monkey should be quick to apply. By acting swiftly and showing himself to be keen, he will often find himself in a strong position to benefit.

For those Earth Monkeys who are seeking work or hoping to move to a different type of work, this is also a year of important developments. Again, though, these Earth Monkeys will need to act quickly when they have chances to pursue. With persistence and determination, many will find their efforts rewarded and their career given a new impetus. April, June, September and October could see some interesting opportunities.

The Earth Monkey also has a talent for coming up with ideas and he should aim to take these further over the Rooster year, particularly if they are related to his work or personal interests. In some cases they could develop in an encouraging manner and be to his benefit.

As far as money matters are concerned, this will be an expensive year and in order to do everything that he wants, the Earth Monkey should manage his resources carefully. He would find it helpful to keep a close watch on his outgoings as well as make allowance for forthcoming expenses. Also, by taking greater control over his finances, he could find that some outgoings could be reduced or that he could move some of his money to higher-yielding accounts. With greater care and control, he will find himself making better use of his money. In addition, where large transactions are concerned, he should carefully check the terms and obligations. Again, this is a year for watchfulness and care.

Although the Earth Monkey will have many demands on his time, it is also important that he does not neglect his recreational pursuits. They will not only give him a break from some of his more usual activities but could sometimes have an enjoyable social element too. Despite pressures on his time, it is important that the Earth Monkey does not deny himself the pleasure his interests can bring. Earth Monkeys, do take note.

THE MONKEY

This will also be an active year socially for the Earth Monkey and with his amiable nature and good repartee, he will often not only enjoy himself but also find his circle of acquaintances widening as the year develops. However, with so much happening, he should be careful not to push himself too far. A succession of heavy days and late nights could, after a time, begin to take their toll. Earth Monkeys, do watch this, and where possible, spread your activities out.

This will also be a busy year domestically, but by setting aside time to be with loved ones and planning projects and activities together, the Earth Monkey will find his domestic life meaning a great deal to him. As he recognizes, maintaining good relations does require effort and, by giving this, he can make the year all the more rewarding. Those Earth Monkeys who are parents will find that by encouraging their children with their interests and schoolwork, they will be able to take pleasure in their progress. However, as with all years, some problems and differences of opinion will arise. When they do, if the Earth Monkey is able to address them and talk them through, he will be able to prevent them from overshadowing what can be an agreeable and positive year.

In so many respects the Rooster year holds fine prospects for the Earth Monkey and by making good use of his strengths, ideas and opportunities, he will be able to achieve a considerable amount and enjoy himself too.

TIP FOR THE YEAR
Do make sure you spend time with those who are important to you as well as on more recreational activities. Also,

do not skimp on exercise or healthy food. To keep yourself on good form, do give thought to your lifestyle. Aim for a balance in all you do.

FAMOUS MONKEYS

Gillian Anderson, Jennifer Aniston, Francesca Annis, Christina Aguilera, Michael Aspel, J. M. Barrie, Johnny Cash, Jacques Chirac, Joe Cocker, Colette, John Constable, Alistair Cooke, David Copperfield, Patricia Cornwell, Joan Crawford, Leonardo da Vinci, Timothy Dalton, Bette Davis, Danny De Vito, Celine Dion, Michael Douglas, Mia Farrow, Carrie Fisher, F. Scott Fitzgerald, Ian Fleming, Dick Francis, Fiona Fullerton, Paul Gauguin, Jerry Hall, Tom Hanks, Martina Hingis, Harry Houdini, P. D. James, Pope John Paul II, Lyndon B. Johnson, Julius Caesar, Buster Keaton, Edward Kennedy, Alicia Keys, Don King, Gladys Knight, Bob Marley, Walter Matthau, Kylie Minogue, V. S. Naipaul, Peter O'Toole, Anthony Perkins, Lisa Marie Presley, Debbie Reynolds, Sir Tim Rice, Little Richard, Anne Robinson, Mary Robinson, Mickey Rooney, Diana Ross, Donald Rumsfeld, Boz Scaggs, Gerhard Schröder, Michael Schumacher, Tom Selleck, Omar Sharif, Wilbur Smith, Rod Stewart, Jacques Tati, Elizabeth Taylor, Dame Kiri Te Kanawa, Justin Timberlake, Harry Truman, Venus Williams.

22 JANUARY 1909 ~ 9 FEBRUARY 1910	*Earth Rooster*
8 FEBRUARY 1921 ~ 27 JANUARY 1922	*Metal Rooster*
26 JANUARY 1933 ~ 13 FEBRUARY 1934	*Water Rooster*
13 FEBRUARY 1945 ~ 1 FEBRUARY 1946	*Wood Rooster*
31 JANUARY 1957 ~ 17 FEBRUARY 1958	*Fire Rooster*
17 FEBRUARY 1969 ~ 5 FEBRUARY 1970	*Earth Rooster*
5 FEBRUARY 1981 ~ 24 JANUARY 1982	*Metal Rooster*
23 JANUARY 1993 ~ 9 FEBRUARY 1994	*Water Rooster*
9 FEBRUARY 2005 ~ 28 JANUARY 2006	*Wood Rooster*

THE
ROOSTER

THE PERSONALITY OF
THE ROOSTER

Take calculated risks. That is different from being rash.
George Patton, a Rooster

The Rooster is born under the sign of candour. He has a flamboyant and colourful personality and is meticulous in all that he does. He is an excellent organizer and wherever possible likes to plan his various activities well in advance.

The Rooster is highly intelligent and usually very well read. He has a good sense of humour and is an effective and persuasive speaker. He loves discussion and enjoys taking part in any sort of debate. He has no hesitation in speaking his mind and is forthright in his views. He does, however, lack tact and can easily damage his reputation or cause offence by some thoughtless remark or action. The Rooster has a very volatile nature and should always try to avoid acting on the spur of the moment.

The Rooster is usually very dignified in his manner and conducts himself with an air of confidence and authority. He is adept at handling financial matters and organizes his financial affairs with considerable skill. He chooses his investments well and is capable of achieving great wealth. Most Roosters save or use their money wisely, but there are a few who are the reverse and are notorious spendthrifts. Fortunately, the Rooster has great earning capacity and is rarely without sufficient funds to tide himself over.

Another characteristic of the Rooster is that he invariably carries a notebook or scraps of paper around with him.

THE ROOSTER

He is constantly writing himself reminders or noting down important facts lest he forgets – the Rooster cannot abide inefficiency and conducts all his activities in an orderly, precise and methodical manner.

The Rooster is usually very ambitious, but can be unrealistic in some of what he hopes to achieve. He occasionally lets his imagination run away with him and while he does not like any interference from others, it would be in his own interests to listen to their views a little more often. He also does not like criticism, and if he feels anybody is doubting his judgement or prying too closely into his affairs, he is certain to let his feelings be known. He can also be rather self-centred and stubborn over relatively trivial matters, but to compensate for this he is reliable, honest and trustworthy, and this is appreciated by all who come into contact with him.

Roosters born between the hours of five and seven, both at dawn and sundown, tend to be the most extrovert of their sign, but all Roosters like to lead an active social life and enjoy attending parties and big functions. The Rooster usually has a wide circle of friends and is able to build up influential contacts with remarkable ease. He often belongs to several clubs and societies and involves himself in a variety of different activities. He is particularly interested in the environment, humanitarian affairs and anything affecting the welfare of others. He has a very caring nature and will do much to help those less fortunate than himself.

He also gets much pleasure from gardening and while he may not spend as much time in the garden as he would like, his garden is invariably well kept and productive.

The Rooster is generally very distinguished in his appearance and if his job permits he will wear an official uniform with great pride and dignity. He is not averse to publicity and takes great delight in being the centre of attention. He often does well at PR work or any job which brings him into contact with the media. He also makes a very good teacher.

The female Rooster leads a varied and interesting life. She involves herself in many different activities and there are some who wonder how she can achieve so much. She often holds very strong views and, like her male counterpart, has no hesitation in speaking her mind or telling others how she thinks things should be done. She is supremely efficient and well organized and her home is usually very neat and tidy. She has good taste in clothes and usually wears smart but very practical outfits.

The Rooster usually has a large family and takes a particularly active interest in the education of his children. He is very loyal to his partner and will find that he is especially well suited to those born under the signs of the Snake, Horse, Ox and Dragon. Provided they do not interfere too much in the Rooster's various activities, the Rat, Tiger, Goat and Pig can also establish a good relationship with him, but two Roosters together are likely to squabble and irritate each other. The rather sensitive Rabbit will find the Rooster a bit too blunt for his liking, and the Rooster will quickly become exasperated by the ever-inquisitive and artful Monkey. He will also find it difficult to get on with the anxious Dog.

If the Rooster can overcome his volatile nature and exercise more tact, he will go far in life. He is capable and talented and will make a lasting – and usually favourable – impression almost everywhere he goes.

THE FIVE DIFFERENT TYPES OF ROOSTER

In addition to the 12 signs of the Chinese zodiac there are five elements and these have a strengthening or moderating influence on the sign. The effects of the five elements on the Rooster are described below, together with the years in which the elements were exercising their influence. Therefore those Roosters born in 1921 and 1981 are Metal Roosters, those born in 1933 and 1993 are Water Roosters, and so on.

Metal Rooster: 1921, 1981

The Metal Rooster is a hard and conscientious worker. He knows exactly what he wants in life and sets about everything in a positive and determined manner. He can at times appear abrasive and he would almost certainly do better if he were more willing to reach a compromise with others rather than hold so rigidly to his beliefs. He is very articulate and most astute when dealing with financial matters. He is loyal to his friends and often devotes much energy to working for the common good.

Water Rooster: 1933, 1993

This Rooster has a very persuasive manner and can easily gain the co-operation of others. He is intelligent, well read and enjoys taking part in discussions and debates. He has a seemingly inexhaustible amount of energy and is prepared to work long hours in order to secure what he wants. He can, however, waste a lot of valuable time worrying over minor and inconsequential details. He is approachable, has a good sense of humour and is highly regarded by others.

Wood Rooster: 1945, 2005

The Wood Rooster is honest, reliable and often sets himself high standards. He is ambitious, but he is also more prepared to work in a team than some of the other types of Rooster. He usually succeeds in life but does have a tendency to get caught up in bureaucratic matters and attempt too many things at the same time. He has wide interests, likes to travel and is very caring and considerate towards his family and friends.

Fire Rooster: 1957

This Rooster is extremely strong-willed. He has many leadership qualities, is an excellent organizer and is most efficient in his work. Through sheer force of character he often secures his objectives, but he does have a tendency to be very forthright and not always consider the feelings of others. If he can learn to be more tactful he can often succeed beyond his wildest dreams.

THE ROOSTER

Earth Rooster: 1909, 1969

This Rooster has a deep and penetrating mind. He is efficient, perceptive and particularly astute in business and financial matters. He is also persistent and once he has set himself an objective, he will rarely allow himself to be deflected from achieving his aim. He works hard and is held in great esteem by his friends and colleagues. He usually enjoys the arts and takes a keen interest in the activities of the various members of his family.

PROSPECTS FOR THE ROOSTER IN 2005

The Chinese New Year starts on 9 February 2005. Until then, the old year, the Year of the Monkey, is still making its presence felt.

The Year of the Monkey (22 January 2004 to 8 February 2005) will have been a variable one for the Rooster and in what remains of it he will need to tread warily. In Monkey years things do tend to happen quickly and this can sometimes be unsettling for one who likes to follow carefully laid plans. However, provided the Rooster is prepared to make the most of the prevailing situations, the remaining months of the Monkey year can go well.

In his work, flexibility is the key. If the Rooster has the opportunity to do something extra, including possible training, he should make the most of it, as it will often be helpful to his future prospects. For those Roosters currently looking for a position or wanting to further their career, September and October could see some interesting opportunities.

The Rooster needs to be careful in his relations with others, though, and in any awkward situation he should watch his words, otherwise an ill-considered remark could cause problems. However, while there is this need for tact and keeping his candid nature in check, the closing months of the Monkey year will certainly not be without some pleasing family and social occasions, with the Rooster often playing a full part. November and December will see much socializing.

The Year of the Rooster starts on 9 February and will be a significant one for the Rooster. In his own year he will feel more in control of his situation and better able to proceed with his plans. As a result, he will reap some well-deserved rewards. This is very much a year when his organized and determined approach will pay off.

For those Roosters who start the year concerned about their present situation, this can mark an important turning-point. As their own year starts, these Roosters should draw a firm line under the past and regard this as a time to move forward. The Rooster knows he has many fine talents and he should resolve to make something of his own year.

One area which is especially promising is work and those Roosters who are keen to advance their career should actively pursue any opportunities they see. With their experience and reputation, many will find themselves strong candidates for promotion. Those who feel it would be useful to broaden their experience in other areas, would welcome a change or are seeking work will also find this is a year for taking the initiative. By making enquiries and pursuing opportunities, they will often be rewarded with a position which will give their career a welcome boost. For work opportunities, the months from March to May and August and November are especially favourable, but with the aspects as they are, interesting developments could happen at almost any time.

The progress the Rooster makes in his work will also lead to a rise in income. The Rooster's earning abilities will certainly be in good form over the year. Some Roosters may even be able to supplement their earnings with some additional work or by putting a skill they have to profitable use. However, while the Rooster can look forward to an improvement in his financial situation, he would do well to monitor his outgoings. Without care, these could quickly mount up, with his money not always being put to the best possible use. The Rooster would do well to keep a watchful eye over his purse strings (some Roosters are notorious spendthrifts) and set money aside for specific requirements. The more control he has over his situation, the better.

Over the year the Rooster's personal interests will bring him pleasure and he should look to extend these in some way, possibly by setting himself a new project or challenge, enrolling on a course or joining other enthusiasts. With his keen and curious nature, he will find his interests very satisfying as well as providing a balance to his other activities.

As far as the Rooster's domestic life is concerned, this will be an active year. There will often be a great deal to plan and think about as well as organize, with all the various schedules of everyone in the household. The Rooster's ability to oversee a great deal will stand him in good stead during the year and he will do much to ensure that his home life runs smoothly. Also, he will be effective in bringing everyone together, and whether discussing events, making arrangements or suggesting family activities, his input will be both considerable and appreciated.

The Rooster will also value his rapport with his loved ones and whenever he has any concerns, feels under pressure or would like additional help, he should be open and ask. He does so much for others and he must not deny them the chance to reciprocate. Domestically, this will be an active but potentially rewarding year.

This will also be a promising year for social matters, although how the Rooster fares will be very much in his own hands. With everything else that is going on, some Roosters will choose to keep their social life low-key this year. Being selective in the social events they attend will, however, often mean that they will appreciate them all the more. For those Roosters who choose to enjoy more social activity, the Rooster year can again go well, with April and the months from July to September offering many opportunities to go out. For the lonely and unattached, the year can also move in fortuitous ways, with a chance meeting leading to an important new friendship. Some Roosters will even meet their future partner during the year. The prospects for the Rooster in his own year are promising and this can be a special and significant time.

Overall, the Rooster's own year is a time of growth and by using his talents well and making the most of the chances that arise, he will enjoy himself as well as succeed in a great deal. For the Rooster, his own year is one of the best.

The Metal Rooster

This is a year of wonderful opportunity for the Metal Rooster, with important developments in both his personal and working life.

For many Metal Roosters this will be a year to remember, with good reason to celebrate, perhaps as a result of becoming being engaged or married, seeing an addition to the family, graduating or enjoying some other personal achievement. The Rooster year will certainly contain some memorable events. Those Metal Roosters with partners too will enjoy the love and support they give to each other and will delight in setting about various projects and activities together. Whether this involves setting up home or adding improvements to their accommodation, sharing interests or just spending time enjoying each other's company, the year will contain some very special moments.

The Metal Rooster will also benefit from the support he receives, and should he have any problems or be considering a major undertaking, he would do well to run it past those he knows and trusts, including more senior relations. Often, with the experience they have behind them, they will be able to give him good advice. Similarly, should the Metal Rooster feel under pressure or need additional help (especially if he has a young family), he will find others can be of great assistance. The Metal Rooster may not always like to bother those around him, but at times during the year he will be thankful for their help and advice.

The Metal Rooster will also value his social life over the year, especially any parties and celebrations to which he is invited. On a social level he will be in demand and will enjoy himself a great deal.

For those Metal Roosters who are unattached or who have had recent problems in their personal life, the Rooster year again holds great promise. Sometimes a chance meeting will transform their life, with some Metal Roosters meeting their future partner or someone who will become a significant friend during the year. Those who move over the year and find themselves alone and in a new area should also aim to get involved in activities they enjoy. By meeting those with similar interests, they will quickly establish a new and often rewarding social life. With his wide interests and genial nature, the Metal Rooster will find his personal life can go well. For socializing and personal matters, April, July to September and December are particularly favourable times.

The year will also be significant as far as the Metal Rooster's work is concerned. He certainly possesses an ambitious streak and over the year many Metal Roosters will be looking to make more of their skills and potential. By setting about their work in earnest and maintaining their high standards, many will find their achievements leading to new responsibilities as well as making them strong candidates for promotion. Similarly, those who are keen to widen their experience, to change what they do or are seeking work should actively follow up any openings that appeal to them. By remaining persistent, many will be successful in securing a position which will not only allow them to add considerably to their skills but could also set their career off an important new track. The months from March to May and August and November could see some interesting work opportunities.

The progress the Metal Rooster makes at work will lead to an increase in income, but with many commitments to meet, he will need to manage his money well. This includes budgeting for requirements and setting funds aside for forthcoming activities. However, by being his resourceful self, he will be pleased with all he is able to do with his money and will also be able to enjoy himself.

There will also be chances for the Metal Rooster to travel over the year, in some cases considerable distances. While these trips can lead to some memorable experiences, the more the Metal Rooster can prepare for his time away, the better he will fare. Here his fine organizational skills will be a great asset.

The Rooster year certainly holds excellent prospects for the Metal Rooster and with the love and support of others, he will enjoy it as well as lay significant foundations for his future success.

TIP FOR THE YEAR

Make the most of opportunities to further your skills. What you learn now can prove helpful and in some cases open up important possibilities for the future.

The Water Rooster

This will be an important year for the Water Rooster, though it will not be without its pressures or demands.

Those Water Roosters born in 1933 will, as always, have plans and ideas they are eager to carry out. For many, these will relate to their accommodation. They may be keen to install new comforts and equipment, change the layout of certain rooms or even move altogether. While these Water Roosters will be eager to get their ideas underway, it is important that they proceed steadily and avoid launching too many undertakings all at once. In 2005 they will need to keep their sometimes over-zealous nature in check! Also, the Water Rooster should make sure he discusses his plans, thoughts and any concerns he may have. Although he may have his own ideas, he will gain a great deal from the input of others and will often find his plans progressing more smoothly as a result. Also, in view of the practical nature of many of his activities, he must be realistic in what he tackles. If anything strenuous or hazardous is involved, it is important that he seeks assistance and in some cases professional help. This is not a year to take risks or jeopardize his well-being.

Those Water Roosters who move should again pace themselves and spread out their various tasks whenever possible. In particular any sorting and clearing out they can do early on would be helpful. And should they have any questions or uncertainties about any aspect of the moving process, they should get these resolved before proceeding. Usually the Water Rooster is thorough in such matters, but throughout the year it is important that he draws on the help available to him when necessary.

However, while the Water Rooster's domestic activities will often take up much time, there will be a great deal for him to enjoy. In particular he will find that interests that can be shared will mean a great deal, as will other joint activities, including trips out and entertaining friends. Some Water Roosters could also find that enrolling on a course with another person will lead to some interesting times.

Many Water Roosters have a literary streak and those who enjoy writing might also enjoy researching and writing about something that means a great deal to them, whether about the past, their family history, a story they have in mind or some knowledge they would like to share. By acting upon their ideas, they will find them leading to some absorbing and satisfying times. Similarly, for those Water Roosters who are keen on other pursuits, whether creative, practical or connected with the outdoors (including gardening, a key interest for many Water Roosters), this is a year to spend time on what they enjoy.

The Water Rooster will also value his social life over the year, especially the chances to meet up with friends as well as the various social occasions, including celebrations, parties and some more local events that appeal to him. The Rooster year can be quite a busy one and there will usually be something for the Water Rooster to look forward to. Those Water Roosters who would welcome more companionship will find that by joining in with local groups or enrolling on a course, they will get to meet others with similar outlooks, and new friendships will be born. The Rooster year is very supportive of its own sign, but to benefit the Rooster does need to take action.

As far as money matters are concerned, the Water Rooster would do well to keep a watchful eye over his outgoings, and when involved in any costly transaction, he should take his time, compare terms and consider what best suits his requirements. Large purchases and important transactions should not be rushed.

For those Water Roosters born in 1993 the year will also see much activity. With more advanced schoolwork, these Water Roosters will find a lot being expected of them. By making an effort and rising to the challenge, many will acquit themselves well and make good progress. Indeed, with his able and inquisitive nature, the Water Rooster is a good learner and over the year will impress many people. In addition, the various activities and interests he gets involved with could lead to him discovering new strengths and skills, and he will enjoy taking these further.

Generally, whether born in 1933 or 1993, this will be an active year for the Water Rooster and by setting about his activities with his usual keen but firm resolve, he will derive much satisfaction from what he accomplishes. This will be both a rewarding and positive time for him.

TIP FOR THE YEAR

Do follow up on your ideas. By doing something practical, you will find that your plans can soon start to take shape and often result in positive developments.

The Wood Rooster

This is the Wood Rooster's own year and it promises to be a significant one. With it being his sixtieth year, he will be keen to mark it in fine style, forging ahead with some of his ideas.

At work this will be a year of opportunity. Some Wood Roosters will choose to retire or opt to work fewer hours and will enjoy the chance to spend more time on activities they have long wanted to do. For those who continue working, their own year can bring some interesting developments. Although many will be content in their present role, their experience will often mark them out for further responsibilities or more specialist duties. Sometimes opportunities could arise with little warning and if the Wood Rooster is able to make the most of them, his career could receive an important fillip. Also, by virtue of his experience, he could find others looking to him for advice and guidance and some of his duties may well involve him training and mentoring others. Many Wood Roosters will find this a rewarding aspect of their work.

In addition to the opportunities that come his way over the year, the Wood Rooster should make the most of his ideas and specialist knowledge. His input will often be welcome and in some cases his suggestions will be taken further. In such an encouraging year, action is the key. The months from March to May and August and November could see some particularly fine opportunities, but, as the Wood Rooster will find, situations can change quickly and it is a case of acting swiftly in order to benefit.

For those Wood Roosters seeking work, or perhaps a position involving fewer hours or less travelling, again the Rooster year could have some surprises in store. Although these Water Roosters may need to undertake some searching, with persistence many will secure an excellent position which will suit their requirements well and often be a welcome contrast to what they have been doing before.

The year is also well aspected for financial matters, with many Wood Roosters receiving an additional sum of money or a bonus over the year, perhaps as the result of a gift, a maturing policy or work done previously. Rather than being tempted to spend this extra money too readily, the Wood Rooster should take the time to plan what he is going to do with it. This way, what he does will be more satisfying. Also, while he is usually so efficient, he should deal with financial paperwork promptly this year. Although he may find certain forms tiresome, to be slow in returning them could result in additional correspondence as well as possibly being to his disadvantage. Wood Roosters, take note, and do not let your normally high standards slip.

To mark their sixtieth year, many Wood Roosters will decide to take a special holiday over the year, perhaps visiting an area they have long wanted to see. By planning their travels in advance and going well prepared, these Wood Roosters will find their times away can prove a high point of the year. In addition, many Wood Roosters will enjoy the company of fellow travellers, and for those who travel alone, an important new friendship could result. Travel is certainly well aspected.

The Wood Rooster will also get much pleasure from his interests over the year. Whether he chooses to spend more time in his garden, carry out projects on his home or develop his recreational interests, he will find this another positive aspect of the year.

In so much of what he does, the Wood Rooster will be grateful for the support of those around him and domestically this will be a pleasing year. However, the Wood Rooster should be forthcoming with his ideas and listen carefully to the views of those who are dear to him. By pooling ideas and talents, he will find that more can be achieved as well as enjoyed. Shared activities can also help with the rapport and understanding the Wood Rooster so values.

The year will also contain some memorable family occasions which the Wood Rooster will not only enjoy but also help to organize. These can include the marking of his own sixtieth birthday as well as the achievements of younger members of his family, including, for some, a wedding, birth or graduation. The Rooster year will certainly contain events that will be long remembered.

The Wood Rooster's social life is also pleasingly aspected and many Wood Roosters will find that their interests and travels will lead to them making some new friends and acquaintances over the year. April, July to September and December could see much social activity.

Overall, this is a year for action and for making the most of the opportunities that arise. With his many talents and keen nature, the Wood Rooster can certainly help to make his own year a memorable and successful one.

TIP FOR THE YEAR
This is a year for seizing the initiative and for making things happen. Act upon your ideas and opportunities and you will soon find your positive approach bringing significant results.

The Fire Rooster

This will be a year of considerable opportunity for the Fire Rooster and one which will see positive developments in many areas of his life.

At work his prospects are especially encouraging, and with his drive and commitment, he is set to make excellent progress. In recent years many Fire Roosters will have accomplished a great deal as well as considerably added to their experience and in 2005 they will find their achievements being rewarded. Some will be offered greater responsibilities or, as more senior colleagues move on, will find themselves ideally placed for promotion. This is very much a time for the Fire Rooster to advance and he should make much of his opportunities. He will find some colleagues especially helpful, both in giving good advice and in speaking highly of him to others. Over the year he will certainly have much in his favour.

For those Fire Roosters seeking work or hoping to change their duties, this can also be a significant year. Their quest may not always be easy, but with persistence, their efforts will pay off and many will be successful in securing a job which will give them greater chance to develop their strengths. The months from March to May and August and November could see important developments, but given the encouraging nature of the year, whenever an opportunity strikes the Fire Rooster should act quickly.

This is also an excellent year for the Fire Rooster to develop his skills. If his employer offers him training or if he is seeking work and is eligible for retraining, he should follow this up. Keeping his skills up to date and acquiring new ones will not only help him now but also widen his scope for the future. Again, this is a year to make the most of the chances that arise.

The Fire Rooster's development need not be restricted to his work but can include his interests and well-being too. If there is a subject that he is keen to find out more about, he should make enquiries. Similarly, if he feels he is lacking exercise and there is some sport or outdoor pursuit that appeals to him, he should seek appropriate advice on how best to proceed. This is very much a year for acting upon his ideas.

The progress that the Fire Rooster makes in his work will often lead to an increase in income, but with his many obligations and plans, he does need to manage his money well. Controlling his outgoings and keeping a close watch on his financial position will allow him to do more. He would also do well to consider setting a regular amount aside for a holiday over the year. The rest and change of scene can do him a lot of good and by choosing his destination with care, he could find a holiday he takes this year could turn out to be one of the best he has had for a long time.

The Fire Rooster will also value his domestic life over the year and his organizational ability will be appreciated. Not only will he do much to ensure the smooth running of his home but he will also be active in advising and encouraging his loved ones, with his thoughtfulness and considered views being valued. However, while the Fire Rooster will do so much for others, he should also make sure that they do their share of household tasks as well. There is, after all, a limit to what he can do!

The year will also give rise to some pleasing family occasions, and in addition to the pleasure shared interests and activities will bring, there will be some fine family successes to celebrate, including the Fire Rooster's own progress. His home life will mean a great deal to him over the year.

He will also enjoy his social life and by following up the invitations he receives as well as going to events that appeal to him, he can make this another pleasing and often beneficial aspect of his life. Many Fire Roosters will find their interests will bring them into contact with other enthusiasts, and those who may be lonely or have had recent sadness to bear will find that by going out more, enrolling on courses and getting involved in activities and interest groups, their social life will pick up and important friendships can be made. Again, the Rooster year does favour its own sign, but to benefit the Rooster needs to act.

Overall, the year holds excellent prospects for the Fire Rooster and by making the most of his abilities, ideas and opportunities, he can make this a time of considerable progress as well as personal happiness.

TIP FOR THE YEAR
Manage your time and resources well. If you set yourself specific goals and go after them, you will find yourself doing and enjoying far more as a result.

The Earth Rooster

The Earth Rooster possesses a very determined nature and when he has decided on a particular course of action, he will do his best to follow it through. In 2005, his determination and strong sense of purpose will lead to some impressive results.

The aspects are especially encouraging as far as his work is concerned. Although many Earth Roosters will have achieved a great deal in recent years, there will be some Earth Roosters who feel unfulfilled in their present position and wish to make more of their skills. By taking action now, they will often find themselves benefiting from a fortuitous turn of events. Thomas Jefferson wrote, 'I'm a great believer in luck, and I find the harder I work, the more I have of it,' and this will certainly be true for many Earth Roosters this year.

In view of their recent achievements at work, many Earth Roosters will be well placed to put in for positions with greater responsibilities. The period from March to May and August and November could see some interesting opportunities, but with the aspects as they are, whenever a chance comes his way, the Earth Rooster should be quick to act.

For those Earth Roosters who are seeking work or hoping to move their career in another direction, again the Rooster year holds excellent prospects. By making enquiries and actively following up openings that appeal to them, many Earth Roosters will be successful in securing an excellent position with potential for the future.

However, while the aspects are encouraging in work matters, the Earth Rooster will need to exercise care with his money. With his many obligations, as well as the plans he is keen to carry out, he would do well to keep a watchful eye over his outgoings. In some cases greater control over the purse strings could help. Also, if he has any sizeable purchases or costly activities in mind, including travel, he would do well to save for these in advance. The more control he can take over his finances, the better he will fare.

Although the Earth Rooster will have many demands on his time, it is also important that he does not let his recreational pursuits suffer. With the pressures he faces, he does need to have time to relax, unwind and just enjoy himself. If he can set aside a regular time each week for his own activities, he will find this particularly beneficial.

This will also be a favourable year for family matters, with the Earth Rooster often doing much to help both younger and more senior relations. Over the year others will often look to him for advice and guidance and will value his judgement and understanding. The Earth Rooster will also often be active in suggesting various activities for everyone to enjoy, and again his ideas will lead to some pleasurable occasions.

With his practical nature the Earth Rooster will also be keen to go ahead with certain projects on his home and garden. However, despite his eagerness, he should avoid starting too much all at once and where possible should try to spread more practical undertakings out over the year.

The year will also be an important one socially. With his interests and work contacts, the Earth Rooster will have many chances to go out and add to his circle of friends. For the unattached, a significant new friendship could result from a chance meeting or introduction.

Overall, the Rooster year is an encouraging one for the Earth Rooster and by making the most of his opportunities and pursuing his aims, he can look forward to making significant progress. On a personal level the year will contain many rewarding times, with the Earth Rooster's loved ones meaning a lot to him as well as giving him much valuable support.

TIP FOR THE YEAR
Although you may be eager to do a great deal, do make sure your life has balance and that your interests and recreational pursuits do not suffer. Where possible, try to spread out your activities.

FAMOUS ROOSTERS

Mohamed al Fayed, Francis Bacon, Dame Janet Baker, Enid Blyton, Sir Michael Caine, Enrico Caruso, Christopher Cazenove, Eric Clapton, Joan Collins, Rita Coolidge, Craig David, Daniel Day Lewis, Sacha Distel, the Duke of Edinburgh, Gloria Estefan, Roger Federer, Bryan Ferry, Errol Flynn, Benjamin Franklin, Dawn French, Stephen Fry, Steffi Graf, Melanie Griffith, Richard Harris, Deborah Harry, Goldie Hawn, Katherine Hepburn, Lleyton Hewitt, Catherine Zeta Jones, Quincy Jones, Diane Keaton, Søren Kierkegaard, D. H. Lawrence, David Livingstone, Ken Livingstone, Jayne Mansfield, Steve Martin, James Mason, W. Somerset Maugham, Paul Merton, Bette Midler, Van Morrison, Willie Nelson, Kim Novak, Yoko Ono, Dolly Parton, George Patton, Michelle Pfeiffer, Priscilla Presley, Mary Quant, Nancy Reagan, Joan Rivers, Kelly Rowland, Paul Scofield, Jenny Seagrove, George Segal, Carly Simon, Britney Spears, Johann Strauss, Barbara Taylor Bradford, Sir Peter Ustinov, Verdi, Richard Wagner, Serena Williams, Neil Young.

10 FEBRUARY 1910 ~ 29 JANUARY 1911	*Metal Dog*
28 JANUARY 1922 ~ 15 FEBRUARY 1923	*Water Dog*
14 FEBRUARY 1934 ~ 3 FEBRUARY 1935	*Wood Dog*
2 FEBRUARY 1946 ~ 21 JANUARY 1947	*Fire Dog*
18 FEBRUARY 1958 ~ 7 FEBRUARY 1959	*Earth Dog*
6 FEBRUARY 1970 ~ 26 JANUARY 1971	*Metal Dog*
25 JANUARY 1982 ~ 12 FEBRUARY 1983	*Water Dog*
10 FEBRUARY 1994 ~ 30 JANUARY 1995	*Wood Dog*

THE
DOG

THE PERSONALITY OF THE DOG

Whatever is worth doing at all is worth doing well.
The Earl of Chesterfield, a Dog

The Dog is born under the signs of loyalty and anxiety. He usually holds very firm views and beliefs and is the champion of good causes. He hates any sort of injustice or unfair treatment and will do all in his power to help those less fortunate than himself. He has a strong sense of fair play and will be honourable and open in all his dealings.

The Dog is very direct and straightforward. He is never one to skirt round issues and speaks frankly and to the point. He can be stubborn, but he is more than prepared to listen to the views of others and will try to be as fair as possible in coming to his decisions. He will readily give advice where it is needed and will be the first to offer assistance when things go wrong.

The Dog instils confidence wherever he goes and there are many who admire him for his integrity and resolute manner. He is a very good judge of character and can often form an accurate impression of someone very shortly after meeting them. He is also very intuitive and can frequently sense how things are going to work out long in advance.

Despite his friendly and amiable manner, the Dog is not a big socializer. He dislikes having to attend large functions or parties and much prefers a quiet meal with friends or a chat by the fire. He is an excellent conversationalist and is often a marvellous raconteur of amusing stories and anecdotes. He is also quick-witted and his mind is always alert.

THE DOG

The Dog can keep calm in a crisis and although he does have a temper, his outbursts tend to be short-lived. He is loyal and trustworthy, but if he ever feels badly let down or rejected by someone, he will rarely forgive or forget.

The Dog usually has very set interests. He prefers to specialize and become an expert in a chosen area rather than dabble in a variety of different activities. He usually does well in jobs where he feels that he is being of service to others and is often suited to careers in the social services, the medical and legal professions and teaching. He does, however, need to feel motivated in his work. He has to have a sense of purpose and if ever this is lacking he can quite often drift through life without ever achieving very much. Once he has the motivation, however, very little can prevent him from securing his objective.

Another characteristic of the Dog is his tendency to worry and to view things rather pessimistically. Quite often his worries are totally unnecessary and are of his own making. Although it may be difficult, worrying is a habit which all Dogs should try to overcome.

The Dog is not materialistic or particularly bothered about accumulating great wealth. As long as he has the money necessary to support his family and to spend on the occasional luxury, he is more than happy. However, when he does have any spare money he tends to be rather a spendthrift and does not always put his money to its best use. He is also not a very good speculator and would be advised to get professional advice before entering into any major long-term investment.

The Dog will rarely be short of admirers, but he is not an easy person to live with. His moods are changeable and his standards high, but he will be loyal and protective to his partner and will do all in his power to provide a good and comfortable home. He can get on extremely well with those born under the signs of the Horse, Pig, Tiger and Monkey, and can also establish a sound and stable relationship with the Rat, Ox, Rabbit, Snake and another Dog, but will find the Dragon a bit too flamboyant for his liking. He will also find it difficult to understand the imaginative Goat and is likely to be highly irritated by the candid Rooster.

The female Dog is renowned for her beauty. She has a warm and caring nature, although until she knows someone well she can be both secretive and very guarded. She is highly intelligent and despite her calm and tranquil appearance she can be extremely ambitious. She enjoys sport and other outdoor activities and has a happy knack of finding bargains in the most unlikely of places. She can also get rather impatient when things do not work out as she would like.

The Dog usually has a very good way with children and can be a doting parent. He will rarely be happier than when he is helping someone or doing something that will benefit others. Providing he can cure himself of his tendency to worry, he will lead a very full and active life – and in that life he will make many friends and do a tremendous amount of good.

THE FIVE DIFFERENT TYPES OF DOG

In addition to the 12 signs of the Chinese zodiac there are five elements and these have a strengthening or moderating influence on the sign. The effects of the five elements on the Dog are described below, together with the years in which the elements were exercising their influence. Therefore those Dogs born in 1910 and 1970 are Metal Dogs, those born in 1922 and 1982 are Water Dogs, and so on.

Metal Dog: 1910, 1970
The Metal Dog is bold, confident and forthright and sets about everything he does in a resolute and determined manner. He has a great belief in his abilities and has no hesitation about speaking his mind or devoting himself to some just cause. He can be rather serious at times and can become anxious and irritable when things are not going according to plan. He tends to have very specific interests and it would certainly help him if he were to broaden his outlook and become more involved in group activities. He is extremely loyal and faithful to his friends.

Water Dog: 1922, 1982
The Water Dog has a very direct and outgoing personality. He is an excellent communicator and has little trouble in

persuading others to fall in with his plans. He does, however, have a somewhat carefree nature and is not as disciplined or as thorough as he should be in certain matters. Neither does he keep as much control over his finances as he should, but he can be most generous to his family and friends and will make sure that they want for nothing. The Water Dog is usually very good with children and has a wide circle of friends.

Wood Dog: 1934, 1994

This Dog is a hard and conscientious worker and will usually make a favourable impression wherever he goes. He is less independent than some of the other types of Dog and prefers to work in a group rather than on his own. He is popular, has a good sense of humour and takes a keen interest in the activities of the various members of his family. He is often attracted to the finer things in life and can obtain much pleasure from collecting stamps, coins, pictures or antiques. He prefers to live in the country rather than the town.

Fire Dog: 1946

This Dog has a lively, outgoing personality and is able to establish friendships with remarkable ease. He is an honest and conscientious worker and likes to take an active part in all that is going on around him. He also likes to explore new ideas and providing he can get the necessary support and advice, he can often succeed where others have failed. He does, however, have a tendency to be stubborn.

Providing he can overcome this, he can often achieve considerable fame and fortune.

Earth Dog: 1958

The Earth Dog is very talented and astute. He is methodical and efficient and is capable of going far in his chosen profession. He tends to be rather quiet and reserved but has a very persuasive manner and usually secures his objectives without too much opposition. He is generous and kind and is always ready to lend a helping hand when it is needed. He is also held in very high esteem by his friends and colleagues and is usually most dignified in his appearance.

PROSPECTS FOR THE DOG IN 2005

The Chinese New Year starts on 9 February 2005. Until then, the old year, the Year of the Monkey, is still making its presence felt.

The Year of the Monkey (22 January 2004 to 8 February 2005) will have been an active one for the Dog and there will be little respite as it draws to a close. Almost all areas of his life will see activity, with him being in great demand.

One area which features prominently for Dogs in Monkey years is accommodation, and quite a few Dogs will move or carry out projects on their home over the year. These Dogs should allow plenty of time for their plans to be realized. Accommodation changes can work out well, but should not be rushed.

With much outlay likely in the closing months of the year, the Dog would also find it helpful to make early provision for what could be an expensive time and if possible spread out some of his purchases. Money-wise, this is a time for careful control.

The closing months will also be busy as far as the Dog's work is concerned. However, his tenacity, loyalty and many talents will have impressed others and for those seeking a position or looking to further their career, there will be some excellent opportunities as the year draws to a close.

Domestically and socially, this can also be a pleasing time, with December being a full and sometimes exciting month. The Dog too will appreciate the chance to get in contact with someone he has not heard from for some time and there could be some surprising news in store.

The Year of the Rooster starts on 9 February and will be a variable one for the Dog. Progress will not always be easy and he could also face some disappointments, but this does not necessarily mean it will be a bad year. There will be some happy times in between some of the vexations and the year will also leave a powerful legacy which the Dog will be able to build on in the future.

In setting about his activities the Dog does, though, need to liaise closely with others as well as be mindful of their views. He does have set ways and often firm ideas and he could sometimes find himself at odds with others as a result. The Rooster year does require him to tread carefully.

This particularly applies to his work. Although the Dog will continue to set about his activities with commitment and verve, he does need to be aware of prevailing attitudes as well as adapt to any changes that may be introduced. This is not a year for digging his heels in or appearing too inflexible. However, while there is this need for care, the Dog can still do himself a lot of good. Whenever there is an opportunity for him to further his experience, whether through training, taking on other duties or covering for colleagues, he should make the most of it. Not only will it be helpful now but it could also open up possibilities for the future.

For those Dogs who are seeking work or keen to change the type of work they do, this will be a significant year. Although obtaining a new position will not be easy and many will face disappointments in their quest, with persistence, they may well secure what can prove to be an important position. In some cases this will be very different from what they have done before, but it will give them a good chance to extend their skills as well as discover new strengths. Again, what is accomplished this year can be important in the longer term. March, May, August and October could see some interesting work developments.

This will also be a good year for the Dog to further his personal interests, and whether developing existing interests or taking up new ones, he will again find what he does satisfying and beneficial. Activities which allow the Dog to draw on his ideas and express himself in some way could be especially pleasurable, while Dogs with musical interests (and many Dogs do have a good ear for music) will find this an excellent year to further their talents.

As far as money matters are concerned, though, this is a year for care. In particular, whenever he is involved in any large purchase or transaction, the Dog does need to check the terms carefully as well as be aware of the obligations he may be taking on. Similarly, when dealing with financial forms, he needs to be thorough and prompt. To delay or not give the matter adequate attention could result in problems and in some cases additional expense. The Dog should also be wary of lending to others or being too trusting in certain situations. This is a year for keeping his wits about him and managing his resources carefully.

This need for care also extends to the Dog's home life and throughout the year he would do well to be open with his thoughts as well as prepared to discuss any matters concerning him or any arrangements that need to be made. By consulting others, not only will he find they are better able to help, but he may also avert a possible difference of opinion. Also, a certain openness on his part will lead to a better rapport with others. Over the year there will certainly be much in his home life that will bring the Dog pleasure. This includes interests and projects that can be carried out with others as well as entertaining friends or relations, going to social events or away for a short break or holiday. Busy though the Dog's family life might be, it will contain many rewarding times.

As usual, the Dog may be selective in his socializing over the year, but when he does go out, whether to meet friends, attend parties or go to other social occasions, he will often thoroughly enjoy himself as well as welcome the chance to unwind and have a good time. However, if at any time he should find himself in a tricky social situation, he does need to watch what he says. There is a danger that an inadvertent comment could cause problems, and in some situations tact and discretion would be wise.

For the unattached Dog and those who are seeking more companionship, there will certainly be many opportunities to meet others, but where affairs of the heart are concerned, the Dog would do well to let any new relationship develop gradually rather than be too hasty. This way both people will have more time to get to know the other and the relationship will have a stronger basis as a result. For meeting others and socializing, February and June to August are particularly favourable times.

Overall, although the Rooster year may not be the easiest for the Dog, by setting about his activities carefully and maintaining good relations with those around him, he will find most of it satisfying. And with his prospects especially encouraging in 2006, what he accomplishes now will often have a significant bearing on his future.

The Metal Dog

This will be a demanding year for the Metal Dog, but while progress will not be easy, the year can still be significant. Not only will it give him the opportunity to broaden his experience and build up new strengths, but it can also pave the way for some important developments over the next few years.

In his work the Metal Dog will find much being expected of him and others will often look to him to take on further responsibilities, become involved in new initiatives or handle complex matters. As a result, his workload will sometimes be heavy and there will be times when he will feel frustrated by the length of time certain activities are taking or the delays caused by bureaucratic matters.

However, while the year will bring its pressures, by keeping himself well organized and concentrating on his priorities, the Metal Dog will find his accomplishments can still be considerable. Also, by working hard and rising to the challenge, he will find himself learning new techniques and strengthening his skills as well as gaining experience, all of which will stand him in excellent stead for the future.

The Metal Dog can also help his position by maintaining good relations with his colleagues. Showing himself an effective team member and building up contacts will help his prospects considerably. However, while his relations with colleagues will often be positive, the Metal Dog does need to remain on his guard. With some of the pressures of the year, he should be careful if at any time he gives vent to his feelings or finds himself in a fraught situation. An unfortunate remark could undermine some of the good relationships he has built up and he must watch this in tense and volatile situations.

Although opportunities for progress will be limited, if the Metal Dog does see an opening that appeals to him, he should act quickly, before the opportunity is lost. Any headway he can make now will often be an important step towards his future success. March, May, August and October could see interesting work developments.

This also applies to those Metal Dogs seeking work or eager to move from their current position. Although chances may not be plentiful and it could take considerable effort to secure a new role, once they do gain a new position, many will find it will give them important new experience as well as open up future possibilities.

THE DOG

As far as money matters are concerned, this is a year for care. Over the year the Metal Dog will have many outgoings, especially with regard to acquisitions for his home, travel costs and family expenses. In view of this, he does need to manage his resources carefully and where possible save towards some of the plans he has in mind. The more disciplined he is, the better he will fare. He also needs to be careful when dealing with financially related forms and should check the terms of any new obligations he may take on. This is not a year to be dilatory over financial matters or take unnecessary risks.

Although the Metal Dog will have much to occupy him over the year, it is also important that he allows time for his recreational pursuits. These will not only be a good way for him to relax but can often provide him with the chance to get additional exercise and meet others as well as take his mind off his more usual concerns.

As far as his domestic life is concerned, this will be a busy year with many calls upon his time. In particular he will do much to assist both younger and more senior relations, with the advice and support he gives being appreciated. However, with a lot to do at home, as well as work and other pressures, the Metal Dog should not hesitate to ask for help with certain household tasks when necessary as well as be forthcoming about any concerns he may have. It really will be helpful for him to be open rather than keep his worries to himself.

The Metal Dog should also make sure he spends time with his loved ones on activities that everyone will enjoy rather than constantly conduct life at such a hectic pace. Joint activities will often give rise to some pleasing family occasions.

With the busy nature of the year, the Metal Dog may decide to keep his social life relatively low-key. However, it is important that it does not get neglected and he should aim to keep in regular contact with friends as well as go to any events that appeal to him. His social life can provide an important balance to his lifestyle.

For those Metal Dogs who are lonely and would welcome more companionship, their interests will be a good way to meet others and by joining a local group and getting to know other enthusiasts, they can make some important new friendships over the year.

Although this will be a demanding year for the Metal Dog, it will be a constructive one, particularly in the way that it will allow him to extend his skills and experience. And what he does now will stand him in excellent stead for the success he can look forward to in following years. His long-term prospects are exciting indeed!

TIP FOR THE YEAR
Manage your time well. In spite of everything you have to do, make sure you spend quality time with those dearest to you and do not neglect your interests and social life. Do try and keep your life in balance.

The Water Dog

This will be an important year for the Water Dog. Events will often happen quickly and to benefit he will need to keep his wits about him. While the year will not be without its pressures or difficulties, he will learn a great deal during it as well as enjoy a full and active personal life.

THE DOG

As far as the Water Dog's work is concerned, this will be a significant year. Those Water Dogs already in work should regard this as a year for widening their experience rather than looking to make major advances. The Water Dog may have his ambitions, but by improving his skills and becoming more established in his area of work, he will find himself better placed when opportunities do arise. Also, by tackling what can be a heavy workload and overcoming some of the pressures the year will bring, he will find himself becoming more disciplined in his approach and this too will be to his future benefit. As so many Water Dogs will find, the Rooster year may be demanding but it can be highly instructive.

The Water Dog should also make the most of any training opportunities he is given, or if there is a chance to cover for colleagues or assist in another capacity, he should take it up. Anything he can do to learn more about his work and develop his skills will be helpful.

As many Water Dogs will find, the real benefits from their efforts will follow in succeeding years, but if the Water Dog does have the chance to move his career forward in the Rooster year, he should make the most of it. March, May, August and October could see some interesting developments.

For those Water Dogs seeking work again the Rooster year will not be the easiest. In some cases the Water Dog will face much competition and there could be disappointments when certain applications do not go his way. However, with each application he makes he will be learning more about what is required and improving his interview techniques and the way he presents himself. And when he does secure a position, it will offer him useful experience now as well as possibilities for the future.

For those Water Dogs involved in study the year will again demand a lot, with much to learn as well as preparation for what will be important exams. However, by focusing on what they have to do, these Water Dogs will find their efforts being well rewarded and having an important bearing on their future. Again, the Rooster year can leave a powerful legacy.

As far as money matters are concerned, this could, though, be a tricky year. With his many plans and ideas, as well as accommodation and other expenses, the Water Dog will have many demands on his resources. As a result he would do well to keep a close watch on his spending and set money aside for specific requirements whenever possible. Also, if he enters into any important transaction or has financial forms to complete, he should be thorough and check the details. Financial matters do need careful attention, otherwise the Water Dog could find he is disadvantaged in some way.

This will, though, be an active year as far as the Water Dog's personal life is concerned. For many Water Dogs the love and support of their partner will mean a great deal and there will be plans to carry out and interests and activities to share. For these Water Dogs the year will contain some wonderful times. However, despite so much going well, the year can still bring its pressures. Tiredness caused by a heavy workload, sleepless nights (if a parent) and sometimes financial concerns could cause difficult moments. At such times, the Water Dog should show understanding and be prepared to talk over any concerns. If need be, talking to more senior relatives may help. Fortunately the Water Dog does recognize the value of dialogue and his openness and sincerity can do much to prevent certain pressures from marring a rewarding domestic life.

For those Water Dogs who are unattached and possibly feeling lonely, perhaps as a result of moving to a new area or a recent disappointment in their personal life, this can again be an important year. Someone met during the year, possibly through their work or interests, will, in time, become very special. For socializing and meeting others February and the period from June to August could be especially promising.

Overall, although the Rooster year will bring its demands, it will allow the Water Dog to develop his skills and discover strengths as well as do much to prepare for his future progress. Personally, the year will contain some rewarding moments, with the Water Dog valuing the love and support of those close to him as well as making new friends.

TIP FOR THE YEAR
Regard this as a year for learning and preparation. You may have ambitions, but often they will need to be worked for and will take time to achieve. Remain persistent and use this year to build up your skills, support and contacts.

The Wood Dog

This will be a reasonable year for the Wood Dog, although attitude will be a crucial factor in how he fares. The Wood Dog can be very self-willed, and without care, there could be times over the year when he does not make as much of his situation as he might. This is very much a year when he will need to show some flexibility and be willing to adapt to prevailing situations.

This is especially true for those Wood Dogs born in 1994. Many will have recently changed their school or class or will do so over the year, and as with any change, there will be certain aspects that the Wood Dog does not like or does not feel comfortable with. However, by being prepared to adapt and make the most of the situations he finds himself in, he will find some of his initial concerns misplaced. Also, in his schoolwork he will often have new subjects to learn, and rather than decide too early that he does not like something, he should keep an open mind. That way he will make better progress as well as find his work more satisfying. The young Wood Dog really can do well in the Rooster year, but it is very much a case of being prepared to adapt and willing to learn.

The young Wood Dog should also remember that others are willing to help and advise, and if at any time he has problems or is worried over some matter, he should let them know about it. By being forthcoming he will find that others can do much to help him deal with his concerns.

The Wood Dog will value his close circle of friends, and those who do change school will soon find themselves making some new and very good friends. The young Wood Dog will certainly value the support and camaraderie. However, a word of warning does need to be sounded. Although the Wood Dog will enjoy some high-spirited occasions over the year, he should be careful not to carry these too far and become involved in situations which he

THE DOG

has misgivings about. Similarly, when engaging in physical or sporting activities, he needs to listen carefully to instructions. This is not a year for personal risks or for being foolhardy. Wood Dogs, do take note.

This will also be a constructive year for the more senior Wood Dog, although attitude will again be important. If he has particular plans he would like to carry out, he should talk them over with others and consider their advice. Although he may have to reconsider some of his ideas, by showing more flexibility, he will gain more as a result.

The plans the Wood Dog has in mind may concern almost any aspect of his life, but one area which will bring him considerable pleasure is improving his home, particularly adding new equipment and comforts. He will often be delighted with the difference these can make. However, should any of his ideas involve anything strenuous, it is important that he seeks help or employs someone qualified to do the task for him. This is not a year to risk his well-being. Wood Dogs, take note.

The Wood Dog will also follow the progress of family members with fond interest and there could be good reason for a family celebration, possibly a wedding, a graduation or the birth of a grandchild. The year will certainly contain moments that will mean a great deal to the Wood Dog. He should also follow up any invitations he receives to visit others living some distance away, as his travels will bring him pleasure.

The Wood Dog will also value the time he spends on his interests and if there is a subject he would like to find out more about or he sees a course advertised which appeals to him, he would do well to follow this up.

Where money matters are concerned, he will, though, need to be careful. When entering into any new agreement he does need to check the terms and implications thoroughly and get any queries resolved before proceeding. Similarly, when completing financial forms, if there is anything he does not understand, he should contact a helpline or seek advice. Financial matters do need close attention over the year.

Overall, the Rooster year can be an encouraging one for the Wood Dog, but he does need to make the most of his situation and be willing to adapt to changes as well as consult others. With a willing and flexible attitude, however, he will gain both satisfaction and pleasure from his activities over the year.

TIP FOR THE YEAR
Make the most of your personal interests and consider setting yourself a particular project to do or skill to learn. Your interests can bring much benefit and satisfaction over the year.

The Fire Dog

This will be a variable year for the Fire Dog and he will need to proceed carefully and steadily.

In his work this will be a busy and demanding year, with a lot being expected of him. He may often have to deal with additional duties or complex issues and his work may not be made any easier by new procedures and additional bureaucracy. As a result, the Fire Dog could find some parts of the Rooster year challenging and a test of his patience.

However, while the year will contain its frustrating times, it will give the Fire Dog the opportunity to extend his skills. While he may be expert in his line of work, he should not let this preclude him from furthering his knowledge or taking advantage of courses that may be available to him. Many Fire Dogs will find what they learn will not only help them now but also give rise to further possibilities in the future.

For those Fire Dogs seeking work or looking to change what they do, the Rooster year can again bring interesting developments. Although there will be times when they will get disheartened when certain applications do not go their way, by remaining persistent many will secure a position which will give them an interesting new challenge. There could be other advantages too, including less travel or more suitable hours. By making the most of any chance they are given, these Fire Dogs will often enjoy their new role. March, May, August and October could see some interesting work developments.

Although many Fire Dogs will enjoy a rise in income over the year, financial matters do need care. The Fire Dog will need to make allowances for his various commitments as well as set money aside for forthcoming plans and activities. Also, if he is able, he could find it helpful to reduce some of his borrowings. He also needs to be careful when taking on any new agreements or dealing with financial paperwork. This is a year for thoroughness and for checking the small print. The extra care and attention the Fire Dog takes in this regard can often prevent problems from arising later.

Despite the many demands on his time, the Fire Dog will get much pleasure from his personal interests and should ensure he sets aside time for them. He will often appreciate the social element involved and will find that meeting other enthusiasts will lead to some enjoyable occasions as well as further his knowledge.

With the demands of the year, he should not ignore his well-being either and if he is sedentary for much of the day or feels that more exercise and modifications to his diet could be beneficial, he should seek medical advice on the best way to proceed. Once again, he can benefit by making the effort and seeking advice.

This will be a fairly active year in the Fire Dog's home life, with those close to him often seeking his views and assistance. While the Fire Dog may sometimes despair of all he has to do, by helping out when he can he will find his efforts greatly appreciated. His rapport with family members too will help, and should any matter be concerning him at any time, he will find that by being willing to talk it over he can do much to sort it out. As he has so often found, it is better to be open than keep his worries to himself or let them linger in the background. The Fire Dog will also find that some of his ideas for family activities will be appreciated and his input into family life will again be valued this year.

He will also enjoy the social occasions he goes to over the year, and whether these are in some way connected with his work or interests or simply involve meeting up with friends, they will often do him a lot of good.

Overall, although the Fire Dog will need to set about his activities with care, by making the most of situations and being mindful of others, he can make this a satisfying and constructive year. Despite some of the pressures, it will still contain many pleasurable times, especially those spent with those dear to him and in furthering his skills and interests.

TIP FOR THE YEAR
Be flexible in your outlook. By adapting to prevailing situations, as well as consulting those who can help you when necessary, you can gain a great deal.

The Earth Dog

This will be a busy year for the Earth Dog and while he will sometimes find it difficult to make the progress he would like, what he does now can be helpful to him in the longer term.

In his work the Earth Dog would do well to regard this more as a year for furthering his skills and expertise than for making major advances. By setting about what may be an often heavy workload in his usual careful manner he will impress many and help both his reputation and prospects. In addition, the pressures he has to face will also give him experience in dealing with other aspects of his work and again he will be able to build on this in the future.

The Earth Dog will also find it helpful to work closely with colleagues over the year and show himself a good team member rather than be too independent. Not only will this be more effective when dealing with certain situations, but it will also allow others to better appreciate his talents.

Although opportunities to advance will be limited over the year, if the Earth Dog does see an opening that appeals to him he should be quick in putting himself forward. Again, any progress he makes now can often be a prelude to further advances in the near future.

For those Earth Dogs seeking work the Rooster year can also be a significant one. Although their quest will not be easy, with persistence many will secure a position which will not only allow them to add to their experience but also lead to other possibilities in the future. Also, if they find they are eligible for training or retraining, they should follow this up. Again, anything they can do to improve their prospects can be helpful and have important implications for the future. March, May, August and October could see interesting opportunities work-wise.

As far as money matters are concerned, this is, though, a year for care. The Earth Dog will face many expenses, especially involving family, education, accommodation and transport, and in view of these and his other obligations, he will need to manage his resources prudently. He should also be wary about succumbing to too many impulsive purchases or expensive treats. To be able to do all he wants, he does need to watch his spending levels and budget carefully. Earth Dogs, do take note and manage your finances well.

This will also be a busy year domestically, with the Earth Dog doing much to help those close to him, particularly younger and more senior relations. While there will be times when he will despair of all he has to do, those around him will be very appreciative of the attentiveness, advice and assistance he is able to give. As always the Earth Dog will play a central and valued role in family life. However, if at any time he feels he has just too much to do, he should not hesitate to ask others for assistance, particularly with certain household tasks. Similarly, if any matter is concerning him or trying his patience, he should discuss this openly rather than let it cast a shadow over family life. His willingness to address issues really can make a difference over the year. However, despite its demands, the Earth Dog's family life will mean much to him, and by setting time aside to share with loved ones, he will enjoy many rewarding occasions. Any short breaks or family holidays will also be appreciated and will do everyone good.

The Earth Dog should also make sure his interests and social life do not suffer due to the busy nature of the year. Keeping in regular contact with friends and setting aside time for his recreational pursuits will again do him a lot of good. Those Earth Dogs who have let their social life lapse in recent years will find that by going out more and meeting those who share similar interests, they can make their leisure time much more enjoyable. For socializing, February and the period from June to August could be interesting and pleasurable.

Although this will be a busy and often demanding year for the Earth Dog, by rising to the challenges it will bring and taking the opportunity to further his skills, he will learn a great deal. What he does now will often be an important factor in the success he can look forward to in following years. Overall, an important, challenging but very constructive year.

TIP FOR THE YEAR
Pay close attention to your relations with others, whether family, friends or colleagues. Their support, advice and assistance can be of great value to you.

FAMOUS DOGS

André Agassi, King Albert II of Belgium, Elizabeth Arden, Jane Asher, Brigitte Bardot, Gary Barlow, Candice Bergen, David Bowie, Bertolt Brecht, George W. Bush, Kate Bush, Laura Bush, Naomi Campbell, Mariah Carey, King Carl XVI Gustaf of Sweden, José Carreras, Paul Cézanne, Cher, Sir Winston Churchill, Bill Clinton, Leonard Cohen, Jamie Lee Curtis, Matt Damon, Charles Dance, Claude Debussy, Dame Judi Dench, Blake Edwards, Sally Field, Joseph Fiennes, Robert Frost, Ali G, Ava Gardner, Judy Garland, George Gershwin, Lenny Henry, O. Henry, Victor Hugo, Barry Humphries, Holly Hunter, Michael Jackson, Al Jolson, Felicity Kendal, Jennifer Lopez, Sophia Loren, Joanna Lumley, Shirley MacLaine, Madonna, Norman Mailer, Barry Manilow, Freddie Mercury, Liza Minnelli, David Niven, Sydney Pollack, Elvis Presley, Tim Robbins, Lord George Robertson, Paul Robeson, Andy Roddick, Linda Ronstadt, Gabriela Sabatini, Susan Sarandon, Jennifer Saunders, Claudia Schiffer, Dr Albert Schweitzer, Sylvester Stallone, Robert Louis Stevenson, Sharon Stone, Jack Straw, David Suchet, Donald Sutherland, Chris Tarrant, Mother Teresa, Uma Thurman, Donald Trump, Voltaire, Prince William, Shelley Winters.

30 JANUARY 1911 ~ 17 FEBRUARY 1912	*Metal Pig*
16 FEBRUARY 1923 ~ 4 FEBRUARY 1924	*Water Pig*
4 FEBRUARY 1935 ~ 23 JANUARY 1936	*Wood Pig*
22 JANUARY 1947 ~ 9 FEBRUARY 1948	*Fire Pig*
8 FEBRUARY 1959 ~ 27 JANUARY 1960	*Earth Pig*
27 JANUARY 1971 ~ 14 FEBRUARY 1972	*Metal Pig*
13 FEBRUARY 1983 ~ 1 FEBRUARY 1984	*Water Pig*
31 JANUARY 1995 ~ 18 FEBRUARY 1996	*Wood Pig*

THE
PIG

THE PERSONALITY OF THE PIG

> Life is a series of experiences, each one of which makes us bigger, even though sometimes it is hard to realize this.
> *Ralph Waldo Emerson, a Pig*

The Pig is born under the sign of honesty. He has a kind and understanding nature and is well known for his abilities as a peacemaker. He hates any sort of discord or unpleasantness and will do everything in his power to sort out differences of opinion or bring opposing factions together.

He is also an excellent conversationalist and speaks truthfully and to the point. He dislikes any form of falsehood or hypocrisy and is a firm believer in justice and the maintenance of law and order. In spite of these beliefs, however, the Pig is reasonably tolerant and often prepared to forgive others for their wrong-doings. He rarely harbours grudges and is never vindictive.

The Pig is usually very popular. He enjoys other people's company and likes to be involved in joint or group activities. He will be a loyal member of any club or society and can be relied upon to lend a helping hand at functions. He is also an excellent fundraiser for charities and is often a great supporter of humanitarian causes.

The Pig is a hard and conscientious worker and is particularly respected for his reliability and integrity. In his early years he will try his hand at several different jobs, but he is usually happiest where he feels that he is being of service to others. He will unselfishly give up his time for the common good and is highly valued by his colleagues and employers.

THE PIG

The Pig has a good sense of humour and invariably has a smile, joke or some whimsical remark at the ready. He loves to entertain and to please others, and there are many Pigs who have been attracted to careers in show business or who enjoy following the careers of famous stars and personalities.

There are, unfortunately, some who take advantage of the Pig's good nature and impose upon his generosity. The Pig has great difficulty in saying 'no' and, although he may dislike being firm, it would be in his own interests to say occasionally, 'Enough is enough.' The Pig can also be rather naïve and gullible; however, if at any stage in his life he feels that he has been badly let down, he will make sure that it will never happen again and will try to become self-reliant. There are many Pigs who have become entrepreneurs or forged a successful career on their own after some early disappointment in life. Although the Pig tends to spend his money quite freely, he is usually very astute in financial matters and there are many Pigs who have become wealthy.

Another characteristic of the Pig is his ability to recover from setbacks reasonably quickly. His faith and his strength of character keep him going. If he thinks that there is a job he can do or he has something that he wants to achieve, he will pursue it with a dogged determination. He can also be stubborn and, no matter how many may plead with him, once he has made his mind up he will rarely change his views.

Although the Pig may work hard, he also knows how to enjoy himself. He is a great pleasure-seeker and will quite happily spend his hard-earned money on a lavish holiday or an expensive meal – for the Pig is a connoisseur of good food and wine – or taking part in a variety of recreational activities. He also enjoys small social gatherings and if he is in company he likes he can very easily become the life and soul of the party. He does, however, tend to become rather withdrawn at larger functions or when among strangers.

The Pig is a creature of comfort and his home will usually be fitted with all the latest in luxury appliances. Where possible, he will prefer to live in the country rather than the town and will opt to have a big garden, for the Pig is usually a keen and successful gardener.

The Pig is very popular with others and will often have numerous romances before he settles down. Once settled, however, he will be loyal to his partner and he will find that he is especially well suited to those born under the signs of the Goat, Rabbit, Dog and Tiger and also to another Pig. Due to his affable and easy-going nature he can also establish a satisfactory relationship with all the remaining signs of the Chinese zodiac, with the exception of the Snake. The Snake tends to be wily, secretive and very guarded, and this can be intensely irritating to the honest and open-hearted Pig.

The female Pig will devote all her energies to the needs of her children and her partner. She tries to ensure that they want for nothing and their pleasure is very much her pleasure. She can be a caring and conscientious parent and has very good taste in clothes. Her home will either be very clean and orderly or hopelessly untidy. Strangely, there seems to be no in between with Pigs – they either love housework or detest it! The female Pig does, however, have considerable talents as an organizer and this, combined with her friendly and open manner, enables her to secure many of her objectives.

The Pig is usually lucky in life and will rarely want for anything. Provided he does not let others take advantage of his good nature and is not afraid of asserting himself, he will go through life making friends, helping others and winning the admiration of many.

THE FIVE DIFFERENT TYPES OF PIG

In addition to the 12 signs of the Chinese zodiac there are five elements and these have a strengthening or moderating influence on the sign. The effects of the five elements on the Pig are described below, together with the years in which the elements were exercising their influence. Therefore those Pigs born in 1911 and 1971 are Metal Pigs, those born in 1923 and 1983 are Water Pigs, and so on.

Metal Pig: 1911, 1971
The Metal Pig is more ambitious and determined than some of the other types of Pig. He is strong, energetic and likes to be involved in a wide variety of different activities. He is very open and forthright in his views, although he can be a little too trusting at times and has a tendency to accept things at face value. He has a good sense of humour and loves to attend parties and other social gatherings. He has a warm, outgoing nature and usually has a large circle of friends.

Water Pig: 1923, 1983

The Water Pig has a heart of gold. He is generous and loyal and tries to remain on good terms with everyone. He will do his utmost to help others, but sadly there are some who will take advantage of his kind nature and he should, in his own interests, be a little more discriminating and be prepared to stand firm against anything that he does not like. Although he prefers the quieter things in life, he has a wide range of interests. He particularly enjoys outdoor pursuits and attending parties and social occasions. He is a hard and conscientious worker and invariably does well in his chosen profession. He is also gifted in the art of communication.

Wood Pig: 1935, 1995

This Pig has a friendly, persuasive manner and is easily able to gain the confidence of others. He likes to be involved in all that is going on around him but can sometimes take on more responsibility than he can properly handle. He is loyal to his family and friends and derives much pleasure from helping those less fortunate than himself. He is usually an optimist and leads a very full, enjoyable and satisfying life. He also has a good sense of humour.

Fire Pig: 1947

The Fire Pig is both energetic and adventurous and he sets about everything he does in a confident and resolute manner. He is very forthright in his views and does not mind taking risks in order to achieve his objectives. He can, however, get carried away by the excitement of the moment and ought to exercise more caution in some of the enterprises in which he gets involved. He is usually lucky in money matters and is well known for his generosity. He is also very caring towards the members of his family.

Earth Pig: 1959

This Pig has a kindly nature. He is sensible and realistic and will go to great lengths in order to please his employers and to secure his aims and ambitions. He is an excellent organizer and is particularly astute in business and financial matters. He has a good sense of humour and a wide circle of friends. He also likes to lead an active social life, although he does sometimes have a tendency to eat and drink more than is good for him.

PROSPECTS FOR THE PIG IN 2005

The Chinese New Year starts on 9 February 2005. Until then, the old year, the Year of the Monkey, is still making its presence felt.

The Year of the Monkey (22 January 2004 to 8 February 2005) will have been a mixed one for the Pig and in the remaining months he will need to proceed with care.

In his work the Pig should aim to work closely with colleagues and as part of a team rather than being too independent. Also, with his prospects looking so promising in the Rooster year, any additional experience he can obtain or skills he can improve on will stand him in good stead. For those Pigs currently seeking work or keen to progress, October could see some interesting opportunities.

As far as money matters are concerned, the Pig will need to be careful, and with the closing months of the year being expensive ones, he could find it helpful to make to early provision for some of his purchases and activities. Also, if entering into new commitments he should check the terms and obligations carefully. Where finances are concerned, this is a time to be thorough.

More positively, the Pig's relations with both family and friends are well aspected. His domestic and social life will be busy, with plenty of activities to arrange and enjoy and many opportunities to go out and meet others. The Pig, so sociable and outgoing, will certainly revel in all the activity. Affairs of the heart are also splendidly aspected and could make the closing months of the Monkey year a special time.

The Year of the Rooster starts on 9 February and will be a rewarding one for the Pig.

His personal life is especially well aspected. For those enjoying romance, perhaps started in the previous Monkey year, this will continue to blossom, with many marrying or deciding to settle down together over the year. And for those who are unattached or who have had some recent disappointment in their personal life, the Rooster year holds some truly exciting prospects and can mark quite a transformation in their lives. Sometimes these Pigs will meet someone purely by chance and fall deeply in love. For affairs of the heart this can be an especially significant year, and while the Pig could feel the effects of Cupid's arrow at almost any time, the period from late March to June and August could offer many chances to meet others.

For those Pigs with a partner, this will be an important year. The Pig will value the love and support he is shown and should set aside time to share with his partner. He will also delight in following the progress of those close to him and the year could give rise to a family celebration, possibly a promotion, engagement, marriage or addition to the family. For quite a few Pigs, the year will be marked by some memorable and gratifying events. And, as ever, these Pigs will take pleasure in helping to organize the celebrations.

However, while the aspects are so encouraging, no year is ever free from its more difficult moments and whenever a problem arises, the Pig would find it helpful to talk the matter through and see how best it can be resolved. Although he may dislike awkward scenes, his willingness to address such matters in an open way can do much to ease problems and prevent them from overshadowing what can be such an agreeable year.

His social life is pleasingly aspected and once again he will be much in demand, with many invitations to parties and other social occasions. He could also find his work and interests lead to him going out fairly often and having the opportunity to make new friends and acquaintances.

Work prospects are promising too, and with the year's emphasis on commitment and hard work, the Pig is set to do well. In view of their recent undertakings, many Pigs will find themselves with the right experience to put themselves forward for promotion or a position with greater responsibilities. They will often be helped by the good contacts they have built up. Throughout the year, the Pig should continue to use his personal skills well, meeting others in his line of work and networking effectively. As he will find, becoming better known will be helpful to his career.

He should also take advantage of any ways in which he can develop himself over the year. Whether this is through training or by taking on other duties, again what he learns now can often make his work more fulfilling as well as widening his scope for the future.

This also applies to those Pigs seeking work, either as the year begins or during it. By actively following up positions that interest them as well as taking advantage of any retraining schemes that may be available, many will be successful in obtaining an interesting new position which will widen their experience. Work-wise, this is a highly encouraging year, and by working hard, maintaining good relations with colleagues and developing skills, many Pigs will find their efforts being well rewarded. The months from February to April and July and November could see some particularly good work opportunities.

The Pig's progress at work will often lead to a rise in income and he could also benefit from funds he receives from other sources. Money-wise, this is an encouraging year, although the Pig must be careful not to take his spending too far. In particular he would find it helpful to set funds aside for more sizeable purchases and make allowance for other plans, including holidays. With care and good sense, this will be a generally positive year for financial matters.

Overall, the Pig will have much in his favour in the Rooster year and by using his talents well and making the most of the opportunities that arise, he can look forward to making well-deserved progress. His personal life is most promising, with him being in demand and enjoying the love and support of those who are special to him. In so many respects, this will be a positive *and* rewarding year.

The Metal Pig

This will be a year of considerable opportunity for the Metal Pig, allowing him to make good use of his talents as well as enjoy many aspects of his life.

In his work he will find the experience he has built up serving him well, and this, together with his ability to relate so effectively with others, will help him to advance his career. Over the year there will be chances for him to take on greater responsibilities or apply for promotion. In addition, his willingness to play such an active role will be appreciated and if he has ideas or suggestions, he should put them forward. This is a year when effort and initiative can make an important difference.

For any Metal Pig who is feeling staid or unfulfilled in his present role, this is a year to take action and look for a more suitable position. By making enquiries and following up opportunities, many Metal Pigs will be successful in securing a position which can set their career off on a new and promising track. It could take several attempts to make the breakthrough they desire, but with persistence, their efforts can ultimately lead to success. February to April, July and November could see some interesting work opportunities.

This also applies to those Metal Pigs seeking work. With faith in their abilities, many will again secure what can be a good position for them and, importantly, one that can lead to other possibilities in the future.

Another benefit of the Rooster year is the way in which it encourages the Metal Pig to build on his skills. Whether this comes through taking on new duties or through training, by being willing to learn, he will do much to help his current position and future prospects. Also, if there is a particular skill or qualification he feels it would be useful to obtain, he should follow this up. Again, this can be helpful in the longer term.

This is also a positive year for money matters, with many Metal Pigs enjoying an increase in income. Some may also be able to supplement this by an enterprising idea or putting a skill to additional use. Certainly the Metal Pig's earning abilities will be in fine form over the year. However, while he will welcome this improvement, he does need to keep a close watch on his outgoings, otherwise he could find them mounting up and eating into his resources. This may be an encouraging year as regards earnings, but the Metal Pig still needs to manage his money well and whenever possible set funds aside for specific requirements as well as consider adding to his savings. Generally, the more control he has over his finances, the better he will fare.

As far as the Metal Pig's home life is concerned, this will be an active year. With his own commitments and those of other family members, life will often be conducted at a hectic pace. However, with organization and a willingness to help out at busy times, the Metal Pig will find his home life going well. He will particularly value the times spent with those dear to him and some of the more pleasurable occasions that take place. Also, he will do much to help both younger and more senior relations over the year and the time and advice he gives will be particularly valued. In addition, if any family member has problems or concerns, the fact that the Metal Pig is so approachable and can relate so effectively will count for a great deal.

Although demands on the Metal Pig's time may prevent him from socializing as much as in some years, he should still keep in regular contact with his friends as well as go to any events that appeal to him. His social life can be a good way for him to relax and unwind as well as help keep his lifestyle in balance. And, for those who desire more companionship or even romance, the Rooster year holds excellent prospects, with the period from March to June and August bringing some particularly good chances to meet others.

Overall, this is a well-aspected year for the Metal Pig and by making the most of his chances to further his skills, he can make it a successful and fulfilling time. And personally, the love and support he receives will give him a lot of encouragement.

TIP FOR THE YEAR

With this being such an active year, do make sure you spend time on more relaxing pursuits and interests. It is important that your lifestyle has balance. Despite your keen nature, you cannot expect to be on the go all the time!

The Water Pig

This is a year of excellent opportunity for the Water Pig and will allow him to make effective use of his many skills and qualities.

Work prospects are especially promising. The Water Pig takes a lot of pride in what he does and his care and industry, as well as his ability to get on with others, will be very much to his advantage over the year. In addition, his willingness to master new duties will count for a great deal and when new openings arise, he will often find himself well placed to benefit. With a positive and determined outlook, the Water Pig can move his career forward this year, and for some, one advance can quickly lead to another.

With the Water Pig being in the early stages of his career, he should also make the most of any chances he has to extend his experience. Whether this is by taking on new duties or going on training courses, what he does now can be helpful to his future prospects. Also, some Water Pigs may not yet have fully decided on the type of career they wish to follow and by being willing to try out various possibilities, they may discover types of work they find more satisfying and are keen to develop further. As well as being a year of advancement, this can also be one of discovery.

Those Water Pigs seeking work, either as the year starts or during it, will again find themselves benefiting from the year's favourable aspects, and sometimes some strokes of good fortune too. In some instances a close friend could advise them of a possible opportunity or they could learn of a vacancy by chance. By acting quickly, many will be successful in securing an interesting new position. The months from February to April and July and November could see some interesting work developments.

For those Water Pigs involved in academic work and studying for qualifications this can also be a significant year. While their workload may sometimes be considerable, by organizing what they have to do and working steadily, these Water Pigs will often find their efforts well rewarded, with many securing qualifications that can help with entry into their chosen profession.

The Rooster year is also a promising one for recreational pursuits and again the Water Pig should make the most of his ideas and opportunities. Those Water Pigs who are keen on travel will find that by deciding on places they would like to visit and making enquiries, their plans can proceed well. Many Water Pigs will get to visit some interesting destinations over the year. The Water Pig will also be pleased with the way in which he is able to further his personal interests, and whether these are of an outdoor nature or more creative, by giving time to them, he will find this another rewarding aspect of the year.

A more challenging area will concern finance. Although the Water Pig's progress and enterprise will often lead to an increase in income, this will be an expensive year. With accommodation and travel costs and some of his personal plans, he will have many demands on his resources. As a result, he should manage his finances with care. To be tempted by too many personal treats or expensive shopping sprees could leave him short of money for other activities and throughout the year he would find it helpful to keep a firm control over the purse-strings. Also, if entering into any long-term agreement, he should check the terms and obligations thoroughly, and if he has any doubts, he should resolve these before proceeding. This is not a year for risks.

As far as the Water Pig's personal life is concerned, this will often be a memorable year, with some Water Pigs getting engaged or married or seeing an addition to their family. For those with a partner, the year will bring many happy moments. Backed by the support and encouragement of someone special, these Water Pigs will feel much more positive in outlook and this will be another important factor in their progress.

However, while the Water Pig will often be eager to set about his various plans and projects, especially if setting up home, he would do well to allow plenty of time for carrying them out. To do too many things at once, to rush projects or tackle something that is over-ambitious could lead to pressures and strains. Despite the Water Pig's willing nature, he must be realistic in some of his more practical activities.

Also, the Water Pig should not hesitate to draw on the support of more senior relatives. Although he may wish to set about his activities in his own way, there are others he can call on who would be delighted to help. Water Pigs, do take note.

The Water Pig's social life is well aspected and he will often have many invitations and opportunities to go out. Both his interests and work can lead to him meeting many new people, some of whom will become close friends. For those Water Pigs who are currently unattached, a significant romance can beckon, with the period from March to

June and August offering good opportunities to meet others.

Overall, the Rooster year holds much promise for the Water Pig and if he makes the most of his ideas, qualities and opportunities, this will be a year of important progress as well as considerable personal happiness.

TIP FOR THE YEAR
Look to develop. With the ambitions and hopes you have for the future, the ways in which you are able to further your skills and interests can be important.

The Wood Pig

The Wood Pig will celebrate either his tenth or seventieth birthday this year and both younger and more senior Wood Pigs can look forward to a pleasant and rewarding year.

For those born in 1935, the Rooster year will be a constructive one. With plenty of ideas about what he would like to do, the more senior Wood Pig will set about his plans in earnest. As the saying goes, *There is no time like the present*, and the Wood Pig will feel this is very much a year for action.

With the year's emphasis on order, many Wood Pigs will feel inspired to tackle projects on their home, particularly ones that would make it better organized and more efficient. As a result, quite a few Wood Pigs will decide to sort through accumulated paperwork and other items they may no longer need. While these projects may take longer than anticipated, the Wood Pig will be satisfied with how much tidier certain areas have become as a result.

The Wood Pig will also be keen to go ahead with other ideas for his home, and whether these involve changing décor and furnishings or adding new comforts, he will enjoy considering the various possibilities and seeing his ideas unfold. His plans need not be restricted to his home – those Wood Pigs with gardens will often be tempted to try out different stock or add a new feature. Gardening is another activity which will bring quite a few Wood Pigs considerable pleasure over the year.

As well as enjoying the practical nature of the year, the Wood Pig can look forward to some memorable family events. In addition to the marking of his seventieth year, there will be other milestones to celebrate, particularly the achievements of younger relations. The Wood Pig's ability to relate so effectively to others, regardless of age, will mean a great deal and the bonds he has with younger relations will often be special and important. And if at any time there is a close relative or friend who would benefit from some encouragement or advice, again the Wood Pig's ability to empathize will be valued.

The Wood Pig will enjoy the chances he has to travel over the year and if he sees any offers that appeal to him or receives any invitations to visit others, he would do well to follow them up. His trips will often be pleasurable as well as do him good.

As far as money matters are concerned, this will be a generally positive year. However, with the Wood Pig's many ideas and plans, he could find it helpful to budget in advance and before making any sizeable purchase he should take the time to compare what is available. In some cases, waiting for sale times could save him considerable

THE PIG

expense. Also, should he have any uncertainties about a transaction or financial matter, including any financially related forms, he should seek advice rather than make assumptions. This may be a good year financially, but it is not one for carelessness. Wood Pigs, take note.

For those Wood Pigs born in 1995 the year also holds fine prospects, particularly as it will give them the chance to make more of their interests. By taking advantage of the opportunities available to them, they will often be pleased with how they are able to master new skills.

As far as his schoolwork is concerned, the young Wood Pig will often have a great deal to learn, and while he will often take it in his stride, if he should ever be worried about any matter or have problems with certain subjects, he should tell others rather than struggle on in bewilderment. However, by doing his best, furthering his interests and enjoying the comradeship of his friends, the young Wood Pig will be able to make much of the year.

Overall, this will be a positive year, and by following through their ideas and opportunities, both younger and more senior Wood Pigs will be pleased with how it develops. And they will be well supported in their activities too.

TIP FOR THE YEAR

Extend your personal interests in some way, either by taking up something new or by setting yourself a particular project to do or skill to master. Your interests can bring you pleasure and often be beneficial in other ways too.

The Fire Pig

This will be a pleasing year for the Fire Pig, especially in the way that he will be able to put his skills and ideas to good use.

However, in order to benefit from the encouraging aspects, the Fire Pig would do well to give some thought to what he wants to do over the next 12 months and talk his ideas over with those close to him. Not only will he benefit from the advice he receives, but with some plans in mind, he will be better able to direct his energies towards what he wants and will achieve far more as a result.

The Fire Pig's ideas could concern several different aspects of his life, but as far as his work is concerned, this will be a year of interesting developments. Some Fire Pigs, having been in the same occupation for some time, will feel the time is now right for a change and quite a few will decide to look for another position over the year, sometimes one that is nearer to where they live. With the aspects as they are, many of these Fire Pigs will discover such a position almost through chance, either by being advised by a friend or alerted by something they read or hear. And once in a new position, they will often revel in the opportunity to do something different and develop their skills in new ways.

For those Fire Pigs who are content in their present position, the Rooster year again offers fine prospects. In view of their considerable experience, they will often find themselves being given more specialist duties or having the chance to make further progress. By making the most of the opportunities that arise, these Fire Pigs will often find their work becoming more fulfilling as a result. The

Rooster year rewards the industrious and the months from February to April and July and November could see some particularly interesting developments.

The Fire Pig will also take much pleasure from his interests over the year and by setting himself some projects to do and following up his ideas, he will again enjoy what he does.

The year is also positively aspected as far as money matters are concerned, with many Fire Pigs benefiting from an unexpected bonus or a maturing policy, or discovering an additional source of income through an idea or skill. However, while anything extra that the Fire Pig receives will be welcome, he should manage his situation with care. Where large acquisitions are concerned, time spent comparing possibilities and waiting for offers will often lead to more satisfactory purchases. Also, if the Fire Pig is able to set funds aside for future activities, reduce his borrowings and add to his savings, he could find this helpful.

With his genial nature, the Fire Pig always sets much store by his relations with others and both his domestic and social life will bring him considerable pleasure over the year. In his home life he will find himself being helped by the advice and encouragement of those close to him, and by involving others in what he does, he will enjoy many special occasions as well as strengthen the rapport and understanding he so values. He too will do much to assist those dear to him and should any close relation have a problem or feel under pressure, the Fire Pig's advice will often do much to help. If a grandparent, he will also enjoy the chance to spend time with his grandchildren and will follow their progress with fond interest. Family-wise, this can be a pleasant and rewarding year.

The Fire Pig will also appreciate his social life, and for those who desire more companionship or who have had some recent personal sadness to bear, the Rooster year can certainly bring an improvement in their situation, with new friendships and a more active social life. For the unattached, romance too could beckon and the Fire Pig could well meet someone special while away on holiday or pursuing one of his interests. In this respect, too, the Rooster year is a fine one for the Fire Pig.

Overall, this will be a year of opportunity for the Fire Pig and by making the most of his experience and personal strengths, he will derive much satisfaction from it.

TIP FOR THE YEAR

Make the most of your ideas. With the support of others and the chances available to you, these can often develop well. This is very much a year for following through on your plans.

The Earth Pig

This will be an eventful year for the Earth Pig and, while often busy, it will reward him well. It is a year of challenge, but also opportunity and substantial progress.

One area which will see considerable activity will be Earth Pig's work. In view of his considerable experience and the fine reputation he has built up, he may well find himself ideally placed to advance his career. Whenever he sees an opening that appeals to him or has the chance to take on greater responsibilities, he should act swiftly. With his willingness and desire to make more of himself, he will often be able to make important advances.

Some Earth Pigs will remain with their present employer over the year and benefit from their in-house knowledge. However, for those who feel there may be better prospects elsewhere or who wish to develop their experience in other areas, the Rooster year will bring some excellent opportunities. Again, by following up suitable opportunities and making enquiries, these Earth Pigs will find their efforts rewarded and often leading to what will be an interesting and important new position. The months from February to April and July and November could see some interesting work opportunities.

The positive aspects also apply to those Earth Pigs seeking work. Again, by remaining active and persistent, many will be successful in securing a position which will set their career off on an interesting new track.

Another important aspect of the year will be the way the Earth Pig is able to add to his experience. This will partly come through taking on other duties, but if he has the chance of further training or can enrol on a suitable course, he should follow this up, as it will not only be helpful now but also widen his future possibilities. As far as the Earth Pig's development is concerned, this can be a significant and far-reaching year.

However, while so much can go in the Earth Pig's favour, some parts of the year will be busy and at such times the Earth Pig will need to remain well organized and focus upon his most important tasks. If he tries to spread his energies too widely, problems could start to mount.

Earth Pigs, take note, and remember that the Rooster year is one when good organization can make an important difference.

The progress that the Earth Pig makes in his work will often lead to an increase in income and some Earth Pigs may also be able to supplement this by freelance work or putting some knowledge or skill to good use. However, while the Earth Pig's earning abilities will be good, he does need to manage his financial situation well. In particular, rather than spend any extra money too readily, he should plan his more substantial purchases and control his budget. Also, if he is able to reduce any borrowings and add to his longer-term savings, he could find this will be to his benefit.

The Earth Pig's personal interests will be important to him over the year, and while he will have many demands on his time, he should still set a regular time aside for activities he enjoys. If he can encourage his loved ones to share in his interests or can join other enthusiasts, he will find his activities all the more rewarding. Some Earth Pigs could become inspired by a new hobby and enjoy the opportunity to master some new skills. Again, the Earth Pig would do well to follow his ideas through this year. He should also aim to go away at some time. With his busy lifestyle, a break and change of scene will do him good. By choosing their destination with care, many Earth Pigs will get to visit some interesting places during the year.

The Earth Pig will also be pleased with how his family life goes over the year and in addition to encouraging those around him to share his interests and hopes, he will enjoy some very pleasurable times with his loved ones. Again, he

THE PIG

will do much to help both younger and more senior relations, and while there may be times when he will be concerned about some of their ideas, by talking to them and offering advice, he will find his words will be of value. Again, his ability to relate so effectively will help.

The Earth Pig will also value his friendships over the year and will not only enjoy chatting with his friends but also the chance to run through certain matters he has on his mind. Knowing the Earth Pig as they do, some of his friends could offer particularly helpful advice. The Earth Pig will also enjoy many of the social events he goes to, and with his friendly and outgoing nature, he will find himself popular company. His social circle is set to increase as the year progresses and for any Earth Pig who would welcome more companionship, the Rooster can bring quite a transformation! The months from March to June and August could be particularly busy socially.

Generally, the Rooster year holds promising prospects for the Earth Pig and by making the most of his opportunities, he can make good progress. He will also be encouraged by the support of his loved ones and the many who think so highly of him.

TIP FOR THE YEAR
With much happening over the year, stay well organized and keep tabs on everything that is going on. The better informed you are and better you manage your time, the more effective and successful you will be.

FAMOUS PIGS

Bryan Adams, Woody Allen, Julie Andrews, Marie Antoinette, Fred Astaire, Sir Richard Attenborough, Hector Berlioz, David Blunkett, Humphrey Bogart, James Cagney, Maria Callas, Richard Chamberlain, Hillary Rodham Clinton, Glenn Close, David Coulthard, Noël Coward, Oliver Cromwell, Billy Crystal, the Dalai Lama, Ted Danson, Dido, Richard Dreyfuss, Ben Elton, Ralph Waldo Emerson, Sven-Goran Eriksson, Henry Ford, Emmylou Harris, Audley Harrison, William Randolph Hearst, Ernest Hemingway, Henry VIII, Conrad Hilton, Alfred Hitchcock, Sir Elton John, Tommy Lee Jones, Carl Gustav Jung, Boris Karloff, Charles Kennedy, Stephen King, Nastassja Kinski, Kevin Kline, Hugh Laurie, Nigella Lawson, David Letterman, Jerry Lee Lewis, Ewan McGregor, Marcel Marceau, Ricky Martin, Johnny Mathis, Meat Loaf, Wolfgang Amadeus Mozart, Camilla Parker Bowles, Michael Parkinson, Luciano Pavarotti, Iggy Pop, Prince Rainier of Monaco, Maurice Ravel, Ronald Reagan, Ginger Rogers, Salman Rushdie, Françoise Sagan, Carlos Santana, Arnold Schwarzenegger, Kevin Spacey, Steven Spielberg, Emma Thompson, Holly Valance, Jules Verne, Michael Winner, the Duchess of York.

APPENDIX

The relationships between the 12 animal signs, both on a personal level and business level, are an important aspect of Chinese horoscopes and in this appendix the compatibility between the signs is shown in the two tables that follow.

Also included are the names of the signs ruling the hours of the day and from this it is possible to find your ascendant and discover yet another aspect of your personality.

Finally, to supplement the earlier chapters on the personality and horoscope of the signs, I have included a guide on how you can get the best out of your sign and the year.

PERSONAL RELATIONSHIPS

KEY

1. Excellent. Great rapport.
2. A successful relationship. Many interests in common.
3. Mutual respect and understanding. A good relationship.
4. Fair. Needs care and some willingness to compromise in order for the relationship to work.
5. Awkward. Possible difficulties in communication with few interests in common.
6. A clash of personalities. Very difficult.

	Rat	Ox	Tiger	Rabbit	Dragon	Snake	Horse	Goat	Monkey	Rooster	Dog	Pig
Rat	1											
Ox	1	3										
Tiger	4	6	5									
Rabbit	5	2	3	2								
Dragon	1	5	4	3	2							
Snake	3	1	6	2	1	5						
Horse	6	5	1	5	3	4	2					
Goat	5	5	3	1	4	3	2	2				
Monkey	1	3	6	3	1	3	5	3	1			
Rooster	5	1	5	6	2	1	2	5	5	5		
Dog	3	4	1	2	6	3	1	5	3	5	2	
Pig	2	3	2	2	2	6	3	2	2	3	1	2

APPENDIX
BUSINESS RELATIONSHIPS

KEY
1 Excellent. Marvellous understanding and rapport.
2 Very good. Complement each other well.
3 A good working relationship and understanding can be developed.
4 Fair, but compromise and a common objective are often needed to make this relationship work.
5 Awkward. Unlikely to work, either through lack of trust, understanding or the competitiveness of the signs.
6 Mistrust. Difficult. To be avoided.

	Rat	Ox	Tiger	Rabbit	Dragon	Snake	Horse	Goat	Monkey	Rooster	Dog	Pig
Rat	2											
Ox	1	3										
Tiger	3	6	5									
Rabbit	4	3	3	3								
Dragon	1	4	3	3	3							
Snake	3	2	6	4	1	5						
Horse	6	5	1	5	3	4	4					
Goat	5	5	3	1	4	3	3	2				
Monkey	2	3	4	5	1	5	4	4	3			
Rooster	5	1	5	5	2	1	2	5	5	6		
Dog	4	5	2	3	6	4	2	5	3	5	4	
Pig	3	3	3	2	3	5	4	2	3	4	3	1

YOUR CHINESE HOROSCOPE 2005
YOUR ASCENDANT

The ascendant has a very strong influence on your personality and, together with the information already given about your sign and the effects of the element on your sign, it will help you gain an even greater insight into your true personality according to Chinese horoscopes.

The hours of the day are named after the 12 animal signs and the sign governing the time you were born is your ascendant. To find your ascendant, look up the time of your birth in the table below, bearing in mind any local time differences in the place you were born.

11 p.m.	to	1 a.m.	The hours of the Rat
1 a.m.	to	3 a.m.	The hours of the Ox
3 a.m.	to	5 a.m.	The hours of the Tiger
5 a.m.	to	7 a.m.	The hours of the Rabbit
7 a.m.	to	9 a.m.	The hours of the Dragon
9 a.m.	to	11 a.m.	The hours of the Snake
11 a.m.	to	1 p.m.	The hours of the Horse
1 p.m.	to	3 p.m.	The hours of the Goat
3 p.m.	to	5 p.m.	The hours of the Monkey
5 p.m.	to	7 p.m.	The hours of the Rooster
7 p.m.	to	9 p.m.	The hours of the Dog
9 p.m.	to	11 p.m.	The hours of the Pig

RAT: The Rat ascendant is likely to make the sign more outgoing, sociable and careful with money. A particularly beneficial influence for those born under the signs of the Rabbit, Horse, Monkey and Pig.

OX: The Ox ascendant has a restraining, cautionary and steadying influence which many signs will benefit from. This ascendant also promotes self-confidence and willpower and is especially good for those born under the signs of the Tiger, Rabbit and Goat.

TIGER: The Tiger ascendant is a dynamic and stirring influence which makes the sign more outgoing, action-orientated and impulsive. A generally favourable ascendant for the Ox, Tiger, Snake and Horse.

RABBIT: The Rabbit ascendant has a moderating influence, making the sign more reflective, serene and discreet. A particularly beneficial influence for the Rat, Dragon, Monkey and Rooster.

DRAGON: The Dragon ascendant gives strength, determination and ambition to the sign. A favourable influence for those born under the signs of the Rabbit, Goat, Monkey and Dog.

SNAKE: The Snake ascendant can make the sign more reflective, intuitive and self-reliant. A good influence for the Tiger, Goat and Pig.

HORSE: The Horse ascendant will make the sign more adventurous, daring and on some occasions fickle. Generally a beneficial influence for the Rabbit, Snake, Dog and Pig.

GOAT: The Goat ascendant will make the sign more tolerant, easy-going and receptive. It could also impart some creative and artistic qualities to the sign. An especially good influence for the Ox, Dragon, Snake and Rooster.

MONKEY: The Monkey ascendant is likely to impart a delicious sense of humour and fun to the sign. It will make the sign more enterprising and outgoing – a particularly good influence for the Rat, Ox, Snake and Goat.

ROOSTER: The Rooster ascendant helps to give the sign a lively, outgoing and very methodical manner. Its influence will increase efficiency and is good for the Ox, Tiger, Rabbit and Horse.

DOG: The Dog ascendant makes the sign more reasonable and fair-minded as well as giving an added sense of loyalty. A very good ascendant for the Tiger, Dragon and Goat.

PIG: The Pig ascendant can make the sign more sociable, content and self-indulgent. It is also a caring influence and one which can make the sign want to help others. A good ascendant for the Dragon and Monkey.

APPENDIX

HOW TO GET THE BEST FROM YOUR CHINESE SIGN AND THE YEAR

Each of the 12 Chinese signs possesses its own unique strengths and by identifying them you can use them to your advantage. Similarly, by becoming aware of possible weaknesses you can do much to rectify them and in this respect I hope the following sections will be useful. Also included are some tips on how you can get the best from the Year of the Rooster. The areas covered are general prospects, career prospects, finance and relations with others.

THE RAT

The Rat is blessed with many fine talents, but his undoubted strength lies in his ability to get on with others. He is sociable, charming and a good judge of character. He also possesses a shrewd mind and is good at spotting opportunities.

However, to make the most of himself and his abilities, the Rat does need to impose some discipline upon himself. He should resist the (sometimes very great) temptation of getting involved in too many activities all at the same time and should decide upon his priorities and objectives. By concentrating his energies on specific matters he will fare much better as a result. Also, given his personable manner, he should seek out positions where he can use his personal relations skills to good effect. For a career, sales and marketing could prove ideal.

The Rat is also astute in dealing with finance, but while often thrifty, he can sometimes give way to moments of indulgence. Although he deserves to enjoy the money he has so carefully earned, it may sometimes be in his interests to exercise restraint when tempted to satisfy too many expensive whims!

The Rat's family and friends are important to him and while he is loyal and protective towards them, he does tend to keep his worries and concerns to himself and would be helped if he were more willing to discuss his anxieties. Others think highly of him and are prepared to do much to help him, but for them to do so the Rat does need to be less secretive and guarded.

With his sharp mind, keen imagination and sociable manner, the Rat does, however, have much in his favour. When he has commitment, he can be irrepressible and, given his considerable charm, often irresistible as well! Provided he channels his energies wisely, he can make much of his life.

Advice for the Rat's Year Ahead

GENERAL PROSPECTS
This will be an active year for the Rat, with plans and ideas often moving ahead quickly. By making the most of his talents and opportunities, the Rat can make good headway as well as enjoy himself.

CAREER PROSPECTS

This is a year to look to advance, and with his experience, contacts and opportunities, the Rat will have much in his favour. This is very much a time for positive action and the Rat should not allow himself to be discouraged if setbacks do occur. These are almost inevitable on the path of progress, and with persistence, the Rat can make important headway.

FINANCE

While the Rat's income may increase and he could also enjoy some good fortune, finances do need to be managed carefully. Accommodation costs could be particularly high, with some Rats moving during the year.

RELATIONS WITH OTHERS

A busy but rewarding year. By giving time to others and sharing plans and activities, the Rat will find his relations with others going well and meaning a great deal to him. For some, new friendships and romance will beckon. With his outgoing and sociable nature, the Rat will find himself in great demand.

THE OX

Strong-willed, determined and resolute, the Ox certainly has a mind of his own! He is persistent and sets about achieving his objectives with a dogged determination. In addition he is reliable and tenacious and is often a source of inspiration to others. The Ox is a doer and achiever, and he often achieves a great deal. However, for him to really excel, he would do well to try and correct some of his weaknesses.

Being so resolute and having such a strong sense of purpose, the Ox can be inflexible and narrow-minded. He can be resistant to change and prefers to set about his activities in his own way rather than be too dependent on others. His dislike of change can sometimes be to his detriment and if he were prepared to be more adaptable and adventurous he would find his progress easier

The Ox would also be helped if he were to broaden his range of interests and become more relaxed in his approach. At times he can be so preoccupied with his own activities that he is not always as mindful of others as he should be and his demeanour can sometimes be studious and serious. There are times when he would benefit from a lighter touch.

However, the Ox is true to his word and loyal to his family and friends. He is admired and respected by others and his tremendous willpower usually enables him to achieve a great deal in life.

Advice for the Ox's Year Ahead

GENERAL PROSPECTS

An encouraging year and one in which the Ox should act upon his aims and ambitions. With his strengths, fine qualities and firm Ox resolve, he will find that much can be accomplished over the year. This is a time for positive action.

CAREER PROSPECTS

The Ox knows he has much to offer and in the Rooster year he will find his experience and determination well rewarded. This is a year when he should make the most of his chances, particularly in areas which will allow him to take his career in the direction he wants. With good use of his skills and a willingness to put himself forward, he can enjoy significant progress.

FINANCE

In money matters the Ox will need to remain his vigilant and cautious self. When entering into financial agreements, he should check the details and implications carefully and not take information at face value. Without care, he could find himself at a disadvantage. This is a year for watchfulness.

RELATIONS WITH OTHERS

While the Ox may be quieter and more reserved than some signs, he can look forward to a pleasant social life with the possibility of new friendships and romance. Domestically, this will be a meaningful year, with the Ox particularly valuing the support and affection of others.

THE TIGER

Lively, innovative and enterprising, the Tiger enjoys an active lifestyle. He has a wide range of interests, an alert mind and a genuine liking of others. He likes to live life to the full. However, despite his enthusiastic and well-meaning ways, he does not always make the most of his considerable potential.

By being so versatile, the Tiger does have a tendency to jump from one activity to another or dissipate his energies by trying to do too much at the same time. To make the most of himself he should try to exercise a certain amount of self-discipline. Ideally, he should decide how best he can use his abilities, give himself some objectives and then stick to them. If he can overcome his restless tendencies, he will find he will accomplish much more as a result.

Also, in spite of his sociable manner, the Tiger likes to retain a certain independence in his actions, and while few begrudge him this, he would sometimes find life easier if he were more prepared to work in conjunction with others. His reliance upon his own judgement does sometimes mean that he excludes the views and advice of those around him, and this can be to his detriment. The Tiger may possess an independent spirit, but he must not let it go too far!

The Tiger does, however, have much in his favour. He is bold, original and quick-witted. If he can keep his restless nature in check, he can enjoy considerable success. In addition, with his engaging personality, he is well liked and much admired.

Advice for the Tiger's Year Ahead

GENERAL PROSPECTS
Much can go in the Tiger's favour in the Rooster year, but to benefit he will need to be flexible in outlook and prepared to adapt to the situations that arise. This is not a

year when he can afford to be stubborn or too set in his ways.

CAREER PROSPECTS
The year will contain some excellent chances for the Tiger to make progress and develop his skills, but he does need to concentrate on the areas with which he is familiar rather than become involved in new and less familiar areas.

FINANCE
A generally positive year, with the Tiger's earning abilities being on good form. However, he would do well to plan his more substantial purchases carefully as well as keep track of his overall financial position. The more care and attention he can give to money matters, the better he will fare.

RELATIONS WITH OTHERS
A pleasing year, with the Tiger meeting and impressing many people, especially those connected with his work or interests. His domestic and social life will see much activity, but throughout the year he does need to consult others and listen closely to their views.

THE RABBIT

The Rabbit is certainly one who appreciates the finer things in life. With his good taste, companionable nature and wide range of interests, he knows how to live well – and usually does!

However, for all his finesse and style, the Rabbit does possess traits he would do well to watch. His desire for a settled lifestyle makes him err on the side of caution. He dislikes change and as a consequence can miss out on opportunities. Also, there are many Rabbits who will go great lengths to avoid difficult and fraught situations, and again, while few may relish these, sometimes in life it is necessary to take risks or stand your ground. At times it would certainly be in the Rabbit's interests to be bolder and more assertive in going after what he desires.

The Rabbit also attaches great importance to his relations with others and while he has a happy knack of getting on with most people, he can be sensitive to criticism. Difficult though it may be, he should really try to develop a thicker skin and recognize that criticism can provide valuable learning opportunities, as can some of the problems he strives so hard to avoid.

However, with his agreeable manner, keen intellect and shrewd judgement, the Rabbit does have a lot in his favour and invariably makes much of his life – and usually enjoys it too!

Advice for the Rabbit's Year Ahead

GENERAL PROSPECTS

This will be a demanding year, with the Rabbit having to work hard to make headway. However, despite the pressures and a need for care, he will gain a great deal and will lay important foundations for his future. This may be a challenging year, but it can leave a valuable legacy.

CAREER PROSPECTS

Progress will not always be easy and to make headway the Rabbit will need to keep putting himself forward and make the most of situations as they arise. His greatest gains will come from extending his experience and skills. Any training or study he undertakes will be very helpful to his future prospects.

FINANCE

This requires care. The Rabbit will need to remain vigilant and thorough when dealing with financial matters, especially when taking on new commitments. His usually cautious nature will help, but this is not a year for risks or giving money matters insufficient attention.

RELATIONS WITH OTHERS

The Rabbit's domestic and social life can be rewarding over the year, but to benefit he does need to liaise closely with others and be forthcoming with his views. In potentially awkward or delicate situations, he would do well to watch his words carefully.

THE DRAGON

Enthusiastic, enterprising and honourable, the Dragon possesses many admirable qualities and his life is often full and varied. He always gives his best and even though not all his endeavours may meet with success, he is nonetheless resilient and hardy, and is much admired and respected.

However, for all his many qualities, the Dragon can be blunt and forthright and, through sheer strength of character, sometimes domineering. It would certainly be in his interests to listen more closely to others rather than be so self-reliant. Also, his enthusiasm can sometimes get the better of him and he can be impulsive. To make the most of his abilities, he should give himself priorities and set about his activities in a disciplined and systematic way. More tact and diplomacy might not come amiss either!

However, with his lively and outgoing manner, the Dragon is popular and well liked. With good fortune on his side (and the Dragon is often lucky), his life is almost certain to be eventful and fulfilling. He has many talents and if he uses them wisely he will enjoy much success.

Advice for the Dragon's Year Ahead

GENERAL PROSPECTS

The active nature of the Rooster year will suit the Dragon and he should make the most of his ideas and opportunities. This is a year to advance and the Dragon's initiative and effort will be well rewarded.

CAREER PROSPECTS

A year of considerable opportunity. With the Dragon's experience, commitment and drive, he is capable of making important strides. This is a time to move forward and make the most of his considerable talents. In 2005 fortune will certainly favour the bold.

FINANCE

The Dragon's efforts can lead to an increase in income over the year, but he does need to manage his finances carefully and control his outgoings. He would find it helpful to save towards any major expenditure, including travel costs.

RELATIONS WITH OTHERS

A pleasing year, with the Dragon benefiting from the support and advice of those around him. There will be many chances to meet others and the Dragon's social circle is set to grow. At busy times he should, however, make sure his domestic life and personal interests do not suffer. With the busy nature of the year, he does need to keep his lifestyle in balance.

THE SNAKE

The Snake is blessed with a keen intellect. He has wide interests, an enquiring mind and good judgement. He tends to be quiet and thoughtful and plans his activities with considerable care. With his fine abilities he often does well in life, but he does possess traits which can undermine his progress.

The Snake is often guarded in his actions and sometimes loses out to those who are more action oriented and assertive. He can also be a loner and likes to retain a certain independence in his actions, and this too can hamper his progress. It would be in his interests to be more forthcoming and involve others more readily in his plans. The Snake has many talents and possesses a warm and rich personality, but there is a danger that this can remain concealed behind his often quiet and reserved manner. He would fare better if he were more outgoing and showed others his true worth.

However, the Snake is very much his own master. He invariably knows what he wants in life and is often prepared to journey long and hard to achieve his objectives. He does, though, have it in his power to make that journey easier. Lose some of that reticence, Snake, be more open and assertive, and do not be afraid of the occasional risk!

Advice for the Snake's Year Ahead

GENERAL PROSPECTS

The Rooster year holds much potential, but the Snake will need to put himself forward and make the most of the chances that arise. This is a year for purposeful action.

CAREER PROSPECTS

There will be some excellent opportunities for the Snake to further his position over the year, but he does need to be quick in acting upon them. He should also make the most of his ideas and often original approach. With determination and persistence, he can make this a highly successful year.

FINANCE

The Snake's earning abilities will be on good form, but with family expenses, travel and other commitments, he does need to watch his outgoings. He could find it helpful to regularly review his position. Some modifications too could make a difference.

APPENDIX

RELATIONS WITH OTHERS

Domestically, this will be a pleasing year, with the love and support of those close to him giving the Snake the encouragement and reassurance he needs. Some fine family occasions will mean a great deal to him. However, throughout the year, the Snake does need to remain attentive to others and careful when expressing his views.

THE HORSE

Versatile, hardworking and sociable, the Horse makes his mark wherever he goes. He has an eloquent and engaging manner and makes friends with ease. He is quick-witted, has an alert mind and is certainly not averse to taking risks or experimenting with new ideas.

The Horse possesses a strong and likeable personality, but he does also have his weaknesses. With his wide interests he does not always finish everything he starts and he would do well to be more persevering. He has it within him to achieve considerable success, but to make the most of his talents he does need to overcome his restless tendencies. When he has made his plans he should stick with them.

The Horse loves company and values both his family and friends. However, there will have been many a time when he has lost his temper or spoken in haste and regretted his words. Throughout his life, he needs to keep his temper in check and be diplomatic in tense situations. If not, he could risk jeopardizing the respect and good relations he so values.

However, the Horse has a multitude of talents and a lively and outgoing personality. If he can overcome his restless and volatile nature, he can lead a rich and highly fulfilling life.

Advice for the Horse's Year Ahead

GENERAL PROSPECTS

This will be a demanding year for the Horse and while progress may not be easy, by making an effort and rising to the challenge, he will learn a great deal. Experience gained now can have longer-term benefits.

CAREER PROSPECTS

The Rooster year favours the hardworking and industrious, and by setting about his tasks in his usual committed way and taking advantage of the chances to learn and add to his skills, the Horse will not only impress others but also do his future prospects a lot of good.

FINANCE

This will be an expensive year for the Horse and he would do well to manage his resources carefully and take his time with more expensive purchases or transactions. Careful budgeting and control will pay off. With travel well aspected, the Horse could find it helpful to set something aside for holidays and breaks.

RELATIONS WITH OTHERS

The Horse may have his independent tendencies but this year he really will gain a great deal by involving others in his plans and activities. Their support and help can make a big difference to how he fares. Socially, this will be a promising year and meeting others who share similar interests can result in some important new friendships.

THE GOAT

The Goat has a warm, friendly and understanding manner and gets on well with most people. He is generally easy-going, has a fond appreciation of the finer things in life and possesses a rich imagination. He is often artistic and enjoys the creative arts and outdoor activities.

However, despite his engaging manner, there lurks beneath his skin a sometimes tense and pessimistic nature. The Goat can be a worrier and without the support and encouragement of others can feel insecure and be hesitant in his actions.

To make the most of himself the Goat should aim to become more assertive and decisive as well as more at ease with himself. He has much in his favour, but he really does need to promote himself more and be bolder in his actions. He would also be helped if he were to sort out his priorities and set about his activities in an organized and disciplined manner. There are some Goats who tend to be haphazard in the way they go about things and this can hamper their progress.

Although the Goat will always value the support of others, it would also be in his interests to become more independent and not be so reticent about striking out on his own. He does, after all, possess many talents, as well as a sincere and likeable personality, and by always giving his best he can make his life rich, rewarding and enjoyable.

Advice for the Goat's Year Ahead

GENERAL PROSPECTS

This year holds good prospects, but to do well the Goat will need to put himself forward and make the most of his skills and opportunities. It is a year when effort, determination and good planning will pay off.

CAREER PROSPECTS

This is a year to advance and the Goat would do well to follow up any opportunities which would further his position. For some this can be a year for setting their career off on a positive new path. What is accomplished in 2005 can often have long-term significance.

FINANCE

The Goat will have many demands on his resources over the year, particularly in view of some of the plans he has for his accommodation, and he will need to watch his spending and budget accordingly. This is a year when good planning and control can make a difference.

RELATIONS WITH OTHERS

Over the year the Goat will be well supported by his family, friends and colleagues, but he does need to be forthcoming with his plans and ideas. If problems arise, he would do well to deal with them early and effectively, before they start to undermine his good relationships. This is, however, a fine year for widening his social circle and also an excellent time to develop his personal interests.

THE MONKEY

Lively, enterprising and innovative, the Monkey certainly knows how to impress. He has wide interests, a good sense of fun and relates well to others. He also possesses a shrewd mind and often has a happy knack of turning events to his advantage.

However, despite his versatility and considerable gifts, the Monkey does have his weaknesses. He often lacks persistence, can get distracted easily and also places tremendous reliance upon his own judgement. While his belief in himself is a commendable asset, it would certainly be in his interests to be more mindful of the views of others. Also, while he likes to keep tabs on all that is going on around him, he can be evasive and secretive with regard to his own feelings and activities, and again a more forthcoming attitude would be to his advantage.

In his desire to succeed the Monkey can also be tempted to cut corners or be crafty and he should recognize that such actions can rebound on him!

However, the Monkey is resourceful and his sheer strength of character will ensure he has an interesting and varied life. If he can channel his considerable energies wisely and overcome his sometimes restless tendencies, his life can be crowned with success and achievement. And with his amiable personality, he will enjoy the friendship of many.

Advice for the Monkey's Year Ahead

GENERAL PROSPECTS

The Rooster year will contain many fine opportunities for the Monkey and by using his skills well and acting upon the chances that come his way, he can accomplish a great deal. This is a year when effort and determination will be rewarded.

CAREER PROSPECTS

Over the year the Monkey can make some important advances in his career and by developing his skills and experience, he will do his prospects much good. His accomplishments can be considerable and far-reaching.

FINANCE

This will be an expensive year, especially regarding plans for the home. As a result, the Monkey would do well to manage his finances carefully, keeping watch over his outgoings and avoiding unnecessary risks or being lax in financial matters. The extra care and attention *will* be worthwhile.

RELATIONS WITH OTHERS

A pleasing and personally rewarding year, with the Monkey enjoying both his domestic and social life. However, he would do well to overcome his more independent tendencies and be forthcoming with his ideas. This way others will be better able to help and advise him. For the unattached, romance could beckon.

APPENDIX

THE ROOSTER

With his considerable bearing and incisive and resolute manner, the Rooster cuts an impressive figure. He has a sharp mind, is well informed on many matters and expresses himself clearly and convincingly. He is meticulous and efficient in his undertakings and commands a great deal of respect. He also has a genuine and caring interest in others.

The Rooster has much in his favour, but there are some aspects of his character that can tell against him. He can be candid in his views and sometimes over-zealous in his actions, and sometimes he can say or do things he later regrets. His high standards also make him fussy, even pedantic, and he can get diverted into relatively minor matters when in truth he could be occupying his time more profitably. This is something all Roosters would do well to watch. Also, while the Rooster is a great planner, he can sometimes be unrealistic in his expectations. In making plans – indeed, in most of his activities – he would do well to consult others. By doing so, he will greatly benefit from their input.

The Rooster has considerable talents as well as a commendable drive and commitment, but to make the most of himself he does need to channel his energies wisely and watch his candid and sometimes volatile nature. With care, however, he can make a success of his life, and with his wide interests and outgoing personality, he will enjoy the friendship and respect of many.

Advice for the Rooster's Year Ahead

GENERAL PROSPECTS

A year of good fortune, but to benefit the Rooster will need to be bold and act upon his ideas. This is a year when positive action will be well rewarded – and it falls upon the Rooster to act!

CAREER PROSPECTS

This is a year for action and for going after opportunities, and with determination, the Rooster can make important progress. He could also be blessed with a certain amount of good fortune and benefit from the support of those who think highly of him.

FINANCE

A positive year, but as the Rooster will want to do a great deal, he should carefully manage and control his financial situation. This is not a year for acting in haste or being too impulsive.

RELATIONS WITH OTHERS

Over the year the Rooster will find himself much in demand, with others often seeking his views and advice. However, in return, he will gain much from the support they can give. Any interests and activities he is able to share can lead to some pleasing occasions. This is also a good year for romance and making new friendships, and for those who have had recent personal problems, it is a year for moving forward.

APPENDIX

THE DOG

Loyal, dependable and with a good understanding of human nature, the Dog is well placed to win the respect and admiration of many. He is a no-nonsense sort of person and hates any sort of hypocrisy and falsehood. With the Dog you know where you stand and, given his direct manner, where he stands on any issue. He also has a strong humanitarian nature and often champions good and just causes.

The Dog has many fine attributes, although there are certain traits that can prevent him from either enjoying or making the most of his life. He is a great worrier and can get anxious over all manner of things. Although it may not always be easy, he should try to rid himself of the 'worry habit'. Whenever he is tense or concerned, he should be prepared to speak to others rather than shoulder his worries all by himself. In some cases, they could even be of his own making! Also, the Dog has a tendency to look on the pessimistic side and he would certainly be helped if he were to view his undertakings more optimistically. He does, after all, possess many skills and should justifiably have faith in his abilities. Another weakness is his tendency to be stubborn over certain issues. If he is not careful, this could at times undermine his position.

If the Dog can reduce the worrying and pessimistic side of his nature, then he will not only enjoy life more but also find he is achieving more. He possesses a truly admirable character and his loyalty, reliability and sincerity are appreciated by all he meets. In his life he will do much good and befriend many – and he owes it to himself to enjoy life too. Sometimes it might help him to recall the words of another Dog, Sir Winston Churchill: 'When I look back on all these worries I remember the story of the old man who said on his deathbed that he had had a lot of trouble in his life, most of which never happened.'

Advice for the Dog's Year Ahead

GENERAL PROSPECTS

This will be a busy and challenging year for the Dog, but its rewards can be considerable. By being flexible in outlook and making the most of his chances, he can do himself much good. This can be an instructive and significant year.

CAREER PROSPECTS

This is more a year to further skills and experience than to make major changes. A lot will be gained by working closely with others and building up contacts. What is accomplished now can prove very helpful in following years.

FINANCE

Financial matters do need careful attention and risk should be avoided. Where possible, the Dog will find it helpful to make early provision for some of his larger expenses as well as budget for his various commitments. This is a year when watchfulness and good management will make a difference.

RELATIONS WITH OTHERS

Over the year the Dog will do much to help and support loved ones and his thoughtfulness and attentiveness will be much appreciated. However, he does need to be forthcoming with his ideas and listen carefully to any advice given. In any fraught or difficult situation he should watch his words carefully. His personal interests can also help to bring him into contact with others.

THE PIG

Genial, sincere and trusting, the Pig gets on well with most people. He has a kind and caring nature, a dislike of discord and often a good sense of humour. In addition, he has a fondness for socializing and enjoying the good life!

The Pig possesses a shrewd mind, is particularly adept at dealing with business and financial matters, and has a robust and resilient nature. Although not all his plans may work out as he would like, he is tenacious and will often rise up and succeed after experiencing setbacks and difficulties. In his often active and varied life he can accomplish a great deal, although there are certain aspects of his character that can tell against him. If he can modify these or keep them in check then his life will certainly be easier and possibly even more successful.

In his activities the Pig can sometimes overcommit himself and while he does not want to disappoint, he would certainly be helped if he were to set about his activities in an organized and systematic manner and give himself priorities at busy times. He should also not allow others to take advantage of his good nature and it would be in his interests to be more discerning. There will have been times when he has been gullible and naïve; fortunately, though, he quickly learns from his mistakes. However, he possesses a stubborn streak and if new situations do not fit in with his line of thinking, he can be inflexible. Such an attitude may not always be to his advantage.

The Pig is a great pleasure-seeker and while he should enjoy the fruits of his labours, he can sometimes be self-indulgent and extravagant. This again is something he would do well to watch.

However, though the Pig may possess some faults, those who come into contact with him are invariably impressed by his integrity, amiable manner and intelligence. If he uses his talents wisely, his life can be crowned with considerable achievement and he will also be loved and respected by many.

Advice for the Pig's Year Ahead

GENERAL PROSPECTS

The Pig can do well and enjoy the year. However, to benefit, he does need to act upon his ideas and opportunities as well as use his strengths and personal qualities to good effect. With a positive approach, he can achieve a great deal.

CAREER PROSPECTS

The Rooster year favours the industrious and hard-working, and with commitment and good use of his skills, the Pig will find his prospects most encouraging. This is a year to advance, to further his skills and add to his contacts. Positive action and good work *will* be rewarded.

FINANCE

This is a year for good planning and careful management. Given that he will want to do so much, the Pig should plan his purchases and activities with care. The greater his financial control, the better he will fare. Also, if he is able to add to his longer-term savings, this too could be to his advantage.

RELATIONS WITH OTHERS

The Pig will particularly welcome the support and encouragement of others and by discussing his ideas and being forthcoming, he will be helped in a great many ways. Socially and romantically, this can be a pleasing year, and with his amiable and outgoing nature, the Pig will often make the most of the many fine social occasions the year will bring.

Make
www.thorsonselement.com
your online sanctuary

Get online information, inspiration and guidance to help you on the path to physical and spiritual well-being. Drawing on the integrity and vision of our authors and titles, and with health advice, articles, astrology, tarot, a meditation zone, author interviews and events listings, www.thorsonselement.com is a great alternative to help create space and peace in our lives.

So if you've always wondered about practising yoga, following an allergy-free diet, using the tarot or getting a life coach, we can point you in the right direction.

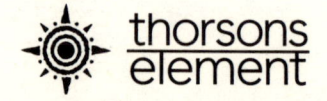

thorsons element